The Lasting South

The Lasting South

Fourteen Southerners Look at Their Home

LOUIS D. RUBIN, JR.

JAMES JACKSON KILPATRICK

Editors

 HENRY REGNERY COMPANY
CHICAGO, ILLINOIS · 1957

For John Dana Wise

Carolinian and Virginian
in affection and respect

Contents

Preface

THIS IS A BOOK ABOUT THE SOUTH: the South that changes, and the South that abides. But particularly it concerns the abiding South, the essential Southernness which permits a region of eleven or twelve States to retain an identity of its own.

This is a book with a thesis: the South's identity is worth preserving. The fourteen writers who contribute their thoughts on the matter share one underlying assumption about the South, and that is, that in an increasingly modern and cosmopolitan world, there is more than ever the need for the persistent individuality of the South, and the need for Southerners to think long before bartering that individuality for the dubious advantages of conformity.

The essayists who contribute to this symposium do not agree about all the ways by which the South should act to retain its individuality. They do not even agree about all the constituent parts of that individuality. With some regret, perhaps, they do not offer to the South a specific platform and bill of particulars such as was so memorably presented nearly three decades ago in that brilliant book entitled *I'll Take My Stand*. Yet it is doubtful whether such a work as that could be written today even if most of the contributors could commune together in a common place of meditation such as Nashville provided the Agrarians. Such are the inroads of thirty years on the South, that it would be next to impossible to find twelve or more reasonably intelligent Southern writers who could approach their subject with the kind of unanimity that characterized the Nashville writers. And it may be noted, too, that the Agrarians have long since gone their separate ways.

What the writers who provide the present volume do agree upon, however, what they insist upon in their essays, is that there *is* a South, that it is possible to talk of the South, and in so doing to mean not merely a geographical grouping but a way of life and a state of mind. What that way of life and state of mind are, these essays attempt to explore.

More so than at any time in a century, the South is today divided by controversy. The issue of school segregation dominates the newspaper headlines and demands the attention of all. It should be pointed out at the outset, therefore, that this is *not* a book about the segregation controversy. Various of the essays refer to it. A good deal of what is contained in this book relates to it directly or indirectly. But there is no single essay on the segregation issue as such. On that issue, there is no unanimity of opinion among the essayists, nor, for that matter, among the editors themselves.

Rather, this volume represents an attempt to look behind and beyond the immediate issues that face the South today, of which educational segregation is but the most dramatic among many. It is an attempt by fourteen Southerners to discover what is enduring in their region, and what changes, and what is to be done about it. Of controversial issues the South has always had its share and more. But the South has gone on being the South, both despite controversy and because of it, and it will continue to go on being the South. "You can't understand it. You would have to be born there," a character in a Faulkner novel tells a Northern friend. Most of the contributors to this book were born there. All have lived there. What they think about their region—its past, present, and future—constitutes this book.

Louis D. Rubin, Jr.
James Jackson Kilpatrick

Richmond, Virginia,
March 1, 1957.

The Lasting South

LOUIS D. RUBIN, JR.

An Image of the South

"IT IS OUT OF FASHION these days to look backward rather than forward," the poet John Crowe Ransom wrote almost thirty years ago. "About the only American given to it is some unreconstructed Southerner, who persists in his regard for a certain terrain, a certain history, and a certain inherited way of living."

Ransom made the remark in an essay composed for a book about the South called *I'll Take My Stand*. The backward-looking Southerner, he said, "feels himself in the American scene as an anachronism, and knows he is felt by his neighbors as a reproach."

Though the States that constitute the region known as the South have changed considerably since Ransom and eleven other Southerners published their symposium in 1930, his observation is still generally true. More than any other region of the United States, the South tends to think about its history, and to live with less regard for the future than for the immediate present, and to do things in certain ways because that is the way such things have always been done before. And, more than any other American region, the South is scolded for being backward and living in the past, without proper regard for progress.

Southerners, except perhaps for some North Carolinians and most Texans, are usually willing to admit this. Even today they will stand in front of a sleek plate-glass store window or a gaudy motel and they will talk about a "Southern way of life," and by that they will mean a kind of relaxed, easy-going acceptance of things, with plenty of time for leisure and with considerable family and social life. And despite the fancy window displays and the motels, they are generally correct.

There *is* a Southern way, a style of its own, and though the motor
court and Chambers of Commerce and the hundreds of new industrial
installations seem to belie it, the way of life still hangs on. It is an
exasperating way of life at times, especially when there is work to be
done, and yet it is the best thing about the South, and in the long run it
counts for more than all the economic expansion so talked about today.

The Southern way of life is now being threatened, as it has not been
threatened since the Civil War. I am not now talking about segregation, or integration, or creeping socialism, or anything so topical as
that. I am talking about the quality which makes a region a region,
instead of a colorless, standardized set of people and places. The South
is in danger today of losing its most precious possession, that regional
quality, and the enemy is just as much within as without. So subtle is
that enemy and so apparently natural and inevitable, that it is mostly
not even recognized for being an enemy. Instead it is being greeted
with enthusiasm by the very people who should be most suspicious
of it.

To understand the South, and to see why modernity is its most
deadly enemy, it is necessary first to understand what constitutes the
South. For before one can decide what is worth keeping about the
South, and how best to defend it, one must know what is being defended. And here the explanation lies in the past as well as in the present, for the South is what it is today because of what happened to it in
the past.

One of the most overworked clichés about the South is that which
involves Gracious Living. "We don't have too much money," the
catch-phrase goes, "but we know how to live," and the Southern
Chambers of Commerce have been tireless in proclaiming that in the
South the living is easy and the hospitality and charm abundant. One
grows weary of such constant prattle, and yet there is some truth in
the boast. The Southern community has *had* to learn to live graciously;
there has never been too much else to do. The South has rarely had
the opportunity to accomplish very much in a materialistic sense;
history and climate have seen to that. It has never been much on pioneering, and it has seldom had much room in its makeup for the
pioneering spirit of America. Early in its history its frontier became

stable. Until quite recently, life for most Southerners has been the business of learning to exist as comfortably and as happily as possible on what was available.

All this has created a sense of the past, an awareness of history. It is seldom something conscious; the Southerner does not go around toting history books. Yet it is there, as it is perhaps not there in, say, New York City or Chicago or Detroit. I doubt, for example, that the resident of Manhattan thinks of his community in terms of history. He thinks of it, from what I can tell, in terms of its material existence, or in terms of the future as it may be affected by the present. Now of course this attitude is itself the product of history. The history of New York City is a history of change, of expansion. Buildings rise and fall; families emerge from the millions of population, then disappear. One must search long and hard for traces of the city of a hundred years ago. Civil War New York has for all intents and purposes been obliterated from the face of the earth. New York is peculiarly a place of the moment; its whole imposing record of success is predicated upon its unparalleled ability to adapt itself to current opportunities and needs. Its welfare has always depended upon its freedom from the restraining and hampering weight of custom. This has been what several hundred years of American history have demanded of New York as the price of leadership, and New York has been able and willing to pay precisely that price—to think in terms of the immediate situation, and to encumber itself with as little historical consciousness as possible.

But the history of the South has been different from New York's. The South has had to find "success" in fields other than the immediately practical aims of material prosperity, economic power, or business leadership. Its history has required of it other goals. So that what has constituted success for the South has not been what New York (or Chicago or Detroit) has considered success.

Where New York has been commercial and industrial, the South has been primarily agrarian. Where New York has expanded, the South has been contained. Where New York has been able to achieve varieties of attainments, the South has had to concentrate on a relatively few activities. Thus where New York has found it most to its advantage to be as adaptive and receptive as possible to new situations, the South has found it most profitable to be able to draw maximum benefit from what it has, since it is all that the South has and has been likely to be all it could expect.

To illustrate this proposition, let me take for an example one aspect of human life—leisure. What is impressive about New York City, what for a hundred years has made it a mecca for the visitor from the hinterlands, is the variety of leisure activities available within it. Contrast this with the opportunities existing in a typical Southern community, and of course this contrast is the more true the smaller the community is. Except for a few cities which in the North would be at best only medium-sized cities, the South has been predominantly a region of towns, villages, and small cities.

The inhabitant of this typical small Southern community finds his choices of recreation limited. It is necessary for him to seek in intensity what is not possible in variety. He must choose his recreation and master it. And where people are concerned, he has no easily accessible group of thousands of persons within the radius of a few blocks. He must get to know and enjoy almost everyone in his community, because by the very nature of small town life he is thrown in with them day after day, at work and at play.

The Southern community is therefore likely to be a much more tightly-knit affair, much more an organic unit, than any Northern metropolis. One has only to examine the society pages of a Southern daily or weekly newspaper to see the range of church, fraternal, and social activities constantly taking place. The local church provides not only a place of worship; it is the scene of numerous other activities. Civic clubs, fraternal orders are well patronized. The roster of organizations whose weekly programs are listed in almost every Southern newspaper is close to incredible, considering the size of the communities involved.

All this may be true, of course, of small communities in the Midwest and the North no less than in the South. The difference lies in the fact that in the South, unlike most other regions, the chief social emphasis still rests upon small cities and towns. They do not exist as auxiliaries to metropolises; they dominate the region's cultural life. Until recently the Southern small town and city has not been an industrial center for which the surrounding countryside acts as feeder of produce and raw materials, so much as a kind of cultural and social seat for the activities of the countryside. Small town and rural life in the South has not developed in terms of dependence upon metropolitan manufacturing centers. And thus to a degree far beyond the life of small towns in other regions, Southern life has developed a distinctive ordering characteristic—a pervading historical sense.

It is easy to see why the emphasis on community, and on the complex social fabric embodied therein, would be conducive to an intensified awareness of the past. The tightly-knit sense of clan and family, which is the woof and warp of the South's complex social fabric, would tend naturally to embrace the past, the ancestral. Family history is traceable in the South, since the region has existed in much the same shape and size for so long a period of time with comparatively little flux and change. And family history can be so clearly tied in with political and social history, that a sense of one involves a sense of the other. Thus an interest in the Civil War, for example, not only involves sectional patriotism; it involves family history. For a community with bases so complex and so firmly placed as that of a Southern town, the awareness of history is the *only* logical ordering device.

The function of the historical sense, however, is not entirely or even primarily one of a mere ordering device for social relationships. It serves an equally useful role for the individual. It is the historical sense which in the South makes the individual identity, the sense of individuality, possible.

This is because the history of the South is one which, for better or worse, has seldom permitted much emphasis on *doing*. The South has seldom afforded its people much in the way of materialistic accomplishment (one excepts the North Carolina multi-millionaire and the Atlanta and Birmingham industrialist from this generalization). It has seldom provided for very long periods of time the kind of expanding economy possible in a metropolis like New York. Save for brief periods during the flush frontier times of the 1820's and 1830's in the Cotton belt, the atmosphere of boom has been generally absent from the South until very recently.

Even that symbol of ante-bellum elegance and material welfare and comfort, the cotton planter, possessed no easily manipulated, easily convertible medium of enterprise. Plantation life, whether with ten or two hundred slaves, was a relatively contained affair. The plantation represented an enormous investment in property, land and labor both, with very little conversion value. And if this were true of the most imposing symbol of Southern material affluence, the plantation, how much more true it has been of the small farm, the merchant, the dweller in the small, relatively static Southern town or city. Take a city such as my own home town of Charleston, South Carolina, for example. In the course of 140 years, from 1790 to 1930, its population increased less than four times. Compare that with any Northern city, and one can see the difference. Boston, for example, increased more than 120 times, Philadelphia more than 67 times, New York more than 300 times during that period. Property values, investment capital, per capita earnings tell a like story. Where industrial capitalism has been dynamic and expanding in the North, providing the citizen an active economic field for his energies, in the South the economic life, with certain exceptions such as Birmingham or Atlanta, has been contained, limited.

What this has meant, among other things, is that there has been relatively little opportunity until recently for the Southerner to derive any solid sense of personal creativeness out of commerce, industry, business activity. To achieve a sense of identity, of worth, the individual Southerner has been forced to look elsewhere than at the *doing of things*. There have been relatively few things, and not too much to do about them. Instead, the Southerner has concentrated on *being*.

The emphasis has been on personality, on one's existence as a recognizable individual in a social fabric designed above all to provide for the individual identity. The late John Peale Bishop has written that "There is even today among the poorest Southerners a self-respect, a sense of their worth as men, regardless of what they have done or accumulated, that sets them apart from the more successful American who is lost without his bankbook and recognizes no price but that of achievement." It is in the field of leisure, of community activities and social life, that the Southerner has looked for his triumphs, and these are activities encompassing individual rather than mass identity. John Crowe Ransom wrote that "the arts of the section, such as they were,

were not immensely passionate, creative, and romantic; they were the eighteenth-century social arts of dress, conversation, manners, the table, the hunt, politics, oratory, the pulpit. These were arts of living and not arts of escape; they were also community arts, in which every class of society could participate after its kind. The South took life easy, which is itself a tolerably comprehensive art."

Social life—not the occasional exclusive cocktail party, but the going and coming of a complex activity—has always been important to Southern community life. It is not confined to a privileged social class; it exists on all levels and in all circles. Economics has comparatively little to do with it; the hardware clerk is very likely to be a member of the town's oldest family, and an extremely eligible bachelor among the best social set. Particularly is this true among the smaller towns. This is not to deny for a moment that there are strata and classes and social levels: Mrs. Ravenel and Judy O'Grady do not go to the same church or wedding reception, but it would not occur to either of them to look down upon or up at the other for economic reasons. There is a kind of social tolerance in the Southern community that makes class not so much a matter of economic limitation as of personal description. It is precisely this distinction that the outsider coming to live in the South has the hardest time understanding.

I have tried to show how the Southern social and community organization is naturally favorable to a consciousness of history and of the past. However, I do not wish to imply that for the Southerner, history is merely something that grows out of these factors, and that any history would do as well. It is the *particular* history of the South that has been so important in making it what it is.

What is different in the history of the South, what distinguishes it from the history of the rest of the United States, is that it is *a history of defeat*. The South was beaten in war and occupied by enemy troops; alone of American regions, the South has a Lost Cause.

The shock of the Civil War is the paramount historical fact about the South. It is the memory of the Civil War that more than anything else distinguishes the South from other areas of the country. Before the war the South was agrarian; the War fixed that way of life upon it irrevocably, stripping it of what capital goods it possessed, reducing it to a status of colonial dependency upon the Northeast. Before the war the South sometimes tended to vote as a unit on certain issues; the War welded it into a Solid South that acted and thought as one on all things. Before the War the South tended to think of itself as a conscious minority within the Union; the War institutionalized that relationship, making it possible for the North to treat it first as a conquered province and thereafter as a colonial tributary.

Upon the mind of the South (and there is a Southern state of mind, although it does not necessarily involve an addiction to catfish or lynching), the war's impact was devastating and lasting, and it was followed by the act of Reconstruction. The South learned from the Civil War something that most Americans have never had to learn: That defeat is possible, that it is possible to do one's best and to lose. The devastation of the War in the South (twenty years after Appomattox there were ruins in the centers of many Southern cities), the loss of the finest men, the anguish of defeat and of having to eat one's own words, the swift and cataclysmic disappearance of slavery with the millions of dollars of investment it involved—all this came about in four years. Then followed a decade of Reconstruction, of living as a conquered people under military occupation. When finally the troops were removed, what was left was an exhausted, impoverished region lacking the capital required to make its way in what was now definitely an industrially oriented Union, struggling to wrench a living from the soil, and nursing the memory of a desperate fight lost irretrievably.

"For thirty years," Richard M. Weaver has written, "the atmosphere was so suffused with the sense of tragedy and frustration that it was almost impossible for a Southern man to take a 'normal' view of anything." Walter Hines Page, in his thinly disguised autobiographical novel, described "Nicholas Worth's" view of the South on a trip home in the 1880's:

It occurred to me for the first time that this region is yet a frontier —a new land untouched except by pioneers, pioneers who had merely lingered till they thought the land worn out and who thought that their old order of life—now destroyed by Time's pressure of which war was the instrument—had been the crown of civilization. Here was poverty—a depressed population, the idle squalor of the Negro now that slavery was relaxed, and the hopeless inertia of the white man who had been deadened by an old economic error.

Page exaggerated, perhaps; but not too much. Many accounts of visitors to the South after the war paint a similar picture. The South was in a state of shock, physically and psychologically. Memories of the War pervaded everything. Fortune, fame, valor, dead parents and friends and family and lovers, all these lay in the past, come and gone with one historical event. The image of the Confederate soldier was everywhere. To quote Nicholas Worth again as he described the veterans of the War who dominated Southern life for four decades after Appomattox, who held the political offices as well as social distinction, "their speech was in a vocabulary of war; their loyalties were loyalties, not to living ideas or duties, but to old commanders and to distorted traditions. They were dead men, most of them, moving among the living as ghosts; and yet, as ghosts in a play, they held the stage."

Page of course had an axe to grind; he was all for Progress, and he wanted the South to throw off what he considered the shackles of history, and so he both exaggerated and deprecated the Confederate tradition in the South. But if wrong in his analysis of what that memory of the War meant, he was accurate in his evaluation of its pervading influence.

In the twentieth century the South began to "rejoin the Union." It became industrialized to a much greater extent than ever before. Improving communications and transportation began breaking down its isolation, and an era of general economic prosperity permitted the South to begin catching up with the rest of the nation—which she is still busy doing. Gradually the old Confederates died off, and a great war in which the South fought on the side of the Union and as part of it destroyed much of the old feeling of hostility. Though politically there continued to be a Solid South, and though economically the South was still less healthy than the country as a whole, the South was no longer a region significantly apart from the rest of the United States.

But by this time the South's historical sense had long since become firmly imbedded in its consciousness. The social organization, the sense of family, had combined with the historical past of the region to create a place and people with a strongly traditional cast of mind. Decades of things as they are, remaining as they are, changing in no appreciable respect, had built in the Southern mind a strong inbred conservatism. Years of material deprivation had inculcated a strong reliance upon a way of life which, though far from shunning material advantage, tended to value material commodities as accessories, and not as the be-all and end-all. A society widely conscious of history, devoted to the familial and regional past, tending to think in terms of the individual rather than along lines of class—this was still the South, Years and years of enforced stasis had built into the Southern mentality a skepticism of change, a strong inclination to let things be.

It should be emphasized that this is by no means an unmixed blessing. The disinclination to look ahead and prepare for inevitable change has caused much difficulty and travail in the South, especially in recent years as the twentieth century's third and fourth decades brought much adjustment in Southern life. The resistance that much of the rural South offered during the 1920's and 1930's to the introduction of modern farming methods is an example. Because farming had been done in certain ways for generations, Southern farmers faced the increasingly commercialized American economy with a stubborn determination not to give ear to all the talk of conservation, soil replenishment practices, crop diversification and the like that the young agricultural agents were mouthing. Because farmland had always been burned over each year, they wanted to keep right on doing it. Only by the hard lesson of worsening economic deprivation were they made to see that there *was* something to be said for the new way of doing things, and that the boys from the A&M school did know something about making a crop, after all.

The foremost example of the paralyzing effects of this Southern habit of worrying for the present day alone, of course, is the Negro issue. One has only to read the racial arguments offered by Southerners for the past 150 years to realize that they have neither changed, nor yielded, despite the manifest fact that the African slaves brought over from the jungles in the eighteenth century have been changing, learning, growing. What was adequate in 1870 is not adequate in 1957. Had the Southerner been willing, in the 1910's, the 1920's, the 1930's, to adjust his thinking to the Negroes' growing development and to make the necessary accommodations, a situation need never have arisen where a Supreme Court could declare that "separate" and "equal" were contradictory terms.

My own conviction is that though Negroes have suffered for want of decent educational, health, and economic and political treatment, their main grievance is not primarily based on these things. Rather, it is the insult to their pride that most rankles. It is the hundred little things, mass humiliations, that are intended primarily to remind "Them" that they are Inferior. It is the knowledge that in the eyes of the white man who governs their region, even the best and finest that their race produces is in essential things equated with the meanest and most wretched. Because Roosevelt Jones kills and has venereal disease, the refined, well educated wife of the Professor of Drama at the Negro college cannot eat dinner at the local restaurants. There were jeers expressed when a psychology professor at the University of Virginia recently declared that the stigma of complete segregation was largely responsible for the high incidence of schizophrenia in Negro mental cases. On the face of it, the statement does seem absurd. Yet when one examines the writings of so many of today's Negro novelists and poets, one may wonder. The psychic wound of second class status pervades their writings to an extent that it impedes the white reader's aesthetic credibility.

Persons familiar with the history of the Negro in the United States know that in the latter half of the nineteenth century and well into the twentieth, there was a controversy between the supporters of the views held by Booker T. Washington and those typified by W. E. B. Du-Bois and the National Association for the Advancement of Colored People. It was Washington's thesis that the Negroes should strive not for political and social equality, but should bend their efforts toward educating themselves and improving their economic lot. When the Negroes had made themselves economically indispensable to the South, and had elevated their educational and social standards to the level of the best elements of the white race, Washington maintained, then political and social equality would follow automatically. With his hand extended for a symbol, he told a predominantly white audience at the Atlanta Exposition of 1897 that "In all things that are purely social we can be as separate as the fingers, yet one as the hand on all things essential to mutual progress." The followers of DuBois and the N.A.A.C.P. held that the Washington policy was unrealistic and involved acquiescence in a status of permanent inferiority. It would be nice to believe that the South accepted Washington's doctrine, which in essence was that of separation with equality. But the South did not do so. No one can realistically maintain that the "separate but equal" doctrine was seriously followed by the Southern States in the long years that followed. Instead, Southerners looked the other way, temporized, persisted in ignoring the Negroes' steady progress. By refusing to grant deserving, elevated Negroes any more essential social and cultural position and status than the most primitive, benighted specimens of the race, the South helped to build up a situation in which "separation" and "equality" became for practical purposes mutually exclusive terms. There was no room at the top for Negroes who could reach the top. The South threw Negroes into the arms of the agitators of the N.A.A.C.P.

With reasonable foresight, with the willingness to recognize the necessity for change when the necessity plainly existed, with acceptance by thinking Southerners of a responsibility for helping to lead those who needed leadership, the South might have avoided or greatly mitigated the impact of an issue which in the sixth decade of the twentieth century threatens to destroy its schools, divide its people, and create bitterness and hatred that may be generations in the undoing.

Vexing as such issues are, they are only aspects of the larger, over-all problem that confronts the South today. That problem is: How can a region retain the values of a traditional social order, based upon the individual and the community and ordered by a strong historical sense of life, in a modern, increasingly industrial and urban world? For the South is confronted with that world. It has in truth begun finally to "rejoin the Union," and that means full participation in a society of cities, of industrial plants, of mass media and mass pursuits, organized for efficiency and bigness, and based not on intensity but on variety, not on individuality but on mass goals.

The problem is a very real one for the South. Take the average small Southern town where suddenly a large factory is erected, promising employment to a goodly number of townsfolk. What then? Incomes go up, new inhabitants arrive by the droves, townsfolk get well-paying jobs, marginal farmers leave the farm to work at the plant. Property values rise, chain stores expand, the demand for consumer goods grows mightily. The factory payroll vastly increases the cash money in circulation, and this affects the entire economy of the town and the surrounding countryside.

But what of the effect on the small town's life, and on the necessarily strong reliance upon individuality and private satisfactions that had always prevailed? The factory works regular hours, its employees perform routine tasks on an assembly line. They become cogs in what for all the efforts at good employee relationships is still an impersonal industrial machine. Gone is the time when a man could close up shop and go fishing. Gone is the time when a man knew everybody in town, and was known by everybody. The pace of life quickens, becomes more standardized. Conformity becomes the norm. The advent of cash money, the possibility for the first time of business gain, tends to weaken the old reliance on the non-economic, personal values. Gone is the lazy, unhurried tranquillity of small Southern town life, with its personal values, its habitual individualism, its easy-going tolerance of the eccentric, the character, the recluse. Gone, in short, is the small town Southern life as it used to be. In its place is the increasing standardization, the stepped-up tempo, the enforced conformity of modern industrial life, which measures its days by factory whistles and its nights by television channel changes.

All over the South this process is taking place, as Southern industrial development increases, as factory after New England factory transfers its operations South. Mile upon mile of suburban development mushrooms about the Southern cities, those once settled, relatively static communities. Small towns become thriving large towns, large towns become cities, factories spring up everywhere. The rural agrarian character of the South as it was for a hundred years is changing. The values that the South held are threatened by new, urban values. What has been distinctive and Southern about the South threatens to disappear, and the South threatens to become a thriving but undistinguished replica of the North and West, dependent upon the national industrial economy as never before. Factory badges, union cards, television antennae, hardtop convertibles, supermarkets and shopping centers, row upon row of almost identical ranch homes in almost identical housing projects, become the monotonous characteristics of the new South.

It must be granted that from this onset of modernity, the South has much to gain as well as to lose. Consumer goods in themselves are no evil. Better roads, better schools, better homes, better and more varied diet, better health facilities certainly represent no setback to the Southern people. The tenant farmer who trades a precarious, hand-to-mouth existence in a wretched shack for a suburban home of his own and the chance to educate his children and keep them healthy and well, cannot be persuaded that the coming of industrialism to the South is an unfortunate thing. The material gains of an industrialized area do not of themselves constitute a menace. The menace of an industrial South comes from the destructive impact of material gains on what was distinctive and desirable about Southern life before the factories came. Not in the material artifacts of industrialism, but in what they represent, is where the threat to the South lies.

History and economic necessity forced certain virtues upon Southern life. Through no fault of its own, the South evolved a civilization that did not place its reliance upon the material goods of life, but upon the values of individuality, self-reliance, the community arts, a life which did not allow getting and spending to interfere with leisurely, relaxed living. The way of life which permitted a man to enjoy himself, to know the satisfaction of being something more than a cog in a machine—at its typical best this was the attainment of civilization in the South. At its heart was an historical sense of life, an instinctive realization that man was not a creature of chance and the moment. It was a life that emphasized the right relationship of man to nature and the essential dependence of man on nature. It was a life of the spirit as well as the flesh, which provided in its makeup for recognition of the values of the spirit. It was a life of stasis, of acceptance, not one of restlessness and doubt. This is the life that is threatened by the coming of industrialism to the South, and these are the values that the dominance of the industrial community most menaces.

If these values are to be preserved, then the South must find a way to reconcile them with the new order, and to preserve their spirit while the material world changes. The South must find a way to control industrialism, to admit it only on the South's own terms. It must accept the factory, but not allow it to dominate its life. It must find a way to integrate industrial civilization into its communities without destroying the time-honored fabric of the community's life.

It is no easy task. Working against a successful outcome is that characteristic ingrained in Southern life, an almost inevitable product of that life—the willingness to ignore practical problems requiring common effort, planning and foresight, in favor of a concentration on personal, inner satisfactions alone. The Southerner is habitually averse to long-range planning. He is temperamentally opposed to the kind of necessarily abstract analysis that would permit him to work out a long range solution. Yet this is what the South must do, if it is to survive in anything like its present form.

It must overcome its reluctance to mapping out a plan of action, and must work out a considered scheme whereby it will admit industrialism, but only such industrialism as it will need. It must force itself to think in terms of the future, and in terms of eventual rather than immediate advantage. It must be willing to sacrifice present material gains for future spiritual happiness. Where it must adjust its ways to the demands of modernity, it must do so with as good grace as possible. Where it must stand firm for what it believes, it must do so with tenacity and conviction. Above all, it must do what it has never done before—sit down and think out its course, prepare for the future without waiting until the next crisis is upon it.

To do this is difficult. It is also most un-Southern. It may be that it will prove impossible to do. It may be that the very qualities which have made Southern life what it is, contain in this age of greater and greater urbanization the seeds of their own destruction. But if the South believes in its traditional way of life, and if it wishes to preserve in American life a region where the individual, the historical and the spiritual are cherished over the mass, the moment and the material, it must rise to the occasion. At midcentury the South faces its greatest challenge.

RICHARD BARKSDALE HARWELL

The Confederate Heritage

As THE CENTENNIAL of America's Civil War approaches, Confederate history reaches a new high in marketability, and the South faces the possibility of losing the values of an honored tradition in a wave of meretricious commercialism. Northerners and Southerners, for different reasons, speed the process toward the same end. Rootless Americans, seeking an American background they do not have, seize on the Confederacy for its sentimental appeal and, with the zeal of converts, become more Confederate than even the professional Southerner. Southerners, rebelling against an overdose of filiopietism, try to forget that the Civil War ever happened, and ignore the merits the Confederacy left the South in attempting to obliterate the scars it left on the region. Yankee authors remake the story of Robert E. Lee to fit the Lincolnian legend of an America reunited at Appomattox. Northern Civil War enthusiasts tour the Southern battlefields and, between parties, unconsciously mock the thing they seek to honor. Commercialism moves in. The movies treat the War as a glamorous example of a sort of code *duello*. Raider Andrews shakes the hand of Confederate Fuller, and a desperate raid becomes an innocuous myth. Confederate songs are revised into radio commercials, and the mulatto "Yellow Rose of Texas" becomes colorless. Where is the conservative Southerner left? Even his own section betrays him, and the heritage of the War becomes an asset of the Chamber of Commerce, a trap to bait tourists.

The Civil War is only a part of the heritage of the modern South, but it is a focal point in that heritage. Those four and a half years from December 1860 to April 1865 conditioned the Southern version of the American heritage that had gone before. They conditioned succeeding generations to a sectional interpretation of the continuing heritage.

Appomattox did not produce a new nation, thenceforth and forever indivisible. Appomattox was a bitter defeat for the South. The end of the War brought back to the Union eleven beaten States. After two years of steadily ebbing fortunes the Confederacy had been driven to surrender. But there were few who would admit error in their course in fighting the War. The Southern States bowed to might. They were not persuaded to a new conviction. Reunion came later. For Southerners Appomattox brought the "bottom rail on top," not the "year of jubilo." Slaves might rejoice in a new found freedom, but the whites' could only fear that they had themselves changed places with their former servants.

A decade of Reconstruction added insult to injury. There was no Marshall Plan, no Point Four Program to help the South back to its feet after the devastation of the sixties. It is easy for the twentieth-century politician, with economic problems in his own constituency, to win support by crying out against millions and billions for the war-weary of other continents. It is easy for him to appeal thus to voters who remember the struggles of their parents and grandparents to re-build after a war. Misery loves company. But he who has risen from misery wants to make very sure it will never again engulf him. This was the motivation and the appeal of Scarlett O'Hara. Consciously or unconsciously, it is still a regional motivation.

No, the end of the War did not bring forth a new nation. The defeated South clothed itself in the sack-cloth of the Lost Cause. It built a psychological Chinese Wall separating the two parts of the old nation. Memory of the War became the wedge for separation in ways of thinking and of living. The Bourbonism of the last quarter of the nineteenth century was a Southern attempt to live inside the Chinese Wall of the Mason and Dixon line. The New South ideal of Henry Grady was an effort to break down this barrier between the sections. Neither Bourbonism nor the New South was a complete answer. Bourbonism tried to reinstate in a different guise the things the South had lost in defeat. It tried to bring back the ante-bellum South by pretending that the War had changed nothing. Grady, on the other hand, invited long-term regional exploitation by bringing Northern ownership to Southern industry. Both were, however, partial answers. Bourbonism restored to the South a feeling of regional integrity. It helped obscure the scar of carpetbagger rule. The New South movement, though it paid a high price in exploiting Southern labor, in making the region a branch-office province of Northern capital, and in deferring the eventual rise of truly Southern industry, brought money into the area when it was most needed.

But, though Bourbonism is a thing of the past, though the New South is a twentieth-century reality which need no longer parade in quotation marks, the Chinese Wall is still there—battered and broken in spots, but still there. It was the War that built this wall, but it was built with bricks of difference and cemented with mortar of competition that had long been in the making. The heritage of New England had changed as new peoples and new industries changed its make-up. The South, with little infiltration by foreign stock, remained much the same as it had been in the early days of the Republic. The War did not create a new heritage for the South. It solidified into strongly defined lines the heritage that Southerners had accumulated in the difficult years of building first colonies and then a nation.

The War was the great event of its generation—North and South— the great American experience of the nineteenth century. It gave new meaning to human existence for all who participated in it. It gave new urgency to life. It gave new reality to ideas. "In the spring of 1861," wrote Sidney Lanier, "an afflatus of war was breathed upon us. Like a great wind, it drew on and blew upon men, women, and children. Its sound mingled with the solemnity of church-organs and rose with the earnest words of preachers praying for guidance in the matter. It sighed in the half-breathed words of sweethearts conditioning impatient lovers with war-services. It thundered splendidly in the impassioned appeals of orators to the people. It whistled through the streets, it stole in to the firesides, it clinked glasses in bar-rooms, it lifted the gray hairs of our wise men in conventions, it thrilled through the lectures in college halls, it rustled the thumbed book-leaves of the school rooms.

"This wind blew upon all the vanes of all the churches of the country, and turned them one way—toward war."

With its whole effort directed toward war, with war a part of every household, of every life, the Confederacy achieved a unanimity of thought and action the section had never known before. Lincoln's election had in part been due to the earlier division of Southern opinion and to Southern failure to concentrate on one candidate as his opponent. But, despite the defections of the Joe Browns and Zebulon Vances who cried States' Rights at the expense of all rights, despite Alexander Stephens who mouthed pettifogging legalities in a time of revolution, the Confederacy maintained an amazing solidarity of opinion throughout its existence. The prescient hero who knew the Confederacy was foredoomed is more the creation of the novelist than of the historian. There were some who doubted the ultimate success of the Confederacy, but they were few among many, and most of them (including Lee) fought, and sacrificed, and finally surrendered as Confederates because honor and duty demanded that they participate in the cause of their native land. Defeat brought the Solid South and a political solidarity that has been broken only in the last generation.

"The victors forget, the vanquished remember," writes Sir Winston Churchill. *The vanquished remember.* . . . All insults, all offense, all slights the vanquished South remembered and related to the War. Too often the War was a cloak to cover Southern shortcomings. Too often it was an excuse. *The victors forget.* . . . The War became a part of the American past to the North. The North had the wealth and the power to move on. For long the South could honor itself only in defiance and remembrance. The past of the South, for sixty years, became centered in recollection of the War. Men who had been rollicking, roistering soldiers became, in retrospect, knights of a vanished Southern chivalry. Demagogues whose most positive accomplishments had been spitting tobacco juice and shouting became statesmen of the Old South. Filiopietism replaced patriotism. Apology replaced history. The Confederate Heritage had full sway.

But the South had nothing for which to apologize. True, it had lost a war. But the world had admired the way it fought that war. There is honor to both sides in the way Federal General Meade's soldiers saluted the gallantry of John B. Gordon on the surrender field at Appomattox, in the way Northern soldiers looked with reverence and respect on the defeated Lee. There is honor to both sides in the conviction with which each believed the American heritage belonged to it.

Certainly the American heritage had an origin common to both sections. The Plymouth colonists had come to America in a ship of the Virginia Company. Massachusetts and Virginia had stood side by side in opposition to the Stamp Act. Washington had led *Americans,* in New England and in Virginia. The accomplishment of the Revolution had been a united effort. The creation of the Constitution had been constructive compromise. The union of American interests was a splendid inheritance, North and South.

But the seeds of disunion, too, had been sown early. In the same breath that the Virginia Convention of May 1776 had instructed its delegates to the Continental Congress to declare for American independence and to federate with the other colonies it had added: "Provided, that the power of forming government for, and the regulation of the internal concerns of each colony, be left to the respective colonial legislatures." The principle of States' rights was openly set forth in the very beginning, and it was this principle which, carried to its logical conclusion, brought disunion, and which carried to absurdity within the Confederacy itself, wrecked the already slim chance of the South to achieve independence.

Throughout the Federal period of our history there were rumblings and warnings of the war to come. The Nullification Controversy brought threats of disunion and saddled the South with an extreme States' rights view. In *The Partisan Leader* in 1836 Judge Beverley Tucker foretold, in the form of a novel amazingly accurate in its details, a war between the Union and a Southern Confederacy, and, in a stirring speech at the Nashville Convention of 1850, he enunciated the tenet of State loyalty which Lee and others would invoke a decade later: "What Virginia says, I am ever ready to vindicate; what Virginia does, I, at all hazards and to the last extremity, will maintain."

Propaganda for secession snowballed in quantity as 1861 approached. With each speech and pamphlet the Southerner became a little more Southern. It was repeatedly emphasized that the South could be economically self-sufficient, that the South should develop its own intellectual life, that outsiders had no right to interfere in the sociological structure of the region, and—in the words of the banner stretched across Charleston's Broad Street during the meetings of the Secession Convention of 1860: "The South Alone Should Govern the South." There was no cloak-and-dagger conspiracy to take the South out of the Union. There was a gradual building to the decision to invoke the right the States believed they held, the right of voluntary withdrawal from a union voluntarily entered. War was a possibility, but a remote one. And not all who expected war found the prospect distasteful. As Lanier commented: "To obscurity it held out eminence; to poverty, wealth; to greed, a gorged maw; to speculation, legalized gambling; to patriotism, a country; to statesmanship, a government; to virtue, purity; and to love, what all love most desires—a field to assert itself by action."

In achieving a favorable climate of opinion in the South the propagandists had pulled out all the stops: The United States had its origins in the wisdom of Southern statesmen; the right of secession was implicit in the Constitution; mass government was abhorrent to the principles of American republicanism; the rights of the States were paramount. Their arguments became branded on the Southern mind. The Confederates truly believed that they and only they were continuing the traditions and convictions of the founding fathers. The first flag of the C. S. A. was strongly derivative of the Stars and Stripes; its Constitution was a rewrite of the United States Constitution; its seal bore an equestrian portrait of Washington. Defeat did not change the Southern belief that the true American heritage lay in the heritage of the South. Perhaps it strengthened it.

The republicanism of a Federal United States died with the Civil War. The results of the War have led steadily to a stronger and stronger centralized government. The majority of Americans wish it so, and the South cannot change, can only delay, the trend. But the Southerner has an historic claim to Americanism that can be matched by the native of no other region. It is the same as the claim of the old New Englander, but successive waves of immigration have changed New England in a way that the South is only beginning to be changed. This is why the Southerner of today sometimes feels like an embarrassed host in his own home. His America is gone. He is not yet sure he likes the new America. He falls back on the old arguments. They no longer work. He appeals to something he regards as the Confederate tradition. Nobody cares. The old arguments have been voided by a changing America. The Confederate tradition has been swamped in a broader American tradition. For the Confederate tradition was simply the American tradition frozen in time—at its peak perhaps, but frozen, static. Defensively the Southerner endows his Confederate heroes with almost superhuman powers. Demagogues of the present quote demagogues of the Civil War in the guise of statesmen. Novelists glamorize the Confederates till we are ready to say, as George W. Bagby said of John Esten Cooke's extravagant portrayals of the colonial Virginians: "I marvel that such a set of homely, selfish, money-loving cheats and rascals as we are, should have descended from such remarkably fine parents. . . . I'm proud of my grand-daddy, proud of the days and the deeds of his generation; but I don't want to be so plague-taked proud of him as to undervalue myself and my times. The old times may have been mighty good, but there are some first rate days and prime doings left."

Until the conservative Southerner can look on the past with Bagby, the Confederacy will have no meaning in the new American tradition. But when he can relate the Confederacy to the whole American picture—not work it into a mawkish legend in which it does not belong, but relate it properly and objectively to the facts of American history— the Southerner and his Confederate tradition will belong to the nation. Abjuring extravagant ancestor worship on the one hand, yet being proud of his background on the other, the Southerner, the ex-Confederate, can be fully American.

For a generation—two generations—after the War Cooke's pattern of the Confederate tradition held sway. Authors romanticized the days of 1861–65, seeing them through the "rose-colored goggles" Bagby accused Cooke of wearing. A Confederate war record was a *sine qua non* of Southern political success. The hustings speech followed a pattern of tribute to the Confederacy, loyalty to the Democratic party, and a bow to the nobility and purity of Southern womanhood. Shut off from full participation in national life by defeat, the South of the later nineteenth century compensated by emphasizing, and being proud of, its insularity.

The older generation instructed its youth well. The Confederate pattern continued far into the twentieth century. Two world wars have not completely eradicated it. World War I broke down some of the more obvious sectional prejudices. Training camps brought thousands of soldiers from other parts of the country into the South. The American Expeditionary Forces took thousands of Southerners to other parts of the world. Even more than the first world war, the economic changes of the twenties changed the pattern of Southern life. The boll weevil swept from Mexico to the Carolinas, devastating cotton fields and bringing ruin to the one crop society of the old Black Belt. Southerners strained for other means of maintaining their way of life. They embraced the Babbittry that had arisen in the great cities of the Midwest. Atlanta and Birmingham moved to the fore among Southern cities. They pushed. They pushed toward success, and they pushed aside the attitudes that had marked Richmond, Charleston, Savannah, Mobile, Natchez, and New Orleans as charming Southern cities from the past. They strained to take the giant step which would make them the competitors and honest rivals of Pittsburgh, Detroit, Cleveland, and St. Louis. The past was something to be remembered only by old women and college professors. Only when remembrance promised financial gain did the New South take it to its heart. Financiers moved in on the idea of Georgia's women for a monumental memorial to the Confederacy at Stone Mountain. But Southern Babbittry could not see beyond the nose on Lee's face. Two million dollars were wasted, and Gutzon Borglum's noble design was destroyed in a greedy fight for silver dollars. Tourists do not pay to see a gashed and scarred mountainside. The projected memorial stands in the unfinished hackings of Augustus Lukeman, a lost-cause memorial to a Lost Cause.

In the twenties the South tried hard to be a part of the new American prosperity. Despite the boll weevil it was swept along in the pattern of growing national wealth. Inspired in part by religious reasons and by the forces of prohibition, it broke with old political patterns and voted for Hoover in 1928. The Depression was a rude awakening. Not only did the new prosperity fail, the old stays of Southern economy went with it. In the national desperation for recovery the South made new concessions. Historically it had controlled the Democratic party through the two-thirds rule. It relinquished this hold. For economic aid in roads, housing, and schools it compromised its stand on States' rights.

Economic influences were gradually reshaping the South. Not only was it being changed internally—great areas were being lopped off at its borders. The "second Yankee invasion" was making resort country of much of Virginia and of great plantations in the Carolinas and Georgia. Miami was rapidly growing into an outpost of New York, and all Florida was becoming progressively less Cracker. The accumulation of oil money in Texas and Oklahoma was divorcing the interests of the western South from those of the Southeast. Tennessee, with a closer political balance between the two parties than other Southern States, was becoming more national in its outlook. North Carolina was growing less Southern as its industrialization increased. With World War II the pace of nationalization of the South increased even more markedly. It continues, and the Old South recedes to the borders of the old Cotton States, and less. When the Supreme Court coagulated Southern opinion with its segregation decision of 1954 it looked as if the lines had retreated to include only South Carolina, Georgia, Alabama, Mississippi, Arkansas, and Louisiana. Reaction to the Court decision has called back the border States. But for how long? The long term tendency toward nationalization has so far been irresistible.

Grown up in a society with a strong remembrance of the past, yet educated in the pattern of the twentieth-century American, the Southerner of today finds it hard to relate traditional regional attitudes to national attitudes. It is easy to feel that the past wounded the South, that the Yankees carried off the American tradition as booty of war, that—final insult—the Democratic party has become the creature of labor and the big cities, but it is hard not to void the past in participating in the present. Yet it is possible to make the past a part of the present, and the future of America will be a stronger future if the tradition of the South is neither rejected nor set apart but woven into its fabric.

What would have been different if the South had won the Civil War is hard to say. Georgia, for example, was economically a stronger State in 1860 than it would become for another sixty years. Cotton was a tremendously important product for eighty years after the War, and its control would have given an independent South great influence. Slavery most likely would have run its course to a planned end that would have avoided the evils of sudden freedom. The Confederacy might have found in Richmond, Atlanta, Birmingham, or Nashville a city about which its social, political, literary, and commercial life could revolve with less of the taint of provincialism than in a society which directs too many lines to Washington and New York. H. L. Mencken, high priest of American liberal thought in the twenties, speculated: "If the war had gone with the Confederates ... New Orleans, today, would still be a highly charming and civilized (if perhaps somewhat zymotic) city, with a touch of Paris and another of Port Said. Charleston, which even now sprouts lady authors, would also sprout political philosophers. The University of Virginia would be what Jefferson intended it to be. . . . Richmond would be, not the dull suburb of nothing that it is now, but a beautiful and consoling second-rate capital." Mencken blamed much of the ills on the South on its having sold out to social inferiors and to the Yankee dollar, on its having exploited cheap labor, and on its succumbing to "the Chamber of Commerce metaphysic." But Mencken, read in the 1950's, is a period piece. The South is no longer the Sahara of the beaux arts— nor of industry, business, or ideas. Mr. Mencken had too high an opinion of the South's cavalier strain and too low an opinion of its abilities.

Has the South rejected the Confederacy in building a new century? No. Consciously or not, the average Southerner carries with him much of the Confederacy. He does not wave the Confederate flag or insist on calling the War "The War Between the States." He leaves the flag-waving to the Yankee converts to the Cause. And, if he thinks about it at all, he leaves "The War Between the States" to the over fastidious and proudly admits that the War was a civil war. Perhaps he doesn't know that Longstreet was late at Gettysburg, but Lee's ideal of duty is a part of his upbringing. Perhaps he knows no details of Reconstruction, but he probably votes Democratic and considers "Republican" and "Yankee" roughly synonymous.

On each side of the average are more strongly marked types. On one side is the "Ex-Mississippian," a sensitive character who has rejected his own heritage without finding anything with which to replace it.

He denies the South, talks with an accent which belongs nowhere, and belongs nowhere himself. On the other is the neo-Confederate, the belligerent, unreconstructed Rebel who spouts battle statistics as easily as a baseball fan recites batting averages. This type is, however, rarer, as the native sort is generally a poor competitor to the Yankee-become-Southerner.

Fortunately the middle ground includes the great majority. It is this average Southerner that has a dual heritage that he learns to live with and that he will learn to make a truly American heritage. If he thinks about it at all, he realizes that the double lines of his heritage lead to the same beginning. The Confederacy was not an attempt to change the South's ideology but a valiant effort to continue it on the lines that Southerners regarded as American. Fort Sumter was not bravado, not an attempt to scare the nation. Appomattox was not a dignified tea party to reaffirm American unity. Sumter was the breaking point, a challenge thrown and taken. Appomattox was bitter defeat.

It was defeat that lasted many years. Gradually, however, the bitterness of defeat receded. The South was rejoining the Union. But the Supreme Court decision has, unnecessarily perhaps, revived the old bitterness, restruck old attitudes. The Confederate flag has been dragged out to dress Southern opposition, any Southern opposition. It doesn't belong. Perhaps the problems of segregation should have been solved long ago, but they were not. Unsolved, they are our problems now. They are not Confederate problems. Let it rest, the flag that was struck at Appomattox. Leave to it the honor of a lost cause. Understanding, not emotionalism, will solve the problems of today.

It is to the honor of the Southerner that he remembers the past. It is his honor to remember honor—for out of the debris of war and devastation he saved a priceless Confederate and American heritage. As Confederate editor E. A. Pollard wrote with Grant's army about to break the thin-spread lines of Lee: "The glory of history is indifferent to events: it is simply Honour. The name of Virginia in this war is historically and absolutely more important to us than any other element of the contest; and the coarse time-server who would sell an immortal title of honour as a trifling sentimentalism . . . is the inglorious wretch who laughs at history and grovels in the calculations of the brute."

In the centennial years soon coming the South has a second time to vindicate its honor. It is a proud and prideful region, conscious of its past. But it is no longer the self-conscious South that the Wolfes, the Cashes, the Daniels tried to explain away. It will serve its history with dignity. It will not stand by and see the honor of its past distorted into tawdry sentimentality, commercialism, and demagoguery; nor used as a barrier against progress. If it will hew to the line of its Confederate heritage, the South will discover again that its Confederate heritage and its American heritage are one and the same.

CLIFFORD DOWDEY

The Case for the Confederacy

RECENTLY when Bertrand Russell was a speaking-guest of the Richmond Area University Center, its director, Colonel Herbert Fitzroy,
drove the philosopher from Washington to Richmond over Route
One. After some miles the usually voluble Russell grew silent, and
nothing would draw him out. Then, as if emerging from deep reflection, he said, "If all the greatest minds of our time—in arts and
philosophy, pure science and the practical sciences—would collaborate
to produce the most hideous method of transportation, that calculated to create the maximum in mental suffering, they would build
this road."

As an engineering project, Route One is a proudful thing to Virginians long forced to endure the plaints and abuses of travelers over its
poor roads. Now no out-of-state tourist can complain of dust and mud
and curves that once tested the daring skill of young hotbloods in open
roadsters and forced to the speed of a horse's trot the more cautious
oldsters. Nor can stranded motorists belabor the State for the distances
between service stations, and the inadequacy for modern life of those
so-called service stations which consisted of a gasoline pump outside
a shadowy country store, operated by a leisurely rustic to whom the
innards of the automobile were an unfathomable mystery. Indeed, one
of the present phenomena noted by philosopher Russell was the fre-
quency of the shiny stations, which he had counted during his bemused silence.

To accomplish this convenience for travelers, the countryside was
denuded of every vestige of its character and natural beauty, and, between the efficient service stations and the quick service eating places,

the uniform ugliness designed for a people in transit holds the quality of some kind of purgatory, of a vacuum between worlds. It is the debasement of all value to the journey itself.

As such, it serves as a dreary symbol of the attitude that values only the destination and not the manner of going. There is no time for enjoyment of things along the road when the only purpose is *to get there,* and the only standard is to make the trip conform in details as closely as possible to the same way in which everyone else makes it. Thus, in a fluid sameness, humans stream over the white concrete purgatories as if they were de-personalized creatures who inhabit this transition between worlds.

If the Southern States had won their independence, there would be no Route One in the region which comprised the Confederacy. Tourists dedicated to zooming through a mechanized bleakness could again complain of a way of going which intruded on the frozen state of their consciousness, but for those not anesthetized to the journey the rewards would offer something along the way that has vanished from all America. They would partake of a life sustained in being for the passing moment and not for some distant end. For, to the antebellum Southerner the journey of his life was everything, and he loved with a fierce immediacy every detail of the land on which his journey was made.

With all the causes of the Confederate War for Independence, which have been harangued over for nearly a century by supposedly dispassionate scholars and avowedly passionate partisans, the one element beyond all hazard and controversy was the Southerner's devotion to his land. There was nothing of the empty sentimentality of a national anthem in the title, The Land We Love, which General D. H. Hill gave to a collection of Confederate memoirs and records. The Southerner was identified with his land, his country, as the religious are with God. Far more than a legal inhabitant of a political entity, the individual as an immortal soul was *of* his land, his consciousness part of the larger consciousness, so that the man and the Southerner were one.

During the angry debates preceding the Civil War, a Senator from Michigan complained to a Senator from Virginia for referring to himself as "a Virginian."

"I don't refer to myself as a Michigander," the Senator said, "but as an American. Yet, all you Southerners identify yourselves with your State."

The Michigan gentleman was complaining of an emotional attachment to home-place which he did not understand, because such an attachment existed nowhere else in that intensity and completeness of personal identification. The Michigan Senator was, unknowingly, also stating the reason why the Southerners would defend their land against an invader.

By the mid-nineteenth century, Southern life, evolved indigenously to its land and climate, had been formed by 250 years of a regional history that marked in no sense a deviation from what became the mainstream of American history. Virginia, the country's first colony, was different from all others except South Carolina in that its settlers, unique among pioneers, adventured to the wilderness to build a new aristocracy. Neither political nor religious dissidents, but staunch royalists and Church of England Episcopalians, the colonists developed a culture that was essentially an extension of England's with the conditioning of the physical life in Virginia. On the model of the British ruling class, and with skillful adaptation to the local conditions, the successful planters built a society controlled by the personal principalities of plantations. This pattern of society was extended from Virginia, and South Carolina, throughout the region that became the Confederacy.

This extension of these cultures spread through the geographical areas where the similarity of the land and climate made practical the economy of a single money-crop, based on chattel labor. Economic-minded historians have made a great to-do about the inefficiency of slave labor, and listed this wasteful system as a contributor to the South's poorly balanced economy. Actually, the South's economy was poorly balanced for a complex of reasons, dating back to the first 150 years under the restrictions of the British and including the intangible personal elements of pride and conservatism. The extant wills of successful planters reveal that they were men of vast tangible wealth, as well as illimitable power, and the body of Southern people appeared to live poorly only by money standards which were not their own.

Almost all historians, measuring the South by foreign standards, have tried to prove some single point either on a bloodless chart or in the abstractions of human ideals. There is no chart available for the soul of man, and the abstractions are based on *post facto* standards. Because the South is usually studied from the outside for its weaknesses, little is learned about the matrix of a civilization which existed collaterally with the dominant American civilization, though essentially in a quite different character and with far different goals.

At bottom, the explanation of all the South's defects is that it lost— in a war fought for its independence. The North's war of subjugation was fought somewhat listlessly until Lincoln interjected a moral slogan on "freeing the slaves," which, at least by his words, he did not believe in himself. Yet, such is the puissance of a moral issue interjected into arbitration by arms that following generations consider their war as a crusade for human liberty and today, even such a learned and objective journal as *Time* magazine, refers to the Emancipation Proclamation as the act which "freed the slaves" in Lincoln's crusade for human liberty. Just to be factual, slavery was legally abolished in America in 1865, after Lincoln was dead. The revered Emancipation was (admittedly by Lincoln) a war measure and applied only to the unoccupied areas of the South, in which he had at the time no authority whatsoever. Where he might have had the authority to free the slaves, *he did not.*

Because the moral purpose of fighting to free the slaves is nobler than fighting to retain humans in chattel slavery, with its military victory the North inherited also a moral superiority. Thus, while the victor was writing history, he naturally explained his victory in terms of morality and blamed the South's defeat on its sins. It lies in the realm of psychiatrists to explain why the physically victorious North must go on endlessly defeating the South morally, but certainly no defeated people in the world's history have ever been subjected to so much analysis by their conquerors. As a hazard, the analyses and judgments continue because the Southern States did not learn through physical defeat that their conquerors were superior in every way, and the Union part of the United States was compelled to explain the inferiority of a defeated people within its midst who rejected its values.

Of course today, when a defeated people or a potential enemy rejects the benefits of American democracy, the United States tries to coddle them with gifts (in cash and in the presence of some of its enlightened citizens) into loving the amorphous giant of good will. However, in the South's time of defeat, the powers of the Union used the helplessness of a region to establish, as they hoped, a permanent exploitation of its resources and people, while the moralists explained why the South had to lose for its sins. By today (while humanitarians beam benevolently on distant masses of people) the explanation of the South's wickedness has become a habit.

It happened that this habit was formed in the post-Christian era when self-conscious *avowals* of social justice replaced the *practice* of morality. The liberal-minded individual, detached from the traditional forces outside himself (like religion) which gave meaning to his morality and moral discipline to his conduct, found an identity by joining the forces of social justice. However, unlike the older comforts, the new forces imposed no obligation upon the individual. It sufficed that he *declared* himself on the side of social justice. Such declarers conformed to attitudes so standardized that they could readily identify themselves with strangers and recognize a fellow cultist; these attitudes of social justice served, in a lonely world, as the fraternal grip or the convention badge in less sophisticated people.

This need to establish the larger identity was particularly urgent in metropolitan centers, as New York, where the uprooted of 48 States converge in pursuit of money and fame, or notoriety, and the aloneness of the individual, removed from place-attachment, is most acute. In New York these lodge members contain a high proportion of superficially literate individuals, of men and women who practice constantly to sharpen and refine the expression of attitudes; thus it happens that the life of the land-rooted Southerners, with its continuity of home life as the center of the social structure, receives its glibbest analyses from this cult among rootless urbanites. That they are not qualified to judge is beside the point certainly to them. Qualification would imply preparation toward an end to be accomplished. These present day Pharisees ("Thank God I am not as other men") are concerned only with their own personal salvation, in which their confession of faith consists of assuming the verbal attitudes. No church service in the world contains a more formalized litany.

Because these attitudes of social justice impose no responsibility to understand the object most under analysis, the habit of explaining the sins of The South has become something like a game played for its own sake by amateurs.

The game, as played in New York, bears no relation to the business of life, as lived in the South. No Southerner expects it to, and for one simple reason: The Southerner knows that his region is judged outside the context of true history. This does not mean in any sense that he attributes his differentiation to the Civil War and its aftermath, or that he should be explained in terms of the personal losses from the war (that "befoh de wah we had plenty of slaves"). It does mean that he should be explained in terms of his *own* ideals and not those which others might wish to impose from the callous ignorance of distance. The calamitous war affected the South in terms of its historic ideals and conditioning from them, in terms of the intent of its civilization and the degree to which the region attained its intention. For the Confederacy did not represent to Southerners only the dissolution of what they regarded as a confederation of States, but the political fulfillment of the intention of their civilization.

They were at last to be free to form their own society "of its people, for its people, and run by its people." Their attempt to form a separate nation for themselves was, then, to establish as a political entity a homogeneous society which had been 250 years in evolving.

When they were frustrated by force of arms in their attempt at independence and returned forcibly as poor relations to a society whose ideals were alien to their own, the people formed no deeper attachment to the alien ideals forced upon them than they had formed when attachment was a matter of choice. It was, however, the necessity of some conformity to the alien ideals which confused the dislocated and impoverished Southerner. Then, spiteful denunciations of his failure to conform more completely, especially in economic standards, stiffened his resistance to one standard of ideals, and, finally, created in him a determination to conform no more than necessity forced upon him. As of today, he is becoming self-conscious in the articulation and preservation of his historic ideals which failed in the test of war.

Until recently, as a shabby-genteel roomer in an opulent house, the

Southerner clung sentimentally to his heritage as of its climactic hour in destruction. At this distillation of his culture in a struggle for life, he contemplated the heroism and gallantry. Now that he has regained some economic independence—through the Southward shifts of industry, through natively owned operations of some of the region's resources, and through a share of Federal largess—the Southerner is beginning to throw off the mental effects of his defeat as he finally begins to throw off the economic effects.

There was more distortion than even the Southerner realized in thinking conditioned by poverty amongst a people from whom the Southerners were differentiated. Its writers and historians were inclined to write "in accommodation" as one Southern historian recently called it. Fiction writers exploited and sensationalized the less savory aspects of Southern life for Northern audiences; Civil War historians concentrated on the non-controversial military aspects, and other historians became apologists for their region. Some even professed to find springs of democracy, as currently understood, in phases of Southern life, in order to minimize the South's differentiation.

As democracy is understood today (or, at least, as it is talked about), the South was never remotely democratic. All the manifestations of Southern life which, in the past fifty years, have been politically and publicly the most obnoxious, were the results of a clumsy, half-hearted adaptation to "the foreign ideology" of American democracy as now practiced.

The literal meaning of democracy, as the rule of "the crowd," offered a state of affairs which was historically abhorrent to the Southerner. Among our social justice cultists there is enthusiastic lip service for man in the mass as opposed to man, alone, unique. While historically a total society was composed of many divergent elements, including those "minorities" which came into fashion when social justice replaced personal moral values, in the era of mass man any divergence is regarded as a cancer in the body politic. Negroes and Jews must be saved from a status that differentiates them from the mass, and that minority of Southerners who are willful divergents must be forced into the common mould.

More than twenty years ago Ortega y Gasset wrote that "the characteristic of the hour is that the commonplace mind, knowing itself to be commonplace, has the assurance to proclaim the rights of the commonplace and to impose them wherever it will." The switch on that in the United States is that the highly articulate social justice advocates proclaim the rights of the commonplace in order to give themselves personal distinction—though, as individuals, their lives are marked by the utmost strivings to become differentiated from the commonplace. As a political switch within a switch, the converts of Mr. Truman found his successor out-commonplaced by the Republican candidate. The devotees of the day-of-the-common-man rallied to a highly personalized individual like themselves, in Mr. Stevenson, while Mr. Eisenhower, by the act of being, *represented* the commonplace. This turn gives to the practical operation of American democracy something of an aspect of "who's looney now."

In the ante-bellum South, Eisenhower would never have been elected for representing the commonplace nor would Stevenson have been rewarded for preaching it. Theirs was a society dedicated to producing the superior man. The average Southerner did not desire a leader who would be just another man like himself: he wanted some one he could admire, look up to, and trust to be led by.

In wars, the emergency forces the abandonment of democratic lip service, and the average enlisted man wants of all things on earth not to be led by another man like himself, but by an officer especially trained and possessing the habit of leadership. The South did the same in politics all the time.

Yet, in time of war, the South fought with the most democratic army in America's history. Officers did not need to be set apart by rigid rules. To the soldiers it was habitual that some led and others followed, and they gave no less allegiance because they called officers by their first names and went to the same parties between battles. Certainly no leader was ever followed by more selfless devotion than General Lee, whom the men greeted most casually as "Uncle Robert." In this the soldiers expressed a deeper respect than army regulations could instill; it was the traditional respect for the natural chieftain, the patriarch. By the same token it was inconceivable that newspapers would refer to Jefferson Davis as "Jeff," in order to make their president one of the boys.

The separation of the men from the boys, in leadership, had begun very early in the generic Southern colony of Virginia. It began with the concept of an aristocratic republic, with a ruling class similar to Britain's. Because of the over-romanticizing of the Virginia settlers as noble "cavaliers," and the mythical backgrounds attributed to FFV's, beginning with Wertenbaker the fashion swung to the other extreme and lately the early Virginians have been presented as plain people at best and rogues and convicted criminals at worst.

Rogues and convicted criminals certainly came to Virginia, as everywhere else, but they contributed nothing to the formation of the social structure; and plain people, as in any society, far outnumbered those of superior backgrounds. But none *as plain people* rose to positions of power and those whose descendants rose (as Thomas Jefferson) had married into a ruling family. The well known families—such as the Lees and Randolphs, Washingtons and Carters, Ludwells and Burwells—were founded by educated and well connected men of substance. Whether or not their British family trees were as fancy as genealogists would prefer is no consequence; they were natural leaders who came to a new colony to establish a power beyond them at home.

During the cavalier influx enough emigrants of gentle breeding came and intermarried to satisfy anyone wishing to make a point of blood lines. The sociological point of the influx was the influence of families accustomed to position, with the habit of authority and the aristocratic attitude to life. The infusion of these royalists in the first half-century of Virginia's existence articulated and gave physical form to the emerging concept of an aristocratic republic with its ruling class.

During the first century-and-a-half of the formation of Virginia's republic, its relations with other American colonies were remote. As its society was modelled on that of the British country gentry, as it was attached through trade, intermarriages and the Church with the mother country, the true capital of Virginia was London. All planters shopped in London, and London was where the well-to-do "went to town." The disagreements that arose between this Colony and England were largely economic.

From the founding of America at Jamestown, all the colonies had been oppressed by prohibitive British laws designed to protect London merchants and manufacturers. Virginia and New England reacted according to the nature of their land and their climate. Virginia readily conformed to the laws forbidding colonial manufacturing because of the golden leaf of tobacco; but the planters consistently evaded the legal restrictions which forced tobacco growers to sell only to British home markets at British controlled prices.

In turn, New Englanders, having no money crop, consistently defied the legal restrictions on manufacturing. Because each section reacted to the British restrictions "according to its nature," New England founded a society on the industrial pattern which was to belong to the future, while Virginia and the other Southern colonies founded an agricultural pattern which was, in time, to belong to the past. New England was no more aware that its area of legal evasion was to become identified with "progress" than was the South aware that its area of compliance would eventually identify its culture with the anachronistic.

When the two sections allied in common cause against England, their alliance by no means embraced a common culture. Their cultures were becoming increasingly divergent. Because Virginia's was here first, it is inaccurate to consider the South as the divergent element simply because the land of the wilderness yet to be settled was more suited to the New England economy than to the Southern, and that the immigrants who settled it responded more to the New England culture than to the Southern.

To be blunt, the South did not want them. A homogenous society and its rulers abhorred the presence of "a restless proletariat" and any elements of population which could throw political power to numerical majorities. The presence of a Negro slave population established the Southern order of rule indefinitely in time, as far as any man could then conceive.

This order of rule by a specially qualified minority was built in a pyramid from the county level. In an agricultural society, with few cities and none large, the county became the basic political entity, in which the potential rulers were first tried and trained, and, if promising, advanced to the State level. There the process was repeated. This selective process produced, in the early republic, the great Virginia Dynasty, and certainly no American State has ever produced so many giants in such a short period.

At the end of the golden age, with a paradise established, the planters became more parochial and less cosmopolitan. While men of size still entered politics (as Calhoun and John Randolph of Roanoke) there was a drift among the planter class toward the traditionally honored profession of arms. The quality of Southern military leadership during the Civil War attests to the fact that young men formed with the habit of authority, and trained for responsibility on the privately owned communities of a plantation, were qualified to lead in any field which the emergency demanded. Strictly from the planter class, Virginia alone produced Lee, his son Rooney and nephew Fitz; Jeb Stuart, Joe Johnston, Pickett, A. P. Hill and Magruder, Ewell and Early, half-a-dozen outstanding artillerists, and threw in—from outside the planter class—Stonewall Jackson. This, of course, does not include the regimental and brigade commanders of promise who were killed early. As these men represented the generations only once and twice removed from Washington, Jefferson, Mason, Harrison, Madison, Monroe, Henry, Pendleton, John Marshall, and all the others, manifestly the intent to produce superior individuals was achieved.

In this achievement, the emphasis on the individual produced throughout the South a strongly characteristic individualism in all the population. It was in this individualism that the Southerner cherished his hot, slumbrous and violent land. Loving his land with a passionately personal identification, he partook of the pride of the imperious plantation masters, and each man was something of a king in all his prideful uniqueness of soul.

Their society has been called "feudal" and "archaic" and less complimentary things, but chiefly it was regarded as "static" as differentiated from the Northern dynamism. Then, as now, the outside critic could never conceive that the static element in his life was what the Southerner loved. Without desire to get on in the material world and without material standards of success by which he was judged, he regarded life as a journey to enjoy. With Cervantes he would say, "The road is better than the inn."

When the North's industrial, conscience burdened "progress" made the Southern hedonist unendurable on the same continent, and when the Northern mercantile-manufacturing class wanted to duplicate England's policy of operating the agricultural region for its benefit, to the confusion of history ever since there was manufactured the handy "issue" of slavery.

The South was not so static that it would never have abolished chattel slavery. In fact, there is a strong probability that the South would have drifted away from chattel slavery soon after 1860 if the vindictiveness of the irresponsible abolitionists had not retarded the emancipation movement in the South. Scarcely more than ten per cent of Southerners were slaveholders in any case; these were growing yearly less and, even with the setback given native emancipation by self-righteous busybodies, the number of responsible emancipationists within the South was growing.

Of equal importance, in Virginia, North Carolina, and Tennessee, and in the Atlanta area, slavery was in a definite state of decline and there was the steady development of industry. In this development of industry, the South never—then or now—wished to be industrialized. It wished for what the currently more prosperously stable communities have achieved—a balance of small (as opposed to monolithic) industries with agriculture and commerce. That the South could have turned to industry on its own is illustrated by the unsung but heroic ingenuity with which an agricultural people, starting with nothing, produced materials of war, including ships, under incredibly unfavorable conditions.

The issue of slavery, which has stigmatized the South's defense of its soil ever since, was a factor which the South and time would have taken care of. There would have been no sudden "freeing of the slaves" because the Southerner—along with Lincoln—recognized the problem of Negroes in a white society. No one can ever know the extent to which efforts at solving this (as yet insoluble) problem were stopped because the South felt compelled to defend what it was. It is this defense of its existence, with the stress on slavery, that has characterized the South historically, and not what the South was defending *in addition to slavery*. Only a fool would believe that ninety per cent of a population would risk and give their lives, dislocate their world, to save the human property of ten per cent.

For the culture which the alliance of Southern States was defending, its people must be regarded as having a life not crucially related to slavery and certainly unrelated to what has become called "the American dream." With Southerners freed of the necessity of defending *all* their institutions against a majority (whose money men wanted to and did exploit the region), slavery would have passed. With its people in a separate, though friendly country, "the American dream" would not have been expected of them.

Expatriate colonies in Paris and Mexico were not founded by seekers of the American dream, nor are Vienna and Florence visited for the study of their principles of American style democracy. Even Ireland has come into a wan and fey fashion admired by fugitives from the American standard. Indeed, it is doubtful if any prosperous nation in the world's history has sent so many expatriates and visitors to places which represented a culture foreign to their own. The South today receives a surprisingly large quota of upper bracket expatriates and commuters who prefer even the vestigial remnants of the plantation society.

From this it can be assumed that the American, despite his verbal conformity, is not satisfied with the greying standardization of today's so-called democracy. No people have ever been so lonely and none have sought so desperately to find identity in crowds. The day of the mass man, producing mass entertainment and mass education and mass standards, has left the resourceless individual in inarticulated need to lose his most priceless gift from God—his mortal self—in crowds.

In an independent Confederacy of the Southern States, none of this would have happened. The confusion today about the Southern States is that the South is seen only as it exists after its destruction in war, its rule by bayonet-supported exploiters, and its reaction to the impact of American democracy.

The destruction by arms and exploitation by the army of occupation caused far more than physical damage. The whole order of the South's ruling class was destroyed. This destruction opened the way for the Southern demagogues—jeered at by the rest of the country as if the rest had no responsibility in producing them, or, indeed, as if Southerners were the only demagogues.

The rise of the lower classes after the war's destruction turned loose in power those who removed from the traditional Southern life its style—its graciousness and high sense of personal honor. These emergent vulgarians, without honor, were only too happy to unite with carpetbaggers and absentee Northern exploiters to sell their own people into the bondage of a conformity to which they could never adapt.

In trying the adaptation, the charming second-flight world capitals of New Orleans, Charleston and Richmond, and countless delightful small cities and towns, all came under the cultural bulldozer of the American dream and, in pathetic fashion, tried to be "like everybody else." The liberal liquor laws of Louisiana permit that small early part of New Orleans called the French Quarter to offer blandishments to tourists; Charleston, in its desuetude, props up the Battery section like a painted corpse; but Richmond, except to the most knowing, has become almost what Mencken once called it, "a suburb to nothing."

Instead of succumbing to this partial levelling process, Southern cities would have flowered in their individual flavor. Doubtless other of the smaller cities would have grown in their own unique identities. Certainly these towns, which missed the savagery of the preservers of the Union, would have retained the warm quality in which the individual would never be lonely enough to seek crowds. This is a physical thing, illustrative of the whole.

That part of the United States which fought as *the* Union would have as a close neighbor (probably as ally in time of war) a society in which the individual dared to be "different," a Southern civilization dedicated to producing the best it had and not the most commonplace. If the two countries could then have worked together, the conservatism of the South would have offered a healthful balance in politics. Ideally, as the Southerner conceived Union, the two countries could have made a reality out of confederation, and progressive-minded Southerners could have taken their talents northward and static-minded Yankees could have sought comfort beside some stream in the South. Essentially the presence of other Americans with a peculiar culture would have served, above all, as a check for the psychotic compulsion to sameness.

Even if the South, allowed its independence, had returned voluntarily with its minority rights assured, frustrated hustlers and operators could have found a haven where they were judged of themselves as individuals and not by the fit of a gray flannel suit. If a man could look at himself squarely and say, "I really do not care about being a success," he could honorably sustain his peculiar genius for life in his own country. This could have sustained the right of the individual and prevented the need of the crowd. Most significantly, this could have sustained the true minorities in a total society and not created the fashion for differentiated minorities. The Southern white people were actually the first—if most arrogant—minority in America. Calhoun, writing eloquently about minority rights, was really very *avant-garde*. The *Union* was not then interested in minorities. It was interested in the rights of the majority, which it established by might.

As of today, where the apostles of social justice are dedicated to minority rights, minority has come not to mean, as the Southerners conceived it, a group specialized by their intentions and responsibilities, but a people specialized by differentiation from the norm. Under that definition, the Southern white is not a minority. He is a backward fellow American who oppresses a minority—the Negroes.

Sinclair Lewis, not noted for his studies of Southern life, in reviewing Thomas Wolfe very favorably, made the reservation that Wolfe excluded the Negro problem from his books. If Negroes are a social problem of America, so did Lewis exclude them from his work—as do most Northern writers. Or, if Negroes by their existence in large numbers in the South, were excluded artistically, so did Edith Wharton exclude the East Side Jews, and Marquand the Boston Irish, and James Farrell the Gold Coast inhabitants of the Lake shores.

A writer writes from his own environment, as Wolfe did. The Negro is not a dominant part of the personal environment of the Southerner as an individual. Negroes appear in all Southern fiction but, except in dramatized writing of accommodation, they do not influence the life of the white Southerner in such vital areas as love and religion, ambition and adaptation. Doubtless the New England manufacturers were no more influenced by the foreigners they exploited. When the foreigner *rises,* he does provide fictional material, but in the South—as in all of America—the Negro does not rise to the point of becoming a problem to society. He stays still and becomes a problem to society. Why should Tom Wolfe be more aware of this social problem than Sinclair Lewis? The fact that Lewis' people turned loose freed Negroes on Wolfe's dispossessed people should have made Lewis the responsible one.

The non-Southern American, in saddling the Southern people with a problem which the Northerner irresponsibly created, has found his own crutch in a social justice of the mind and not the heart, of a fashion and not of practicality. This the Confederate did not need. The Confederate was not lacking in social justice because members of his society continued chattel slavery after the New Englanders, following the abolition of their slave trade, became pious about a matter which concerned them not at all when they were making money from it.

Chattel slavery is, after all, not the only sin a society can commit. That, as of today, it is regarded as sinful, was as true when New Englanders made money out of the slave trade as when Southern planters used Negroes as chattels in the field. The Southerners were caught with the Negro, while the New Englanders had made their money out of the slave and grown moral about the whole thing. But slave labored plantations did not make all Southerners exist only as oppressors of a minority.

Forcible abolition made the lower class white Southerner, especially in the newer Lower South, hate the Negro freed among them in economic rivalry in their postwar debasement. Even this mutually detrimental circumstance would not have happened if the Confederacy could have handled in its own way the abolition of a dated system of labor. In Southern eyes, chattel slavery was *only* a system of labor, a counterpart of the pre-labor-law mills, and the order of the Southern ruling class could have been sustained with only a change in its labor system.

For refusing to change on outside directions, which the responsible Southerner knew would bring chaos to all, his whole historic society has been viewed in a distortion to its purpose and achievements within that purpose. The Confederacy politically—as of that day and under outside pressure—was formed to remove Southern people from non-Southern interference, specifically as regards slavery. But, more fundamentally, it was formed to preserve the rule of specialized minorities in a society of individualists.

Even the fact that such a purpose can, and probably will be, regarded as monstrous in today's verbal insistence on a neutral equality, presents a case for the Confederacy which believed in a distillation of the best.

After all, it was a Southerner, from his non-egalitarian society, who introduced into political philosophy "the pursuit of *happiness*" as the natural order of man.

Jefferson did, however, say "pursuit." He declared all men equal in that *pursuit;* he never intended the phrase to mean, as the social justice "democrats" have perverted it, a total equality in all things by accident of birth. That is against nature. The Confederacy was formed of very natural people. It is their postwar malformation that is usually observed without compassion. As of their own day, before defensiveness set in and then all the horrors, they were people with the courage to accept politically the natural superiority of the superior, and try to found a country in contempt of the levelling of society by mass man.

Today in the South, we are jeered at by ignorant Northern tourists who possess that peculiar gift of derisiveness for anything different, and we are condemned by the half-educated pontificators who deplore our lack of a "progress" which would—if we would only try—make us undistinguishable from everybody else. It must finally be said: The Confederacy was formed, and fought for its life, in order to avoid becoming Americanized.

It achieved its glory in proportion to its difference and it was a sad day for America when another set of values was removed as a balance to middle class, competitive money standards whose goal is to establish a vast, grey anonymity. And if the United States today wish to be more effectual in world relations, our leaders could well begin by recognizing the (however hateful) fact that other peoples wish, as did the Confederates, to avoid Americanization.

Somebody once said, "Money isn't everything." This is a wry joke to Americans, to whom it *is* everything, but our leaders should understand that other people really mean it. The Confederacy lost its fight for independence because it was poor in comparison to the United States. Yet, with all that has happened to its people since the war—and is happening today—the Southerner did not lose his personal identity with his land. He is still a part of something larger than himself.

You will never have to indoctrinate a Southerner in order to get him to fight for his land. His land and himself are one. Of that land, he is an individual among other individuals who walk proudly among inequalities and diversities in acceptance of the natural order of the world. In acceptance of the natural order, he never has to preach what he does not practice. He lives by his heart, and his heart belongs to his land—in all its purblind, parochial and chauvinistic oneness. The Southerner retains the Confederate heritage of love of a place, to the point of dying for it, and, in his way, he is the most practical of all Americans. He values the journey of the moral individual in its brief span on earth.

Though the doctrine of success has influenced him (balefully in spots), like his Confederate ancestors he is most happy where least American. This is certainly intellectual treason, with nothing about it of that "if" of another Virginian, Patrick Henry, but the Confederacy *is* rising again—for the values it defended and the life it fought for. And there are a lot of Yankee converts.

RICHARD M. WEAVER

The South and the American Union

STRETCHING FROM THE Potomac River across the southeastern quarter of the United States in a broad arc into the plains of Texas is a region known geographically and politically as "the South." That this region has been distinctive by reason of its climate, type of produce, ethnic composition, culture, manners, and speech is known to every citizen of the country. That it existed for four years as an independent, if beleaguered, nation is one of the focal chapters of American history. All the while it has been a challenge, never very well met, to Americans to understand themselves historically.

The chief reason for this is that in the minds of most Americans there exists, like an inarticulate premise, the doctrine of American exceptionalism. This assumption is that the United States is somehow exempt from the past and present fate, as well as from many of the necessities, of other nations. Ours is a special creation, endowed with special immunities. As a kind of millenial state, it is not subject to the trials and divisions that have come upon others through time and history. History, it is commonly felt, consists of unpleasant things that happen to other people, and America bade goodbye to the sorrows along with the vices of the Old World.

It must be owned in fairness that two facts lend some plausibility to this seductive notion. One is that the American Union began at a definite point in time. The dates of its origin can be cited by any schoolboy reasonably well up on his books. Its beginning does not have to be traced sketchily in a mist-shrouded antiquity. It became a republic by *fiat,* as it were, and even the documents involved in its creation survive for our inspection.

The second is that this union of States was formed by men who sat down and discussed among themselves principles and ideals before drawing up a form of government. This was, of course, a rational undertaking, which many find more agreeable to remember than the prior fact that the nation owes its existence to the battlefield. The thought of forming a government *de novo* at a definite point in time does therefore encourage the conclusion that here is an exception to history. Our flag-waving orators—and flag-waving historians too— have seldom failed to make special claims for us on the basis of it. The feeling pleases that to be an American carries qualification and exemption.

The Founding Fathers who worked over the problems of government that hot summer of 1787 in Philadelphia, though conscious of their great opportunity, were on the whole realists. They were under no illusion that their creation would be exempt from the trials of history. A great political thinker has written: "The existence of man in political society is historical existence; and a theory of politics, if it penetrates to principles, must at the same time be a theory of history." Most of the State delegates at Philadelphia had read history soberly, and one lesson they had gathered was that evil continuously arises from the nature of man and is capable of perverting the best of institutions to wicked purposes. They desired a government with greater power, yet the problem of restraining that power was never absent from their thoughts. Abuses of power had recently driven them to armed rebellion, and they wanted no more of these. On the other hand, they thought they saw grave dangers in excessive democracy and the anarchy it might produce.

The device which they created out of an awareness of these two perils is, as is well known, a system of checks and balances, whereby any branch of the government, if it took the road to aggrandizement, could be restrained by one or both of the others. As most of the Founding Fathers felt that man needs to be guarded against his own worse impulses, so they believed that government needs to be protected against itself. It was a brilliant conception, which speaks well of their foresight of things, and their realization that the new government would not be exempt from contingencies or the temptations that might dazzle men in future circumstances.

Not everything was taken care of equally well, however. We must remember the heat, the fatigue, the limits of time, the uncertainties, the pressures of private business, and above all a widespread and determined opposition to the structure of union known to be under design. Some sleeping dogs had to be left alone. What about the principle of rebellion, so recently invoked and blessed with success? The Declaration of Independence certainly suggested that the right to rebel was a right inherent in all peoples. Might it not be asserted again sometime? In such case the American revolutionaries might discover that they did but "teach bloody instructions, which, being taught, return to plague the inventor."

What about the true locus of sovereignty in the new nation? The States claimed it, yet the new instrument of government seemed to gather many sovereign powers to itself. Could sovereignty be divided? Was not the idea of a dual sovereignty just a way of deceiving yourself? Of all the questions left unresolved by the new instrument of union, this was to be the most fateful. Yet it was a question too dangerous for this hour, since most of the States were extremely jealous of their rights, and only the most conciliatory attitude could get them to ratify at all. Despite the great influence of Alexander Hamilton, the important State of New York ratified by the slim margin of thirty to twenty-seven and then stated that it did not regard its ratification as irrevocable. Virginia went even further and spelled out in its ordinance of ratification the right to resume the powers thus delegated if Virginia should ever become convinced that they were being abused. North Carolina stayed out for two years until it could be persuaded that its people were not entering a combine that might be perverted to their injury.

When the issue of the scope of Federal power was raised a decade later, in connection with the Alien and Sedition Acts, the famous Kentucky Resolutions, of which Jefferson himself was the author, affirmed that "free government is founded in jealousy, not in confidence; it is jealousy and not confidence which prescribes limited constitutions to bind down those we are obliged to trust with power."

It was resolved accordingly that "the several States composing the United States of America are not united on the principle of unlimited submission to the General Government." These words and actions fairly indicate the attitude of the States in subscribing to the compact of union. Had they then been told they were entering a door which could never be opened again, it is questionable whether a single one would have entered.

The Constitution was, especially in its bill of rights, a creation of eighteenth century classical liberalism, which looked upon the freedom of the individual from state coercion as the highest political object. As John C. Calhoun was to point out later, the constitution of a free state is primarily a *negative* document in the sense that it consists of prohibitions and restraints imposed upon the authority of the state. It is a fixed obstacle to that government by confidence, to echo the language of the Kentucky Resolutions, under which so much oppression in the Old World had been possible. The ways in which men seek power over other men are almost infinitely various and subtle, and it was felt that if the new government were left to judge the extent of its own powers, there could be no way of forestalling eventual tyranny. The true aim of a constitution, from the standpoint of classical liberalism, is not to create empowerments, but to "bind down the powers of men to do mischief." Several, if not most, of the States desired to preserve some form of veto in case that power should exceed its prescribed bounds.

In essence, what the Founders established was a federal republic of limited delegated powers. How limited those powers were was the subject of diverse interpretations. But even in the North at this time Senator Maclay of Pennsylvania could write in his Journal for March 22, 1790: "Is it to be expected that a federal law passed directly against the sense of a whole State will ever be executed in that State?" Now it is necessary to follow some of the great historic forces that turned these questions of freedom and organization into concrete issues.

Even at the time of the Revolution there was an awareness of important differences between North and South. The leaders of that movement did their best to keep them in the background, but they were often mentioned privately. These differences were not merely in economic life, but also in what may be designated as "regime," or gen-

eral way of life. Historical realism shows that people living side by
side do not necessarily grow to resemble one another. They may grow
apart, and this the North and South did rather rapidly after the second
war with Great Britain.

Many attempts have been made to characterize the Northern and
Southern minds; few of them satisfy our perceptions. I am inclined
to think that no account of the mind of the South can be valid unless
it stresses the extent to which the Southerner is classical man. Even
in the South of today one can find surviving large segments of the
classical-Christian-medieval synthesis. It was not unusual for a Southerner of the upper class to steep himself in Roman history and name
his sons after Roman generals. Here the Greek Revival in architecture
had its inception; and here, in the region influenced by Charleston,
the idea of Greek democracy was not only practiced but articulated in
theory, as Vernon Parrington demonstrated in his great work on
American culture. Here law was an exalted profession, and the Cicer-
onian ideal of rhetoric was admired. The fact that the Southerner
stayed wedded to the idea of classical liberalism in government, with
its fixed limitations of power, may be taken as further evidence of his
classical spirit.

The Southern world-outlook was much like that which Spengler
describes as the Apollinian. It knew nothing of infinite progressions
but rather loved fixed limits in all things; it rejected the idea of cease-
less becoming in favor of "simple accepted statuesque becomeness."
It saw little point in restless striving, but desired a permanent settle-
ment, a coming to terms with nature, a recognition of what is in its
self-sustaining form. The Apollinian feeling, as Spengler remarks, is
of a world of "coexistent individual things," and it is tolerant as a
matter of course. Other things are because they have to be; one marks
their nature and their limits and learns to get along with them. The
desire to dominate and to proselytize is foreign to it. As Spengler
further adds, "there are no Classical world-improvers." From this
comes the Southern kind of tolerance, which has always impressed
me as fundamentally different from the Northern kind. It is expressed
in the Southerner's easy-going ways and his willingness to let things
grow where they sprout. He accepts the irremediability of a certain

amount of evil and tries to fence it around instead of trying to stamp it out and thereby spreading it. His is a classical acknowledgment of tragedy and of the limits of power.

This mentality is by nature incompatible with its great rival, the Faustian. Faustian man is essentially a restless striver, a yearner after the infinite, a hater of stasis, a man who is unhappy unless he feels that he is making the world over. He may talk much of tolerance, but for him tolerance is an exponent of power. His tolerance tolerates only the dogmatic idea of tolerance, as anyone can discover for himself by getting to know the modern humanitarian liberal. For different opinions and ways of life he has not respect, but hostility or contemptuous indifference, until the day when they can be brought around to conform with his own. Spengler describes such men as torn with the pain of "seeing men be other than they would have them be and the utterly un-Classical desire to devote their life to their reformation." It happened that Southern tolerance, standing up for the right to coexistence of its way of life, collided at many points with the Faustian desire to remove all impediments to its activity and make over things in its own image. Under the banner first of reform and then of progress, the North challenged the right to continue of a civilization based on the Classical ideal of fixity and stability. Bruce Catton gives a characteristic expression to this Faustian urge when he writes in an article on the Civil War that "America would cease to have room . . . for a feudal plantation economy below the Ohio, veneered with chivalry and thin romance and living in an outworn dream. . . ."

This Southern philosophy of life, which the North has generally regarded as a stumbling block in the road of progress, may be characterized more directly with reference to three things: the creation, the nature of man, and the ends of living.

To most Southerners the term "creation" comes with its literal meaning. The world is something created for man, but certainly not by him. He can understand some of its intermediate principles and relations, but its ultimate secrets are forever beyond him. He is granted some dominion over it, but not an unlimited one, since that would be setting him on a level with the Creator. Basically nature is right in being as it is. Change for its own sake is not good, and many of nature's dispositions are best left as they are. He has a degree of reverence for the natural order of things and he suspects *hubris* in a desire to change that order radically.

Toward man the Southerner takes an attitude inculcated by orthodox religion and by tragedy also. Man is a mixture of good and evil, and he can never be perfected in this life. The notion of his natural goodness is a delusive theory which will blow up any social order that is predicated upon it. Far from being a vessel of divinity, as the New England Transcendentalists taught, he is a container of cussedness. It is fatuity to suppose that his every impulse is good, for many of his impulses are anti-social and some of them are suicidal. He needs to be protected against himself by the teachings of religion, by law, and by custom. The Southerner has always been *conservative* in his view of man in the sense that he has been pessimistic. Yet this kind of pessimism, just because it refuses to fret over optimistic impossibilities, leaves large room for *joie de vivre*. Laughter and good humor have always been native to the region, with the Negro joining in rather freely.

The South's attitude toward the ends of living has deeply influenced its mores and institutions. In the eyes of its energetic neighbor to the north it has never been sufficiently up and doing. But there is a profound difference between accepting your place and your role and working out the most practicable regimen of enjoyments, and conceiving life as an unceasing struggle which has as its object the reordering of everything. "Southern inefficiency" is a notorious phrase, but then "efficiency" is a term out of science and business. If you set little store by science and business, you will not be much influenced by the rhetorical force of "efficiency." True, life cannot be lived without some sense of making progress, but progress may occur through intensification and elaboration; and the art of living in the South remains a rather complex thing. The saying of John Peale Bishop is worth recalling, that the South excelled in two things which the French deem essential to civilization: a code of manners and a native cuisine. Both are apt to suffer when life is regarded as a means to something else. Efficiency and charm are mortal enemies, and Southern charm indubitably derives from a carelessness about the efficient aspects of life.

One further fact is of great consequence: the South has maintained, generally speaking, a social rather than a business civilization; one can scarcely imagine a Southerner's saying, as Calvin Coolidge once said, that "the business of America is business." This means that the claims of business have usually had to yield precedence to what has been considered socially desirable or important. It probably would have been "good business," in one sense, for the South to have maintained a nonsegregated school system: It might have cost less; but financial considerations have been powerless against social objections. Likewise the Southerner has often been chided for asking "Who are you?" rather than "What can you do?" But in a world that spins on an axis of social relations, who you are is more important than your efficiency rating. For the Southerner, things tend to derive their reality and their importance from social, not business life, where personality counts, and manners are a deference to personality.

In one of the novels of F. Hopkinson Smith there occurs the story of an old Virginia gentleman who lived on a decayed plantation. Whenever visitors came, he insisted on directing the conversation to the past glories of the ancestral hall. On one occasion he mentioned, purely incidentally, that there were coal outcroppings on the estate. This led to the discovery of extensive coal deposits, which eventually launched the old gentleman into prosperity. But he had not thought the matter of coal worth discussing beside what one ancestor had done at Williamsburg and another at Yorktown. His was a world of human relations. The relative incapacity for business of the Southerner has cost him sadly in this acquisitive world. The choice involves, of course, the contentious subject of the order of values.

While these attitudes were growing deep-rooted in the South, the North was developing in a different direction. Its world outlook traces back fairly clearly to the Reformation and the Puritan Revolution. Especially was the Puritan mentality influential upon the North. A reformist type of mind, it was indifferent toward tradition, inclined to be suspicious of the arts and graces as snares set by the Evil One, and proudly conscious of a duty to make the world over. This Northern or "Yankee" mind, which has been received by the world as the typical American mind, is excellently shaped and disciplined for success in the practical sphere. It focuses sharply, knows how to keep feeling under restraint; it is shrewd in estimating practical consequences. There has never been such a mind for getting things done.

But as always in this ambiguous world, positive qualities carry liabilities in their train, and this mind does not always impress others favorably. To some it seems too insistent on the explicit, too lacking in depths and psychic recesses, too deprived of what might be called resonance. To some it appears like a house kept in perfect neatness and order, but lacking in charm. When the Southerner or the European or the Latin American communicates with this dust-free, unencumbered mind, he finds that things which are significant to him strike no response. Especially is this true of matters of sentiment, and he finds shocking the relegation of sentiment to a kind of Sunday-morning observance. The tendency seems to be to think scientifically and hence abstractly in the interest of manipulation rather than concretely out of respect or pleasure in contemplation. Local attachments seem dragweights, and allegiance is given, as Tocqueville pointed out, to something large and grandiose. States' rights do not mean much unless you have learned to know and to prize the special contours of your State.

Nowhere has the Northern mind more clearly embraced the Faustian concept than in the idea of progress. There is the constant outreaching, the denial of limits, the willingness to dissolve all into endless instrumental activity, to which even some American philosophers have supplied theoretical support. Hence the incessant urge to be doing, to be transforming, to effect some external change between yesterday and today. The mood of the Americans, another French critic of a century ago remarked, is that of an army on the march. The language of conquest fills the air. They will "master nature"; they will "attack problems"; they will "control energy"; they will "overcome space and time." The endlessness of progress in these terms is the most generally accepted dogma. And thus enchanted by the concept of an infinite expansion, they reject the classical philosophy as too constricting.

The Southerner, to sum up the contrast, has tended to live in the finite, balanced, and proportional world which Classical man conceived. In Cicero and Horace he has found congenial counsellors about human life. The idea of stasis is not abhorrent to him, because it affords a ground for the identity of things. Life is not simply a linear progression, but a drama, with rise and fall. Happiness may exist as much in contemplation as in activity. Experience alone is not good; it has to be accompanied by the human commentary. From this, I believe, has come the South's great fertility in myth and anecdote. It is not so much a sleeping South as a dreaming one, and out of dreams come creations that affect the imagination.

In this way two civilizations of quite different impulse grew up in the United States. Was it inevitable that one should make war on the other and offer it the alternative of being "reconstructed" or perishing? It was not inevitable if you believe that the coexistence of unlike beings is possible. Diversity is a rule of nature, and it would be ideal if the cultures of the world would practice a doctrine of live and let live. It would also be ideal if empires and large nations would consent to a separation of their parts in times of irreconcilable difference. When personalities begin to clash in a household, it is often best for one party to remove and set up an independent establishment of its own. This is what the Americans did in 1775; and the British, taught by this painful experience and others, have since recognized the right to withdraw from the Empire. The Soviet Union has written the principle of secession into its constitution. But the Americans of the North and West have generally viewed the idea as scandalous—or perhaps as blasphemous against the notion of the perfected millenial state.

The events leading up to the historical separation of the two sections are too well known to need detailed review. Economic and political disagreements arose to accentuate the underlying differences. The first issue to poison the relations between North and South following the "Era of Good Feeling" was the tariff. It is unquestionable that the protective tariff has worked great injury to the South from that date until, as one might say, the South was partly transformed into an image of the North through industrialization. For the interest of the South as a region producing agricultural surpluses has historically lain in free trade. The South sent abroad rice, indigo, cotton, and tobacco and took in exchange the manufactured products of Europe. The North began to use the Federal Union to put an artificially high price upon manufactured goods in order to help its industries. The South was thereby forced into the position of selling cheap and buy-

ing dear. All this meant that the agrarian way of livelihood, characterized by Jefferson as the most innocent form of vocation, could not
be continued except under penalty of a heavy tax. As Abbott Law-
rence of Massachusetts wrote to Daniel Webster regarding the tariff
of 1828: "This bill if adopted as amended will keep the South and
West in debt to New England for the next hundred years." If the
South had ever been able to save and fuse what was taken from it
by the protective tariff system, it could have afforded a Harvard and
a Yale, with a few Amhersts, Dartmouths, and Williamses thrown in
for good measure.

There was of course the curse of slavery. During the Civil War one
ingenious Northern general pronounced the Negroes to be "contrabands." Contrabands they may well have been from the beginning,
and I have often wondered why the sellers of this article were not
held more reprehensible than the users, as is true of those who peddle
cocaine. A large number of these hapless slaves were brought to America in New England bottoms, and more than one fortune in Newport
and New Bedford owes its origin to profits in black flesh. The facts
could be represented thus: New England sold the slaves to the South,
then later declared their possession immoral and confiscated the holding. The morality of the case was less clear to the Southerners than to
the agitators of Boston, and even Lincoln, if we may judge by his less
political utterances, tended to believe in the common guilt of the
nation.

Alienation of the sections was widened by mutual attacks upon
character. Some of these reached an extreme of violence which one
would hardly associate with Victorian America. A few were the
products of reformist agitators giving way to their feelings, but an
appreciable number seem to have been the work of the new journal-
ism, which finds it profitable to stir up strife by assailing character,
even if the character is that of a straw man. The South, which had
more than its share of pride, retorted with frantic boast and foolish
word. It certainly went out of its way to wound Northern vanity. It
charged the North with having the deadly virtues of the middle class
while claiming for itself the virtues of the chivalric age. On the whole,
the South did not have a clear picture of itself or its resources. Being

long on the defensive and seeing the tide running against it, the South created a number of phantasms which were to serve it ill. This is what that dour North Carolinian Hinton Helper tried to point out in his *The Impending Crisis*.

Whether the grievances of these States were sufficient to justify a withdrawal from the Union has been argued long and voluminously. Political separations of this kind, as Jefferson observed in the Declaration of Independence, should not be undertaken for light and transient causes. On the other hand, as Calhoun was later to argue, making the Federal government the sole judge and umpire of its authority would be setting up an engine of government from which there would be no kind of appeal. To take the position that every State remained forever a member of the Union, whether it liked it or not and whether it suffered by the association or not, certainly involved grave assumptions of political authority. There is at least as much idealism in the statement of Lee that "a Union held together by bayonets has no charms for me" as in the claim that the Union is forever indivisible. The Southern position goes back, in political theory, to the principle that there are some matters on which a majority cannot override a minority.

The South has always maintained that in this great quarrel it had the law on its side. Its case for the legality of secession rested upon an interpretation of the Constitution in the light of its creation. This contended that the Federal Union was a compact of limited, delegated authority, to which the States voluntarily acceded between 1787 and 1789. The *Federalist Papers* had referred to the States as "distinct and independent sovereigns." Madison, writing in the *Federalist No. 39*, had said: "The proposed government cannot be deemed a NATIONAL one; since its jurisdiction extends to certain enumerated objects only, and leaves to the several States a residuary and inviolable sovereignty over all other objects." These expressions became common currency of the discussion. It would be cynical to assume that this was mere bait, held out to catch reluctant fish which thereafter would be permanently hooked. Surmises of the kind, however, could have been in the minds of New York, Virginia, and other cautious signers. Later one of the textbooks on political science taught at West Point—

and this has important bearing upon the decisions of Southern officers in 1861—was William Rawle's *View of the Constitution of the United States,* which accepted the doctrine of State sovereignty.

Legally, secession was seen by the Southern States simply as a repeal of the ordinances of ratification they had adopted 70 years earlier. In the Southern continuum, 70 years is nothing. When South Carolina voted 120 to 0 to rescind her ratification, she was repealing in her sovereign capacity what she had enacted in her sovereign capacity. The enactment of secession was not treason under any written law. It might have been treason to a concept, but that is an extra-legal matter, and the concept was not the South's. When Bruce Catton struggles to characterize the heinousness of secession, he can only soar upon wings of metaphor and call it "a wanton laying of hands upon the Ark of the Covenant."

For an American political leader, Abraham Lincoln has a remarkable record of consistency, but on this matter he was not consistent. Speaking in the House of Representatives on January 12, 1848, he made as good a case for the right of secession as the most ardent Southern separatist could have wished for. With reference to Texas and the incidents which had led to the Mexican War, he said:

> Any people anywhere, being inclined and having the power, have the *right* to rise up, and shake off the existing government, and form a new one that suits them better. This is a most valuable —a most sacred right—a right, which we hope and believe is to liberate the world. Nor is this right confined to cases in which the whole people of an existing government, may choose to exercise it. Any portion of such people that *can, may* revolutionize, and make their *own,* of so much territory as they inhabit.

But thirteen years later, when faced with a concrete instance of this, he saw secession in an entirely opposite way. Then a portion of a people of a government, having their own territory, revolutionized and set up a government of their own. He countered their claim of right to do this by saying that he had taken an oath to support the Constitution, and that furthermore every nation has an inherent duty to protect its integrity. The objections to this position, as the South saw them, were that the Constitution was silent on the question of secession, and that the right to revolution was a right inherent in the people if the American Revolution had any ideological basis. It was not without reason that Southerners in 1861 said, "I am no more frightened by the word 'rebel' than were my forefathers in 1775."

During the War, the western counties of the State of Virginia, having been for decades at odds politically with the remainder of the State, withdrew and set up a State of their own. The Federal government showed no compunction about the legality of this secession, for West Virginia was admitted as an independent State in 1863 and has never been "reconstructed" into Virginia. In this instance Lincoln seems to have reversed himself again and to have upheld the right to revolutionize which he had emphasized in his speech on the Mexican War. It begins to look like a matter of whose ox is gored.

Another case in point is the treatment of Jefferson Davis. The passions of the victorious side demanded that he be arrested and tried for treason, and he spent about two years in prison at Fortress Monroe. But when the task of getting up the prosecution was undertaken, it was realized that there was no law under which he could be convicted—this, it should be added, was a pre-Nuremberg doubt, which troubled men in a day when nations were unwilling to invent *ex post facto* law by which to hang defeated enemies. Acquittal would have been a great embarrassment to the victors, who had no desire to lose in court what they had won in war. Therefore Davis, instead of being hanged on a sour apple tree, went free with no other penalty than disqualification for office-holding, which was provided by the newly enacted Fourteenth Amendment.

Thus the South has remained convinced that whatever the differing moral views of slavery and secession, it had the law on its side as the law had come down from 1787. From the standpoint of these considerations, perhaps the best description of the terrible conflict which ensued is that of Gerald Johnson, who called it a war between "the Law and the Prophets." On the side of the South was the law, with its promise of respect for the sovereignty of the States and its recognition of slavery. It was with reference to this that Alexander Stephens, vice-president of the Confederacy, was to entitle his apologia *A Constitutional View of the Late War Between the States*. On the side of the North were the prophets of emancipation, industrialization, and nationalization. Of these the most potent was nationalization, and it should be remembered that Lincoln professed his willingness to preserve slavery if by so doing he might preserve the Union.

The potency contained in the cry "Union" at this time must always be of curious interest to students of political psychology. "Union" became in the North the paramount slogan of the War, and the popular term of opprobrium applied to Confederates was not "slaveholders," but "secesh." Middle Westerners in particular favored "saving the Union," sometimes to the exclusion of all other issues involved. What was there to make the idea of union sacred?

Considered in its essence, union is an instrumentality of power. This fact appears in the common saying that "in union there is strength." But what is this strength wanted for? Unless it has some clearly understood applicability, the mere preservation of union is a means without an end. And because one of the prime purposes of the idealistic founders of the nation was to check the growth of a centralized, autonomous power, the things that have been done in the name of "Union" might lead one to say that it is the darling of the foes rather than of the friends of the American experiment in free government. H. L. Mencken once observed that there are, of course, advantages in union, but that they usually go to the wrong people. They usually go to the ones whose real interest is in power and the wielding of it over other men. The instrumentality of union, with its united strength and its subordination of the parts, is an irresistible temptation to the power-hungry of every generation. The strength of union may first be exercised in the name of freedom, but once it has been made monopolistic and unassailable, it will, if history teaches anything, be used for other purposes.

One cannot feign surprise, therefore, that thirty years after the great struggle to consolidate and unionize American power, the nation embarked on its career of imperialism. The new nationalism enabled Theodore Roosevelt, than whom there was no more staunch advocate of union, to strut and bluster and intimidate our weaker neighbors. Ultimately it launched America upon its career of world imperialism, whose results are now being seen in indefinite military conscription, mountainous debt, restriction of dissent, and other abridgements of classical liberty. We must be "unified" at home so that we can be strong abroad—indeed, there are now those who would outlaw party division over foreign policy. But why does one have to be strong abroad? From the clear perspective which the Founding Fathers seem to have enjoyed, Charles Pinckney of South Carolina observed: "Conquest or superiority among other powers is not, or ought not ever to be, the object of republican systems." But this was not the view of those who were to make use of the great consolidation effected by the Civil War.

To the mass of soldiers in blue and to the Northern civilians, "Union" seems to have been a kind of mystique—a vague attitude against which political and metaphysical demonstrations of reserved rights had no power to make an impression. "Union" was hypostatized and bowed down to, and the question of whether separation does not have some advantages also was ruled out as not in keeping with the times. The material fact is that under this potent cry the union of the United States was shifted in 1865 from a basis of voluntary consent to one of force.

When the Joint Committee on Reconstruction presented its report in 1866, it opened with a terse description. "They [the Southern States] were in a state of utter exhaustion, having protracted their struggle against Federal authority until all hope of successful resistance had ceased, and layed down their arms only because there was no longer any power to use them. The people of those States were left bankrupt in their public finances and shorn of the private wealth which had before given them power and influence."

This might appear a situation dire enough, yet the South still had to face about a dozen years of having its bones picked. To make real what went on during the years of so-called "Reconstruction" demands the pen of a novelist, and it is regrettable in a way that this chapter of our national history has not received more attention from creative writers. Lincoln had taken the view that the States were really never out of the Union, and had mentioned that if in any Southern State ten per cent of the population—surely a curious fraction, but perhaps the best that could be hoped for—were found "loyal," that State might resume its standing and function within the Union. But this was, as Professor E. Merton Coulter has pointed out, a conservative solution, and no such thing was in the minds of the Radical Junto which took over after Lincoln's death. They saw their chance "not only to remake Southerners in many respects that had no direct relationship to the war; they would also remake the Union by not only degrading the Southern States but in the process also depriving all States of much of their power and bestowing it upon the central government. Here was the fruition of a growth in extremism evident in the North long before the war broke out, but now made easy by that war's having been fought."

Under their program the Southern States were to be held in the Union as far as the purposes of rule and exploitation went, but kept out of the Union as far as rights and the ability to protest effectively were concerned. This was a method of having the States and eating them too, and it was highly profitable both politically and financially.

The invading army was in control. Down from the North swarmed carpetbaggers looking for a good thing, and up popped scalawags ready to assist them. The Negro, who, it must be admitted, behaved considerably better than circumstances might have warranted, was a useful auxiliary. State governments were set up consisting of outsiders with various axes to grind, the scum of the local populace, and the misled and eventually victimized freedmen. There ensued a carnival of debauchery, corruption, and political buffoonery such as no other modern nation has witnessed. In a hundred ways, kangaroo legislatures robbed the stricken people not only of their present but of their future substance also. Over the whole affair hangs an aura of unreality, so that even the most cynical might question how this was possible after a hundred years of American traditions. The best verdict on Reconstruction was written by Richard Harvey Cain, a Negro editor of Charleston: "When the smoke and fighting is over, the Negroes have nothing gained, the whites have nothing left, while the jackals have all the booty." It is proof of the public morality which existed in the Southern people as a whole that these States were eventually able to recover, instead of sinking permanently to the level of the worst mismanaged Latin American countries.

William A. Dunning, the Columbia professor of history, expressed admiration for the way in which Reconstruction was carried out against "a hostile white population, a hostile executive at Washington, a doubtful if not decidedly hostile Supreme Court, a divided Northern sentiment with regard to Negro suffrage, and an active and skillfully directed Democratic Party." On the same principle one might express admiration for the way in which the South managed to preserve some remnants of its civilization against an invading army and an alien and partly disaffected race, with a government in which it was not represented claiming authority over it. Some of the means, for example the Ku Klux Klan, were irregular, but essentially it was the political genius of Jefferson, of Washington, of Madison, and Pinckney expressing itself in times of trouble and oppression.

The nightmare of Reconstruction ended in 1877, after the South, in a frank "deal" to get rid of the occupying forces, decided not to contest the election whereby the Republican Hayes had fraudulently won over Tilden. But it was another twenty years before the South was able to struggle back to its feet economically, and it was even longer before it could begin the establishment of an adequate school system. There was no Marshall Plan for the Southern States. Instead, the South's economic disadvantage was prolonged, if not intensified, by even higher protective tariffs and by its contributions to national pensions for a clamorous GAR.

The era of Reconstruction is thus an indelible memory in Southern minds. In effect the period was a forging process which hardened the South's determination not to be assimilated into the national pattern, but to preserve her character and autonomy in all ways that could not be prevented. The palpable unfairness of the era even brought recruits to the South's side, for Kentucky, which had been divided during the war, turned pro-Southern and Democratic in politics as soon as it saw the uses that were being made of the victory. If, as President Edwin Alderman of the University of Virginia wrote, "under the play of great historic forces this region developed so strong a sense of unity in itself as to issue in a claim of separate nationality, which it was willing to defend in a great war," it seems equally true that its experience during the great upheaval confirmed the feeling that is was in spirit and needs a separate nation. It might be viewed as an American Ireland, Poland, or Armenia, not indeed unified by a different religious allegiance from its invader, but different in its way of life, different in the values it ascribed to things by reason of its world outlook, and made more different after the war by its necessary confrontation of the tragic view, which success and optimism were holding in abeyance in the North. The South has in a way made a religion of its history, or its suffering, and any sign of waning faith or laxness of spirit may be met by a reminder of how this leader endured and that one died, in the manner of saints and saviors. It has, in fact, its hierarchy of saints, and the number of public tributes offered up to Lee and Jackson must run to untold thousands. Being a Southerner is definitely a spiritual condition, like being a Catholic or a Jew; and members of the group can recognize one another by signs which are eloquent to them, though too small to be noticed by an outsider.

There are some who will say that this is talk of old, unhappy, far-off things, and battles long ago. But a nation is made what it is by its past; there is no identity without historicity. And the South, far from being ashamed of its past, as a good many outsiders seem to assume, is proud of it just because that past is a story of resistance to many things urged or forced upon it from the outside. If these things are added together, they will be seen to comprise rather completely what is known as modernism or "progress." In the political field the South has resisted nationalization and centralization of authority, sometimes with cannon and musket, and sometimes with political maneuver, as in the case of the States' Rights Party of 1948. In the economic and financial field, there has been an instinctive opposition to industrialism; and if the spirit is not very conspicuous now, it has flourished strongly enough in the past to warn the South against mechanization and standardization. Southerners owe a debt of gratitude to Russell Kirk, who comes from Michigan, for pointing out that "Despite its faults of head and heart, the South—alone among the civilized communities of the nineteenth century—had hardihood sufficient for an appeal to arms against the iron new order, which, a vague instinct whispered to most Southerners, was inimical to the sort of humanity they knew." The historic South has been indeed "unprogressive," but defiantly so and on principle.

Pragmatists have never been able to convince the South that religion is just another one of the cylinders of the engine that produces "progress." The South retains a belief that religion is the expression of man's poetic, tragic, and metaphysical intuitions of life, and that as such religion is tied neither to science nor utility. Hence the South's famous fundamentalism and literalism, the footwashings of the primitive Baptists, the doctrinal rigor of Southern Presbyterians. Believing in the necessity of man's redemption, the people—especially country people—typically like preachers who preach hell fire and damnation better than those who put their faith in psychiatry and socialism. The preference is essentially for the older religiousness, such as one finds before the age of rationalism.

By the same token, the South has never lost sight of the fact that society means structuring and differentiation, and that "society" and "mass" are antithetical terms. It has never fallen for a simple equalitarianism, nor has it embraced the sentimentalism that anyone on the bottom *ipso facto* belongs on top. Its classes have gotten along together with surprisingly little envy because they have been fused into a society by a vision which has kept subordinated the matter of varying degrees of success in the pursuit of money. Because the mass looks with hatred upon any sign of the structuring of society, the South has been viewed with special venom by Socialist and Communist radicals, past and present. One of their prime goals is to break down the South's historic social structure and replace it with a mass condition reflecting only materialist objectives.

These facts and others which could be cited mean that the South remains a great stronghold of humanism, perhaps the greatest left in the Western World. It has opposed by word and deed the kind of future portended by George Orwell's *1984*. In doing so it has developed considerable toughness and resourcefulness, and it has never run from a fight. Its people still have no desire to be pulled in and made to conform to a regimented mass state, by which homes that look like homes, whether in Tidewater or in the Blue Ridge, must give way to the ant-colonies of public housing, and the traditional courtesy of a region must change into "public relations."

Today the South is faced with fresh assaults upon its regime and its order of values. All the while it has known that what grudging respect it has obtained from the North has come because the South has maintained the standards of white civilization. It knows that if it were to accept without reservation the dictates of the Supreme Court, it might be turned into something like those "mixed sections" found in large Northern cities. Such sections are there spoken of in whispers, and those who have the money flee as from the plague when they find a neighborhood beginning to "go." The South cannot learn these facts from Northern newspapers and journals, which maintain a curious attitude of unreality upon the subject. But it notes the behavior of Northerners who come South to live; it learns of the plummeting of Northern real estate values where "integration" is on the march; and if a Southerner happens to journey North, he finds the hotels and resorts conspicuously unmixed. As Bishop Hugh McCandless of New York's Protestant Episcopal Church of the Epiphany recently admitted: "What the North generally has done is to accept the social conventions of the South, while condemning the reasons for those conventions." Naturally the Southerner wonders from what area of the Northern consciousness the great outcry against segregation comes.

For such reasons, the Supreme Court's decretal has to it the look of a second installment of Reconstruction. As the first was inspired by vengeance, so this looks inspired by a desire to impeach the South and to impose upon it conditions which have generally proved impossible even where the obstacles were far less. The South knows that in wide areas a forced integration would produce tensions fatal to the success of education. It believes that the advice of Booker T. Washington to the Negro, though not the easiest, is still the best. Let the Negroes cultivate excellence. When they create something that the world desires, the world will come and ask to have it, and will have to accept it on the Negroes' terms. That is the way other races have raised themselves, and it is the only permanent way. The South's decision to resist the new forward motion of the centralizing and regimenting impulse has won it support in the North among those who see the issue of authority as transcending this particular application.

The question of whether the South deserves separate nationality will today be dismissed as academic. It has not forgotten its tremendous sacrifices in the bid for independence, as its innumerable Confederate monuments, its continuing Confederate pensions, and its odes to the Confederate dead testify. And with the United States insisting on independence for this and that country half way around the world —independence for Czechoslovakia, independence for Indo-China, independence for Korea, independence for Israel—it has certainly been handsome of the South not to raise the question of its own independence again. But putting this aside as one of those considerations which may be logical but are politically fantastic, let us turn to the role of the South in the future of the Union.

Many years ago a Southern speaker in a eulogy of George Washington predicted that at some distant date the nation would again need to look to such a man for its salvation. He based this upon a prophecy that one day the nation would arrive at such an embittered tangle of animosities, brought on by the clashing of pressure groups, the contradictions of opportunistic policy, and the blindness of relativist doctrines that it could no longer save itself by ordinary means. There would be no recourse but to turn to a man of pure, disinterested, and unshakable character to lead it out of the impasse produced by snarling self-interest and the obscuring of principles.

Washington is in many ways the prototype of the Southerner. His image adorned the Great Seal of the Confederacy; he has been, with Lee, the beau ideal of the conservative section.

Broadening this somewhat, I am inclined to believe seriously that the nation may one day have to look to the South for leadership as it once looked to the Virginia planter and soldier. If the future of the world shapes up as a gigantic battle between communism and freedom, there is not the slightest doubt as to where the South will stand. It will stand in the forefront of those who oppose the degrading of man to a purely material being, and it will continue to fight those who presume to direct the individual "for his own good" from some central seat of authority. On this matter, its record is perfectly clear. The South has opposed scientific materialism while the rest of the nation mocked it for being old-fashioned. If it has had little use for evolution, neither has it had any for Marxism. It has maintained a respect for personality while other sections were tending to relegate personality to the museum of antiquities. It has proved its conviction that when principles are at stake, economics is nowhere. Though it believes in coexistence, as I tried to show earlier, it is quick to scent the kind of aggressor that makes coexistence impossible—and hence, I think, its readiness to arm in 1940–41. By all the standards that apply, the South has earned the moral right to lead the nation in the present and coming battle against communism, and perhaps also in the more general renascence of the human way of life. The stone which the builders have so persistently rejected may become the headstone of the building. This would not be a new thing in history, and the present trend of events indicates to me that it is in the making.

One quality of the Southerner has a special relevance here. Over most of the free world today one sees an alarming loss of confidence in self in the upper or guiding classes. They seem weary of the past, disillusioned by the forces that created them, pessimistic about their future. Even a suicidal motif appears, and they are found subsidizing and even fighting for those forces which would avowedly destroy them. They go in for "liberalism," for socialism, even for communism; and if they think of resistance at all, it is usually in terms of appeasement. They seem ready for extinction by the first rude barbarian who says, "I will."

To this the South is an exception. The reverses to which the Southerner has been subjected and the great enginery of propaganda which has been directed against him have never been able to break his belief in himself. His self-confidence, sometimes irritating to those who lack it, comes from a knowledge that he stands in a central human tradition, and that the virtues which stem from this, though they may sometimes pass out of fashion, are never out of season. About certain matters he has an "unyielding stability of opinion," often complained of, but a priceless asset when the foundations of things are being threatened.

It may be that after a long period of trouble and hardship, brought on in my opinion by being more sinned against than sinning, this unyielding Southerner will emerge as a providential instrument for the saving of this nation. With pragmatists and relativists giving away the free world bit by bit, his willingness to fight with an intransigent patriotism may be the one thing that can save the day from the darkness gathering in Eastern Europe and Asia. If that time should come, the nation as a whole would understand the spirit that marched with Lee and Jackson and charged with Pickett.

JAMES McBRIDE DABBS

The Land

LET US BEGIN with a few basic facts.

The Southern economy, originally agrarian, is industrializing at an accelerating pace. This process has been going on more or less steadily since about 1880. Its inception was marked by Henry Grady's popularization of the phrase "the New South"—meaning the industrial South. If a State is to be called industrial when its manufactured products are more valuable than its agricultural products, then some Southern States already are industrial. How far this swing will go, no one knows. Tremendous industrial advances still lie ahead.

There is no reason to believe, however, that in any clearly foreseeable future farming will cease to be one of the main sources of income in the South. The climate is bland; the rainfall is generally sufficient, and annually it is brought under greater control by reservoirs, ranging in size all the way from half-acre farm ponds to the lakes of the TVA; the soil, with better methods of farming, becomes increasingly productive. It is true, this demands enormous quantities of commercial fertilizer, the cost of which puts the Southern farmer at a disadvantage relative to farmers of more fertile areas; but the advantage of a climate suited to a wide variety of crops more than offsets this disadvantage.

The factories, then, will continue to climb the hills and infiltrate the valleys of the South, the role of the farmer will for some time grow relatively less important, but there is no reason to believe that farming will become a marginal activity.

The shift toward industrialization is also a shift toward urbanization. A smaller proportion of the population will live scattered over

69

the countryside, a larger proportion will be concentrated in cities, towns, and villages. This is important, because farm life characteristically reflects the wide-spacing of people in the physical scene. The increase of industries may also be expected to increase the population of the South. It is not yet clear, however, just what residential pattern the coming of the mills will foster. It seemed for a time that the early mill village, company owned and controlled, was on its way out. Industries were selling their villages; workers were driving in from the countryside, over paved roads, for many miles. Now, again, mill towns are being built. They are better mill towns, it is true, but still subject to close company control; and factories, parachuted as it were from flying boxcars into lonely countrysides, find mill houses clustering around them like chickens about the mother hen. To the degree that this happens the coming of industry changes not only the productive efforts of a people but their residential habits.

The process changes also the life of the farmers who are left. The farm is being mechanized and power-driven. Gasoline engines and attached equipment replace human hands and mule power. The industries of the North, and now of the South, build the machines; the farmers buy them to maintain production with less labor or make increased production possible; this increased production throws some farmers and farm laborers out of jobs, and these now landless men flock to the towns to be absorbed into business, the distributive trades, or into industry itself—thus accelerating the movement toward industrialization. It is immediately apparent that those weeded out by the machines are the less efficient, intelligent and able. It is one thing to handle a hoe, though I early learned, watching my father's flashing hoe among the grass and cotton, that there is skill even in that; it is another thing to operate a tractor cultivating two or four rows. And when the tractor-drawn rotary hoes begin to lessen the work of the manual hoes, and the tractor-drawn plows to push aside the single-mule "Dixies," it is the rare hoe-hand or plow-hand who climbs to the tractor seat and takes over. Most of them just can't make it.

The substitution of high priced machinery for human labor raises the capitalization of the farm, and, within limits, gives the edge to the farmer with the most resources. The capital it takes to go into successful farming today has been estimated at from $25,000 up. A Master

Farmer of South Carolina said recently that, if a man wanted to go into farming really to make a business success of it, he should have about $70,000. If the old style farmer had $70,000, he'd already be such a success that he'd retire. It is in a sense an unhappy day when the poor farmer with one lean mule, one wagon, one "Dixie," one sweep, one hog, one cow, one wife and "ten head of chillun" can't go to the banker when spring is in the air, and sign away everything, including the labor of said wife and children, for the chance to farm again. But such "free enterprise" has become increasingly difficult. I sympathize with the poor devil who longs not only to eat but also to walk bare-footed in the fresh plowed furrows of spring. I do not sympathize with the banker who so uses his financial power as to keep the South a low wage area. Too often he doesn't object to the presence in the South of the poor devils with ten "chillun" and a mule; he merely objects to lending this fellow three hundred dollars to go into farming on his own.

But we gain certain benefits from the change. Farming as a whole becomes more stable. In the past, when anybody could get into farm-ing, with a rise in the price of cotton everybody got into farming, and we all went down again. The present higher capitalization of the aver-age farm serves as a control. Such a farmer does not make extreme in-creases or decreases in his planned production: His equipment does not allow for it, and the prudence which his situation indicates he probably possesses does not suggest it.

The question arises here as to whether there is a limit to the increas-ing capitalization of the farm, and if so what it is. If some bigness pays on the farm—as it undoubtedly does—how much bigness pays most? Are we headed for incorporated farms and "factories in the fields"?

No one knows how much bigness pays most. It depends primarily upon the kind of crop produced, secondarily upon the character of the manager. I think it may be said, however, that with all our trend to increasing capitalization, there is no particular tendency to immense incorporated farms. A few of them have existed for decades; but the present consolidation of industry, which has grown for the past fifteen years and has brought continual challenge from the national govern-ment, has no counterpart in farming. One reason probably is that farming is far more complex than industry, and does not lend itself so

successfully to unified control. The extensive farm easily becomes un-
manageable, and begins to yield less on the investment than the
smaller farm.

As for the "factories in the fields," it is true that we have in the
coastal truck areas of the South a good deal of concentration and
streamlining in processing and packing, and the related use of transient labor during the harvesting period. It is exceedingly doubtful,
however, if this type of operation will become widespread in the South.

I said earlier that unskilled laborers and inefficient managers are being driven from the farm. But often it is the better ones who are leaving. One of the standard complaints of the Southern farmer is that as
soon as he has trained a good machine operator, the worker picks up
and goes to town to drive a truck or up North to work at what-you-
please. A farmer friend of mine even philosophizes this situation by
saying, "What do you expect? The farms are supposed to take care of
the trifling people who can't do anything else." Maybe this was true
in the past, but with mechanization the pace grows faster and the old
customs will change. Right now the South is in the position of having
machines too complicated for its operators, for the simple reason that
we have been far more concerned to develop our mechanical resources
than our human resources. But more of this later.

It is not enough to ask, What size farm is the most successful farm?
This masks a more fundamental question: What is a successful farm?
Is success on the farm to be equated with success in business? Can it
be read simply in black and red on a ledger?

The answer is, it cannot. There is more involved than the ledger.
If there were not, farmers would generally quit farming and take up
industrial work, or go into business or a profession. For the ledgers
look better in all of these fields than in farming. You may say, of
course, that farmers haven't generally kept ledgers, and do not realize,
until the sheriff comes, that they are failing. There is some truth in
this. I think, however, that, in spite of the prevalent lack of ledgers,
farmers generally realize that they don't succeed as well financially as
most other groups. Nowadays, the government reports continually remind us of this, and the power of the farm bloc in Washington indicates that we know it; but I seriously doubt if many of us really think

we are going to make as much as other groups in the economy: We simply object to being overlooked.

Farmers can't make as much money simply because they can't produce as much goods. The goods they do produce are essential; their output will not be overlooked. But the rewards they receive will generally be in proportion to the amount of goods produced, and the farm simply cannot be streamlined and controlled to the extent the factory can, and therefore cannot produce as much goods per man as the factory. The areas of production involved are greater, the productive processes more complex, and, because they are concerned with living and not inert matter, far less controllable. It would be fairly safe to say, then, that any man who goes into farming merely to make money, makes a mistake; he would do better elsewhere. Of course, he may be making a mistake in evaluating his own motives; he may be going into farming for something besides money; or he may discover this something as he goes along.

Granted, then, that many people keep on farming from ignorance of the ledger, and also, as must be true, from inertia, and from sheer lack of economic power to make a change, it yet remains that success in farming is more than financial success. The problem, then, is this: As the Southern farmer takes on more of the power, and assumes the mechanical aspects and to some degree the financial aspects of modern industry, how is he to avoid taking on the simple measure of success which industry knows—monetary profit? How far shall he go along the road he is traveling? How can he know when he has reached his proper limit? The answer to these questions lies in the answer to the question, What is the nature of success on the farm? That had better wait until we come to a consideration of farming as a way of life.

So much for the broad economic picture of Southern farming. What are the political implications? The most evident political comments about Southern farming apply also to American farming. American farming is in politics and politics is in American farming. It may be too much in. In that case, the process of extricating the victim is a political question. I am not concerned primarily with the national question of the proper relation of agriculture to the total economy; I am concerned primarily with the Southern question, the relation of Southern agriculture to the economy of the South. We may note in passing the existence of severe political controls upon the growing of cotton, tobacco, and wheat. Such controls may well increase the acre-age of other crops or introduce crops not at present known in the South. However important this possibility may be, it is incidental to the concern of this essay; my concern is the inner nature of Southern farming and its significance as a way of life.

Yet a general observation may be made on agriculture's role in the national economy. We have noticed that the financial rewards of farm-ing tend, for certain economic reasons, to be less than those of indus-try. It appears that these rewards also tend at the present to be less for certain political reasons. Farming is absolutely essential to the safety of the country; armies still fight on their stomachs, as in Napoleon's day, but because they fight faster and more mechanically than they did, there are fewer stomachs and more machines involved; and gasoline is more important than grain. Furthermore, the country is assured, through long experience, that the farmers will produce anyhow; in-deed, it is hard for farmers to stop producing, and given a little urging, as during World War II, they flood the country with food, and create a vast alluvium of surplus crops to plague the politician. But industry will not produce anyhow; having little else to work for, it works mainly for money. Again, the job of retooling factories for wartime production is tremendous, slow, and expensive. Wheat and cotton are wheat and cotton in peace or war; but disk-harrows and tractors have to be converted to shells and tanks. Therefore, the nation, for safety's sake, must favor industry, and give it the greater reward, sharpening thus politically the economic edge industry already possesses. What-ever farmers may have been in the hand-to-hand conflicts of the past, they are now, relatively speaking, men of peace; and it is industry that must prepare to make, and make, the mechanical wars of today.

All this applies to national agriculture. In considering Southern agriculture and its political relations, I think we may gain some insight by turning back one hundred years and looking at the agricultural-political situation then. The ante-bellum South has often been criti-cized for being too much concerned with politics, too little concerned with economics. Even Southerners sometimes made the criticism.

David Rogerson Williams, one-time governor of South Carolina, speaking on the Nullification issue, urged South Carolinans to recede from the political arena, ease the tariff fight, plant less cotton, and "manufacture our own clothes, and be wise enough to wear them." Some two decades later, William Gregg, so-called father of the Southern cotton mill, begged to differ with Mr. Calhoun. Suppose we secede from the Union, he asked; where are the industries to protect us? The South, following Calhoun, made no reply; and, left thus unprotected, was lost. As Bruce Catton has said recently, in *This Hallowed Ground,* the South "needed all the things the rest of the world needed—railroad iron, rolling mills, machine tools, textile machinery, chemicals, industrial knowledge, and an industrial labor force—yet it clung to a peculiar institution which prevented it from producing these things itself, and it relied on the rest of the world to make its deficiencies good."

If it be advisable for the nation now to favor industry through political action, which in turn influences economic action, it would seem to have been advisable, from the point of view of the South, for its political leaders in the 1850's to have favored industry at the expense of farming. The criticism, then, is not mainly that the South engaged in political rather than economic action; it is that its politicians and statesmen bet on the wrong economic horse. They spent their time attempting to bolster a productive system which was not only increasingly in disfavor in the world, but also, as the event proved, was doomed to destruction; they might better have spent their time seeking modifications of that system which might have made it both more productive and more acceptable.

We might take a lesson from their mistake. For what are our Southern politicians doing now? Unless I misread the signs, they are doing exactly what Mr. Calhoun did, and for which Mr. Gregg, with true insight, reproved him. They are striding along the battlements, shouting defiance to the imaginary hordes approaching, swearing to keep forever unchanged the sacred pattern of Southern life. As to what this sacred pattern is, there is considerable doubt. When the politicians are pressed, they finally say "segregation"; but, though the human heart is strange, and has done stranger things than this, it is rather hard to bow humbly before the shrine of segregation. Some of us are doubtless sincere in this worship; but the more modern and sophisticated—and there are sophisticated people even in the South—are inclined to glance slyly from one side to the other to see what the supposed worshippers are really doing.

It turns out that many of them are making a mighty good thing, temporarily at least, out of this worship. The economy of the South is based upon low wages; and the low wages are based upon keeping the Negro in his place—a low economic place. The employers of the South benefit, at least apparently and temporarily, from this situation. Apparently and temporarily—as the slave owners were benefiting apparently and temporarily a hundred years ago.

But, as the time was growing short in 1857, it is growing short now. There will be no war of course. What would be the need? We are already lost, and by our own will. The same Southern politicians, striding along the battlements or—to speak more accurately—filibustering beneath the Capitol dome, if they should glance behind them, and realize the nature of the enemy deployed and deploying across the South, would recognize how futile are their cries. What they would cry then, I don't know; I hope it would be more appropriate. For they, and we, have brought in, and are bringing in—are beseeching to come in—industry, the force which in the long run will make nonsense of the shibboleths of race, and knock the present low-income rulers of the South for a loop. Calhoun defended slavery and the economic well-being of the rulers of the South, and died with the words "the poor South" upon his lips. Our politicians defend segregation and the economic well-being of the present rulers of the South, and will die, not tragically, like Calhoun, the great forerunner of a doomed but splendid cause, but foolishly, defeated by their own confusion without a real battle.

When, in the 1880's, Grady envisaged the smokestacks upon a thousand hills he acknowledged by his vision the victory of the industrial North. But even Grady didn't know what he was doing. Speaking in New York, he thrilled the members of the New England Society with his picture of the new industrial South; speaking in Texas a little later, he called upon his audience "to defend to the last drop of their blood the principle of the white man's domination of the Negro." Poor Grady. Poor South. And now I have to watch my tractor driver, trained because he was a Negro to be only a plow-hand, drive my three thousand dollar tractor up a power-line pole. I hadn't told the tractor that the driver was a Negro and must be treated in a certain way. Come to think of it, I don't know how I could have got this across to the tractor. We have failed to build into our machines the essential knowledge that we have here a sacred pattern of life they must defend. This error is probably due to some hidden wickedness of the Yankees. Or maybe the NAACP. You've got to stay up late to beat that gang.

But, in spite of all these contradictions, the politicians still insist that they are defending our way of life. This brings us to the question: What is the relation, if any, between farming and the Southern way of life?

The phrase "a way of life" connotes moral values. In a sense any custom, say, the common American custom of a 55-mile speed limit, is a way of life; but this is not the usual sense of the term. A way of life is something men are inclined to defend because, presumably, it has moral values. Now, I am not prepared to maintain that segregation has, or at least has had attached to it, no moral values; perhaps it has, though confused and now largely inappropriate. The basic source of moral values, however, is our way of making a living. The way in which we relate ourselves to one another and to the physical world in the necessary task of subsistence is of basic importance in determining our moral values and spiritual insights. Making a living is the one thing which cannot be omitted, and it is through this means that we discover most clearly and convincingly the nature of the world. Livelihood and life are closely bound together.

The Southern way of making a living has been largely, and still is predominantly, farming. We may expect, then, that the Southern way of life will have much to do with farming. It will also have much to do with the association of Negroes and whites, because it is through this association that we have farmed. But to include this total productive association of whites and Negroes and land in the bare term *segregation,* and then to say that this segregation is our way of life, is to fail to see that segregation is rather a principle of dissociation than of association, and as such is a source, not of spiritual value, but of spiritual disvalue. The earlier institution of slavery, largely though of course never entirely accepted by those involved, and existing for the purpose of economic production, did tend to moralize itself; it created obligations, duties, loyalties; it became a way of life. The institution of segregation, never really accepted by the Negroes though necessarily acquiesced in, and existing in part merely to satisfy the desire of the whites for superiority, has developed few moral implications, and is therefore but slightly a way of life. It might more properly be called a way of not-life.

As much, however, as I question the institution of segregation as a primary source of moral values, I also assert the importance for these values of the association of whites and Negroes in the agricultural life of the South. The essential characteristics of Southern life, the things which make us Southern, are chiefly the result of this basic productive pattern: Whites and Negroes farming, in some sense, together. What are the things which make us Southern? This is my guess.

Your Southerner, white or Negro, is put together a little less tautly than most other Americans. He has a slightly greater sense of relaxation, a slightly greater tendency to linger by the way, and, lingering, to observe the oddities of life. (As if there weren't enough already, the South has created, perhaps for its own amusement, a lot of new ones.) Lingering thus, the Southerner tends to see people as three-dimensional, interesting in their own right, significant. He is apt to value personal instead of abstract relationships. He does this partly because of his feudal, personal tradition, which developed from landed estates and Negro laborers, and partly because of large farm families, numerous kith and kin, and his interest, in his so personal world, of claiming these.

All this figures in the farming effort carried on by whites and Negroes together, and all this contributes to the something in Southern farming that is more than financial success. The nature of farming is such as both to discourage the farmer from taking the end, the product, certainly the financial product, too seriously, and to encourage him in taking the means more seriously. The reason for this is partly that the end depends upon a too complex harmony of too many factors, many of which are not known, and some of those known not controllable. Success is therefore to some degree a gift, failure to some degree fate. Character and intelligence are important, but not all important. He does better who sets his mind upon a goal, but winning depends upon

more than skill and perseverance. In addition, the means in farming
are in many cases interesting in themselves. The objects the farmer
deals with are alive and therefore not entirely predictable. They work
by themselves, at night, for instance, when he is resting. If crops, they
are working to his good, if weeds to his ill, but they attend to their
business even while he is away.

All this accent upon the present, these general suggestions not to
take too seriously the future, become stronger when the farming pattern is composed of both whites and Negroes. There is no proof that
Southern Negroes have brought to farming any racial characteristics.
They may have; even from African days they may have tended more
than the whites to be artists, not practical men, interested more in the
full-bodied present than in any theoretical and as yet unbodied future.
There is no need, however, to assume this. The white man himself has
set up a situation which has made the Negro enamoured of the present
and careless of the future. Through much of his American history
success has perched beyond his reach, and because of this the Negro
has sensibly enjoyed the day as it passed, borrowing little trouble from
the future, distilling from the passing moments such immediate
value as they might have. He may have been this way anyhow; but
certainly the productive system tended to make him this way, and certainly also the white man has tended, partly in self-defense, to copy
him; and, even while criticizing him for the impossible things he does,
views these odd doings with amusement not untouched with envy.

The clue to the Southern way of life, then, lies in the farm and in
the Negro—either as he is or as we have made him.

A way of life, it was said, carries moral implications. Farming as a
way of life carries religious implications also.

The basic religious fact about farming is the farmer's sense of dependency. According to Schleiermacher, this is the basic motive in
religion. Whether basic or not, it is surely important. Your real
countryman would never take complete credit for a good crop or complete blame for a failure. There is always that demi-god, the weather.
It is the recognition of so fickle a god as this, upon whom he can lay
at least some of the blame for his failure, which makes it possible for
the farmer to fail so often without despair. "Tomorrow is a new day,"

say the corn-huskers; and the typical farmer, sniffing the fresh turned soil in spring, with puffs of warm air caressing his cheek and torn clouds scudding across the blue, forgets the past. Inspired by his awakening mother, Nature, he begins to believe again that this is the year he will make 200 bushels; this is the year of the Lord. And then, perhaps, the rains come, and the bottoms fill, and the growing crops disappear beneath the muddy water, and there's a loud croaking of frogs from once productive fields. On such an afternoon, perhaps, after a brief brave show of sun, the clouds and rains descend again, and, these having blown away, he meets among the puddles a Negro neighbor who greets him—as one of my tenants once greeted me upon a similar occasion—with the words, "Nice little season, Cap'n."

"Ben," I replied, "if you'd entered the Ark along with Noah at the rising of the flood, you'd have remarked, 'Nice little season, Cap'n Noah.' "

"Ah, Cap'n," he replied, "we must trust the Good Master."

And that's about the truth if you're going to be a farmer.

In addition to this sense of submission to the unpredictable, the farmer is aware, however vaguely, that he deals with great, mysterious forces, in a scene forever attractive, forever changing, blessed by recurring light and darkness, the rising and setting of the sun, the moon, the stars—an illimitable arena through which passes the faultless procession of the seasons. Both participant and observer in this procession, he gains therefrom a sense of inevitability. He leans toward Calvinism; in the fruitful Southern scene it is a confident Calvinism, from which he expects the good more than the bad. "There's more fair days than foul, Cap'n," said Ben in another mild reproof. Even "If winter comes, Can spring be far behind?" Yet fall comes too, the farmer knows, and winter . . . and winter . . . and winter . . . till the final chill overtakes him. He knows too that the years will blaze up and burn down to ashes still, and he not there to see.

I grant that most farmers feel but vaguely these things. If they are too hard-driven—and many of them are—they can hardly lift their eyes from the furrow. Yet even furrows end, in most fields frequently, and the plow-man, turning the mule or wheeling the tractor, sees, though only with a passing glance, the panorama of sweeping field and parallel rows and woods breaking the perspective. It is, I think, the good fortune of the South that many of its fields are small. I could speak for endless plains if I lived and worked there. But Southern fields are friendlier, odd shaped as they are, often surrounded by woods, or flanked by creeks and branches and mile wide shadowy swamps. Friendlier and more exciting. For here the cultivated breaks quickly into the wild; here is continuous frontier. The woods may be narrow, with a neighbor beyond, but they are there, hiding in winter a covey of partridges perhaps and in summer the rattler coiled by a rotting log.

For the most economical tractor farming, such fields are too small. In spite of this, Southern farming is becoming tractor farming. This raises the question of whether mechanization is changing the essential values of farm life. I do not think so. At least, not markedly. One's relation to nature is essentially the same whether one is handling a hoe or guiding a tractor. The man with the hoe is physically more unified with nature; with every stroke he adapts numerous muscles to a changing contour of the earth. The man with the tractor has to be mentally more alert; his mind, reaching through his eye, and his hand on the wheel, cause waves of dirt to flow around the plants. He has replaced a tool with a machine, but he isn't any less a man for doing so. He may be more a man. Certainly, there is possible for him a new sense of exhilaration from the power surging continually beneath his control.

There is an interesting contrast here, between agricultural and industrial mechanization. Industrial mechanization has usually replaced the skilled craftsman with a host of half-skilled or unskilled laborers, whose function is so slight and sometimes so mechanical as to be almost beneath human dignity. Automation may carry us entirely beyond this phase, but this is generally the present phase. Agricultural mechanization, on the contrary, generally tends to replace the simple unskilled laborer with the more highly skilled machine operator. There may be some exceptions to this, as, for instance, in the routine harvesting and packing operations on extensive truck farms; but the general picture seems as I have given it. Farm mechanization itself is no real threat to the Southern way of life.

There is at least one other way in which farm life implies religion. In the ideal farm situation the home and the farmhouse are one; the family is both a social and an economic unit. This is a direct tying together of material and spiritual values. One belongs to the family both because of love and because of economic need. The farmhouse is probably located somewhere on the farm; it may be visible from many points in the surrounding fields. The farmer looks up from his work, then, to glimpse the center of his hopes. He knows now what he is working for. The means he is using fuse with the ends he is seeking. He sees the picture of his life, stretching across the fields and through the days. His work is inwoven with his life, his life inwoven with the family, and, through his work and his family, he is inwoven with larger communities, even with the world, and with the universe, of which this world is an infinitesimal part.

Thus, his daily life continually reminds him that he belongs to a human family, bound to it by ties of affection and interest; he belongs to the natural world, in coöperation with which he-and-the-family gain their livelihood. His life is all of a piece; he is integrated; he has integrity.

When we consider this rich, integrated, personal life which the Southern farmer, white and colored, through the conditions of farming and the complementary relations of the races, has touched, and at moments attained, we wonder whether in our emphasis upon segregation we have not denied the deepest promptings of our hearts. We have lived a rich life, the present redolent of the past and imbued with the future, means and ends entangled, amid people interesting and curious. We have been too busy living thus to achieve great financial success. This is our way of life. But down through the center of this rich scene, which is of course our heart, we draw a sharp line and say: "Segregation." I think our hearts would bear some looking into—if only we could bear looking into them.

Now, this real way of life, the product of the combined farm life of whites and Negroes, will be more and more strained by the increasing influence of industrialism. For the industrial world is, at least up to the present, a world of stress, of drive toward the future, of emphasis upon ends—financial ends. It is geared to the machine, and the only limit to the speed of the machine is what the operative can stand. In this world of getting and spending, we lay waste, as Wordsworth said, our powers. It becomes increasingly difficult to disengage oneself, and observe the oddities and foolishness of men. We are so busy going to a better place that, puritans at heart, we fail to see the excellence of the place we leave behind; and, worse than that, we lose the sense of having any place at all. There is no question that, in the long run and the modern democratic atmosphere, the industrialization of the South will knock the Negro's place into a cocked hat. What we need to worry about is not this, but the fact that the same influence, unrestrained, will knock any man's place into a cocked hat. We shall then be cut loose from ourselves; we shall lose the old integrity of the individual standing with his family amid the elements. We shall lose the sense of belonging. We shall lose the heart out of our religion.

This will happen unless, like the countrymen we are, we take the gift of the factory, the factory method, and the machine with a grain of salt. For these things aren't really gifts; we buy them. It is up to us to ask in each case if the product is worth the price. I have a brother who built a lettuce packing-house. An industrial representative, visiting him, complimented him upon the new structure, and then, after pointing out to him that the same plant could be used successfully to pack cucumbers, squash, beans, urged him to grow these crops and keep the plant running. "No," replied my brother. "No! When I'm through packing a crop of lettuce, I've had enough for a long time. The packinghouse can just stand there and wait till I get ready to use it again."

As long as the South has men like that, so long will it retain its way of life. Men who know that machines are for human use, that it is foolish to be too serious about making a living, know also that we are here to live, and that life is now, infusing both the means and the ends.

That life is now, and interesting. I suppose the South today, raising such a ruckus about segregation, is acting true to form. She can't really be bothered about getting more industry, or raising the standard of living, or even getting an education. She's got a show going that keeps her entranced. To tell the truth, it keeps me entranced, too. Everywhere I look people are acting just like people, and if that doesn't warm the cockles of your true Southerner's heart, what will?

FRANCIS BUTLER SIMKINS

The Rising Tide of Faith

THERE WOULD BE no point in writing about the South unless one assumes that the region below the Potomac in important respects is happily different from the rest of the United States. It varies more than any other region of the country from the woeful standardization described in Sinclair Lewis's *Main Street.*

There are various explanations of the South's differences. One of these is a climate that favored the creation of the kingdoms of tobacco, rice, cotton, and sugar, slowed the tempo of living, and encouraged the employment of Negro labor. Out of the presence of Negroes grew what many regard as the essence of Southernism, the doctrine of White Supremacy. It is the belief that "in the interest of orderly government and the maintenance of Caucasian civilization" the Negro should be kept socially subordinate. Other explanations of the Southern variations from the national norm are the prevalence of the country-gentleman ideal, a powerful nativism largely untouched within the past one hundred and fifty years by European immigration and ideas, and the creation of the ideal of settled life in rural comfort in which more is thought about the past than the future. Psychologically the South is slow in catching up with the nineteenth century ideal of progress.

I am convinced that faith in the Biblical heritage is a factor second only to White Supremacy as a means of conserving the ways of the South. The historians often say revolutionary changes that enveloped the European continent in the last few centuries have stopped with the Pyrenees. Historians of the United States say with equal reason that revolutionary changes in this country stop with the Potomac.

Spain and the South have remained conservative. The reason ascribed for this is the unrelenting piety of the Spanish and Southern peoples.

The hold of orthodox Protestantism upon Southerners of the twentieth century is a likely explanation of why the section, in the face of earth-shaking changes in industry, transportation, and education, has kept its identity as the most conservative portion of the United States. Fundamental convictions in matters of faith account for the difficulty of arousing Southern churches to the need of social reform and for the indifference of Southerners to non-religious agitations except those of a political or purely practical nature. Public forums, even in large cities, are rare, and soapbox orators of the Hyde Park or Union Square variety discoursing on other than religious subjects are unknown. Faith, to expand Karl Marx's adage, is in the South the opiate of the rich as well as the poor. A Southern journalist moving to the secular atmosphere of a Northern university despairingly remarks that the pervading influence of orthodoxy had recreated an Old South unable to grow into a New South.

The modern South has made progress in technology and education, the handmaidens of faith. The growing cities of Nashville and Memphis blaze with the latest neon signs beckoning people to attend the fundamentalist adjurations of the Church of Christ. The radios of the Piedmont textile belt echo with warnings of Holy Roller preachers—even with utterance in the Unknown Tongue. Manger scenes appear during the Christmas season in front of churches stretching from the Rio Grande to the Potomac with an extravagance impossible before the time of spotlights and plastics. A sick South Carolina neighbor of mine hoped, in her distress, that angels would give her signs of comfort. She was satisfied when a minister of her faith soared above her house in an airplane proclaiming through an amplifier the riches of heaven that would be hers when she was gathered to the angels.

The implemention of universal education by the Southern States bids fair to be the means of making Christianity universal. This may happen despite a decree of the United States Supreme Court attempting to restrict the teaching of religion in schools. Educational institutions all over the South resound with daily prayers, hymns, and Bible reading; early in December the school children begin the decoration of their classrooms in preparation for the coming of the Christ Child.

In 1926 some 61 percent of the adult population of the States of the Southeast were enrolled in church. This was the largest proportion of any section of the country. The 39 percent who were not church members were often illiterates, isolated mountaineers, poor whites, and poor Negroes. Among them were persons who might be expected to join the church when they became sufficiently sophisticated to understand the Southern heritage. Or the non-church members were persons who inherited a frontier individualism which caused them to abhor the regimentation of church organizations without necessarily abhorring the faith of their British ancestors. They never went to church and were likely to sit on street corners or behind tobacco barns on Sunday morning and tell scandalous tales about the preacher and the female members of his choir. But they would react furiously if a stray interloper attacked the orthodoxies.

Not since 75 years ago when the crackerbox atheist repeated Tom Paine has there been a native in a typical Southern community who shouts unbelief. Today one seldom finds a native of the middle or upper class who has not in some way affiliated with a Christian communion. Never does a Southerner die so depraved in his conduct or so independent in his thinking that he leaves behind him the request that he not be given Christian burial. Ninety-nine percent of the students of the college in which I teach in rural Virginia are church members; I do not think such a figure could be duplicated anywhere in the world outside the South.

If some Southern parents fail to send their children to Sunday School, it is because they are too lazy to get their children fed and dressed in time for the opening activities of the Sabbath morning. I have known but one Southerner, and he was not native born, who kept his children away from Sunday School because he disapproved of what was taught there. He was a biology teacher who was a convert to the New Decalogue of Science. He believed that the Bible tales were unbiological and hence superstitious. When his views became known, his children were ridiculed and suspected by the neighbors to such a degree that they were shamed into joining a Sunday school.

Urbanization in the South has not, as elsewhere in Christendom, led to a falling away from God. *The Census of Religious Bodies* demonstrates that church membership in Southern cities has grown more rapidly than whole populations. Between 1916 and 1926, for example, the church membership of Memphis grew 62 percent and the whole population, 23 percent; for New Orleans, to cite another typical example, these figures were 35 and 13 percent, respectively.

The things of Mammon have not caused the Southerner to put aside the things of God. "Religion," says Bishop Brown in another essay in this series, "grabbed hold of the coat-tail of secular prosperity and growth." The increasing wealth that has enveloped the South in the 1940's and 1950's has not halted the habit of a greater and greater proportion of the section's people to attend church. It may be that prosperity is an important cause of this trend. In the fashion of their Calvinistic ancestors, Southerners are entering God's house to give thanks for the good things of this earth. The new prosperity has made it possible for more people to have automobiles in which to ride to church, to wear the necessary new clothes, and to give funds with which to build church centers. Church buildings have sprung up in the new cities and new suburbs like mushrooms after a summer rain.

The very rich men—the Candlers, the Dukes, the Belks, and the Cannons—have demonstrated their interest in the faith of their fathers by bestowing great sums on church institutions. A Marxian cast of mind might lead one to suspect ulterior motives in these givings. I examined a biography of Methodist Bishop John C. Kilgo, the father-confessor who persuaded James B. Duke to give millions to Methodist causes, to discover whether or not Duke was trying to destroy Methodist prejudices against cigarettes. But after reading this account of Duke's intimate conversations with Kilgo, I discovered that the tobacco capitalist was more interested in making peace with God than in overflowing his pockets with tobacco money.

Not since before the American Revolution has the South attempted to enforce religious conformity by law; it has absolute religious freedom so far as the state is concerned. But it forces religious conformity in a subtle and effective way, irritating the visiting Englishman by asking, "To what church do you belong?" If the answer is "No church whatever," the Southerner turns away bewildered. Unless he is widely read or widely traveled, he can scarcely conceive of a person who is decent in dress, manners, and morals who has no church inclinations.

After 1830 the Southern mind was captured from the Jeffersonian deists and the liberal politicians by a group of orthodox Presbyterian theologians, the most eminent of whom were James H. Thornwell and Robert L. Dabney. These staunch theologians drove the Unitarian Horace Holley from Transylvania University and the deist Thomas Cooper from the South Carolina College. They were as learned in the traditional church lore as the Catholic doctors of the Middle Ages, but they reconciled the teachings of orthodox Protestantism with the conditions of Southern life. They accepted all the local dogmas from the creation of the world by divine fiat to the belief that the Negro got to be like he was because Ham laughed at his drunken father. The secular leaders of the later years of the Old South from Jefferson Davis to Robert E. Lee did not wrestle with doubts as John C. Calhoun and John Randolph of Roanoke wrestled before them; they accepted without question the faith of their learned theologians.

Then after the Civil War came "the treason of the clerks." Some of the learned among the clergy abandoned the belief that the Word of God as revealed in the Book provided an unchanging and certain truth before which the demonstrations of scientists and sociologists seemed negligible. Instead they turned to the beliefs of the French *philosophes* and certain advanced American thinkers of the late eighteenth century. They saw the necessity of reconciling divine truth with the ever-aggressive teachings of science. They would substitute the facts inferred from experiments for the certainties which had been handed down from God to the Prophets and the Apostles.

The issue revolved around a question of fundamental importance: whether man was miraculously made by God in His own image or whether he evolved by natural processes out of lower species as described by Charles Darwin. To orthodox Southerners Darwinism seemed to usurp a principal prerogative of religion by lowering man to the level of animals without the personal moral responsibilities of Christians. The optimistic side of Darwinism, that man was evolving into something better, did not impress those who believed in original sin.

The issue came to a head in 1884 when James Woodrow, of the

Columbia Theological Seminary in South Carolina, published his address *Evolution*. This graduate of Heidelberg University maintained that "the Bible does not teach science" and that a sympathetic understanding of the theory of evolution did not lead to doubt but to a more profound reverence for God's plan of creation. The writer of this repudiation of the literal words of the Bible as the unquestioned source of knowledge was accused of teachings calculated to destroy divine authority and was removed from his professorship. But the moral victory was Woodrow's. The bold manner in which he advocated the claims of science on faith was the first step in the spread of unorthodox thinking among the theologians of the South. Thereafter for nearly eighty years the advocates of unyielding orthodoxy were in retreat.

The forces of religious subversion moved ruthlessly forward. Robert L. Dabney, the last of the theological titans out of the Old South, in lectures and books fought energetically for three decades against universal education, the industrialization of the South, and such nineteenth century heresies as evolution, positivism, and pragmatism. He found it convenient to retreat from the Union Theological Seminary in Virginia to the more orthodox atmosphere of Texas.

The most devastating attack on the old-time faith came when John T. Scopes, at the behest of individuals largely non-Southern, flouted at Dayton, Tennessee, the law of Tennessee forbidding any institution supported by State funds "to teach the theory that denies the story of divine creation as taught in the Bible." Scopes and his supporters were the aggressors; the law-enforcing agencies of Tennessee had made no earlier attempt to implement the anti-evolution law in classrooms.

The Dayton courthouse became the scene of a memorable battle between the orthodox people of the South and those who demanded academic freedom unhampered by church-motivated laws. Much to the secret gratification of the evolutionists Scopes was convicted; the constitutionality of the anti-evolution law was upheld by the courts. But the real victors were Scopes and his friends. The anti-evolutionary laws of Tennessee and other Southern States fell into disuse. The Scopes case was called the Monkey Trial by the press of this country and of England. The South was ridiculed for allowing such an event to happen.

A most significant fact about the Dayton trial was that there was no one among the learned theologians of the South willing to accept the role of prosecutor. That function was assumed by William Jennings Bryan, a conservative in theological matters, hopelessly naive when confronted with the complexities of Biblical and scientific interpretations. Clarence Darrow, the defense attorney, made a fool out of Bryan.

The reality of the matter was that by 1925 a majority of the high-ranking theological professors of the South and the sophisticated pastors of the big city churches had gone modernist, or they were too tactful to allow themselves to be convicted of obscurantism in the eyes of the Darwinians of the North. By that date the most successful— perhaps the most intellectual—members of the clerical profession in the South were playing down the traditional mission of Christianity, the saving of souls for the bliss beyond the sky; they were emphasizing the social welfare gospel. They were giving advice on everything from how to sleep with a husband or wife to how to clean up the back streets of the home city. They were supplementing or supplanting the conventional Southern belief in two heavens, the one beyond the sky and that of the Old South, by a return to the eighteenth century belief that, by the invocation of the prescriptions of the sociologists, something approximating paradise could be attained on this earth. They thought it was possible to go to heaven without dying.

Scriptural injunctions such as "My kingdom is not of this world," "To him that hath shall be given," and "For ye have the poor with you always," were discounted as cynical aspersions against human improvement. The wisdom of putting whole trust in a divine dictator was set aside in favor of the belief in the innate goodness of man. Moral teachings almost crowded out faith in divinity.

I heard in 1927 a Chicago-educated minister tell students at a distinguished Methodist institution of learning that it was more important to live like Jesus than it was to believe in Jesus. This was ethical culture, a novelty among a people whose faith flowed from that fountain filled with blood first envisaged in seventeenth century England.

To protest against this type of modernism got one nowhere. To do so brought from the ecclesiastical snobs the charge of being a fool, of catering to the unwashed multitude, or of being ignorant of the discoveries of the Darwinians and the social scientists, with their philosophies of progress and democracy. The laity, in whose hands ultimate authority rests in Southern churches, was not offended by the opinions of highly placed ecclesiastics. Southern laymen were not sophisticated enough to make a distinction between ethics and faith. They assumed that because a clergyman lived in charity with his fellowman, it followed that he also believed in the orthodoxies.

I once heard at a laymen's supper the president of a Southern Presbyterian seminary answer well-grounded accusations of unorthodoxy against one of his professors by cleverly evading the issue of heresy. The seminary president proclaimed something that had never been questioned, the good character of the accused professor. "I trusted," said the seminary official, "the custody of my two daughters to Professor Blank while I was away at war, and he was true to his pledge." The proof that Professor Blank was not a seductionist was accepted by the naive laymen at the supper as proof that the professor was not a heretic.

A clerical friend of mine journeyed over Mississippi telling orthodox laymen that some of the clergymen in their employment were doubting the Virgin Birth and the Glorious Ascension. The reply this complaining minister got from the laymen was, "These ministers must be all right; they carry umbrellas when it rains, wear decent clothes, pay their debts, and are not suspected of trying to seduce members of the choirs." Again good character was taken as proof of solid faith.

The people of the Confederacy who were literate enough to leave letters and diaries were convinced that the Confederacy could not fail because the Lord God of Battles had raised up such consecrated men as Marse Robert and Stonewall to defend the Southern cause. But the miracle did not happen; the Confederacy did fail. It did so, suggests E. Merton Coulter, the most complete historian of the Confederacy, because Christianity had not yet become a vital interest of the lower masses of Southerners and therefore did not become a much-needed rallying point around which an invincible morale might have been constructed.

Three divines—Bishop Leonidas Polk and the Reverends Mark P. Lowrey and William N. Pendleton—were fighting generals of the

Confederacy; the few generals who were not already Christians were
converted and baptized; and such powerful divines as James H.
Thornwell and Benjamin M. Palmer went among the soldiers fighting
sin and urging the soldiers to slay the Yankees. But during the war
scarcely 20 percent of the civilian and military population was affiliated
with any church.

Since 1865 this 20 percent has increased to 65 or 70 percent. Still there
are millions of Southerners of both races who are ignorant or indifferent to the saving grace of the Gospel. Many Southerners perhaps have
never heard of Jesus. As revealed by the writings of Erskine Caldwell
and William Faulkner, there is a vast rural underworld of poor whites
and poor Negroes who dance to the beat of juke boxes Sunday night
without knowing about the puritan Sabbath of other Southerners;
they also violate one or more of the Ten Commandments without having compunctions of conscience. If there were, as in Colonial Virginia,
a law compelling church attendance, it would do little good among
unchurched Southerners. The poor whites do not have the clothes or
the manners to make them feel at ease in the church; they are not
sophisticated enough to understand the King James Bible or the "seminary language" of a clergy among whom educational standards are
rising.

Yet the failure of the intellectuals among the clergy to adhere to "the
old-time religion," and of a large part of the lower classes to be impressed by the old-time gospel, does not destroy the claim that the
South is one of the most devout sections of Christendom. The contro-
versies of our intellectuals should not be taken too seriously in an area
essentially rural in its psychology and non-intellectual in its outlook.
Southerners, outside the restricted circles of the professors, the editors,
and clergymen and other speakers, are hardly aware of the controver-
sies that have ruffled the feathers of the pundits.

More than a hundred years ago Harriet Martineau, an observant
English traveler, met an English clergyman in Georgia who said that
his congregation loved him and looked after his every need, but had
not paid enough attention to his sermons to tell him whether they
liked them or not. Southerners in the time of Miss Martineau did not
listen to sermons. This is still true, if the observations of one who has

attended hundreds and even thousands of church services in the South may be taken as valid. My observation is that if a person does not want to be impolite, he had better not after services ask the average worshipper to comment on what the preacher said. If he does so, he will get a shrug of the shoulder or a sharp reply such as, "Why ask me? If you wanted to know what the preacher had to say, why didn't you listen yourself?"

Many of the liberal thinkers of the South in matters of faith have been forced to retreat from their advanced position because their mentors in the theological schools of New York and Chicago in recent years have retreated from their advanced positions. Reinhold Niebuhr, the most eminent of the Northern theologians, has found that "the near moralism of traditional liberalism" of his seminary days has no real answer to the needs of Christian living and Christian thinking. Southern thinkers are slow in catching up with Northern thinkers. But if past performances are a key to future behavior, the Southerners will, before many years, catch up with Niebuhr and other champions of neo-orthodoxy. They will do this or else put themselves in the ridiculous position of imagining themselves "advanced" by holding on to doctrines abandoned in areas intellectually more energetic than the South. Southern liberal theologians are not that foolish. Already they are adopting the new conservatism; already they are growing pessimistic over the hopes of bringing heaven down to earth; already they are reaffirming the old dogmas of the church as man's only certain hope. They are substituting for hopes of progress the expectation of the Second Coming.

The fact that the Southern churches are not democratic enough to make all sorts and conditions of men comfortable has certain advantages. This barrier gives the enterprising among the lower classes something to aspire to: To become well enough dressed, well enough behaved, and well enough informed to give proof that he should become a member of a church made up of people better off socially and morally than the class from which he sprang. Whether or not it fits with American ideals of democracy, climbing the social ladder by way of the church is as dynamic a force in Southern life as getting ahead through money, education, or claims to aristocracy. If a Southern church were to become democratic enough in cultural and social standards to capture that one fourth of the people who are unchurched, it would be faced with the peril of perishing for lack of elevating ideals to which its members could aspire.

The rise of educational standards has reduced illiteracy among Southerners to a minimum; denominational ideals are being aspired to by so many members of the lower classes that before many decades perhaps the number of the unchurched may become as small as the number of illiterates.

The schools of the South have been accused of lowering their standards to suit the tastes of the meaner elements of society. The same accusation has been made against the Primitivist sects that have become so strong in the lower middle classes of the South in the past fifty years. This accusation is only fair from the viewpoint of rationalists who would reduce the emotional and miraculous in Christianity to a minimum. Many trusting souls have been made extremely happy by the acceptance of the belief of the Primitivist churches that faith can do as much for them today as for Christians in the times of the Apostles. Given to prophecy, the Primitivists believe that hidden in the obscurities of the Prophets and the Apocalypse are divinely inspired keys to the future. They are divine healers, believers in heavenly intervention in favor of the sick. They report various experiences with the Unknown Tongue and Pillars of Fire, means through which God converses with the Faithful. Frequently they are Premillenialists, believers that Christ would not postpone indefinitely His Second Coming to save His troubled people.

There is nothing in the beliefs of these so-called off-color faiths not accepted by the high-church Episcopalians and other sincere believers in Divine Providence. Southerners of neither race are lured away from the straight and narrow path by such heresies as those of Father Divine. The shouting, screaming, and jumping in which Primitivists indulge is no more irrational than the shouting, screaming, and jumping in which people of high rank indulge at football games; the events narrated in the New Testament are for the Primitivists still the most exciting news the human race ever had.

The greatest misconception of the Bible Belt that Henry L. Mencken and other critics have propagated is that it is preacher-ridden. The weakness of this charge is revealed through the pathetic stories of the ministers in Ellen Glasgow's *Vein of Iron* and William Faulkner's *Light in August*. Southern churches are vestry- or deacon-ridden, with the ministers approaching the role of puppets rather than that of spiritual dictators. From early Colonial days the South has had a weak church structure, with church installations as a rule modest and the laity in almost absolute control. It is by no means uncommon for love and loyalty to a church by its members to vary in direct proportion to disloyalty, jealousy, and even hatred of the minister. It is not considered entirely improper for respected church members to engage in carping criticisms of their ministers. During the Colonial period the parsons of Virginia were given only one year tenure; today ministers in all Southern States frequently lose their positions because of espousing unpopular causes. Witness the large number punished today for opposing the determination of their congregations that the races be kept apart in the house of God.

This lack of independent power by the clergy has obvious disadvantages. It also has its advantages. The effectiveness of lay pressure has kept the great popular churches in harmony with the conservative sentiments of the majority of the Southern people. In the old days the influence of the magnates of the land made the church pro-slavery and separatist. Today this influence keeps those among the clergy heedful of non-Southern opinion from alienating Southerners from the faith of their fathers. Specifically does it hinder radical experiments in race relations.

The Southern Baptist church is growing faster than any other major denomination in the United States. This is partly because lay control in that church is so complete. The Baptist deacons refuse to give up fundamentalist doctrines at the behest of clerical demands that their church unite with the less orthodox Baptist church of the North.

A powerful factor in the growth of certain church bodies in the South is their willingness to adjust themselves to the consistencies of the Southern environment. Some years ago this fact was sympathetically brought to the attention of the American people by the play *Green Pastures*. This drama may have taken license with prosaic fact by conceiving of God as wearing a frock coat, eating catfish stew, and smoking a fifty-cent cigar. But it is true that in the genuinely popular

churches of the two races activities and ceremonials have gone contemporary. The preacher dresses like a businessman and speaks in the
vernacular. The choir consists of the prettiest girls in town with rouge
on their faces and, until the coming of angel robes, displaying the
latest modes. Traditional musical instruments are often supplemented
by fiddles and even by trombones; the old-time hymns of a treasured
English heritage are often supplemented by tunes that sound like those
of the juke boxes.

Attached to the more recent church structures are hotel-like append-
ages. Even ministers are wont to refer to their church as "the plant."
These make possible the development within sacred precincts of activities that would not have been accepted in more austere ages of
Protestantism. There everything recreational and even frivolous takes
place short of round dancing. There hot dogs in hunks of bread
supplement the anemic wafers of the communion table. As Harry
Golden wrote in *The Carolina Israelite,* future archeologists may
some day excavate the ruins of our civilization and wonder what kinds
of sacrifices were offered in the huge bake ovens and barbecue pits
discovered in our churches.

This compromise with the contemporary worldly attitudes is what
gives the Baptist and Methodist churches advantage in winning the
allegiance of the masses as well as the classes. "The Scotch scotched
themselves," says a wise historian. He means that the Presbyterian
church declined relatively because it would not fully Americanize
itself by dropping to a sufficient degree the customs of Scotland. This
is truer still of the Episcopal church where the surplices, prayer books,
and formal ritual of an English background are strange to the average
Southerner.

Southern churches in ritual and doctrine pursue tactics in important
respects opposite to those of Fifth Avenue. The New York churches
practice a ritual often as old as the middle ages and a doctrine as modern as Charles Darwin and Thomas Huxley. The Southern churches,
except in a few cities and university centers, follow a ritual in harmony
with modern American practices and a doctrine as old as that of the
seventeenth century. This discriminating application of the new and
the old is what gives the Roman Catholic Church strength in such
countries as Mexico, Brazil, and Portugal. In those countries the image

of the Blessed Virgin satisfies local tastes by being an Indian, a Negro woman, or a white woman with a double chin.

Once while addressing a Sunday school class I used the example of the confusion of tongues at the Tower of Babel to describe the division of Southern Christians into so many denominations. This repetition by me of an unoriginal assertion already made by a hundred church journalists was contradicted by the wisest member of my audience. "Religion in the South," said this interlocutor, "is like Joseph's garment, a coat of many colors. It is a flawless ensemble." He explained that the battle of the sects so far as the South is concerned is an event of the ante-bellum past. It is no longer good manners, in pulpit or parlor, to criticize a church other than one's own. The different denominations today are cordial toward each other; every Sunday night in summer in every Southern town they hold union services. A Methodist minister going about the countryside criticizing the Baptists, as did Parson William G. Brownlow in the 1850's, would today be considered a frightful anomaly. Roman Catholics, though suspected and misunderstood in an overwhelmingly Protestant region, have been tolerated since the American Revolution. The fact that the average rural Southerner will not vote for a Catholic is not proof that the Southerner is not willing to allow the Catholic perfect religious freedom.

This last statement must be qualified. Lord Bryce's assertion that in America there is an unofficial union of church and state applies with greatest accuracy to the South. Democratic politicians and old-fashioned liberals were rudely shocked in 1928 when several Southern States refused to support Al Smith's candidacy for the presidency largely because he was a Roman Catholic. Thomas Jefferson's statue in Charlottesville was draped in crepe.

This repudiation of Al Smith was no more than could be expected by those who appreciate the intense Protestant heritage of the South. Jefferson's admonition to segregate religion and politics in different sides of the head may have worked well in an age when Jefferson and other members of the ruling class had little religion to mix with their politics. It is impossible for the devout Southerner of the twentieth century not to vote the same way that he prays. He gets concepts of faith, righteousness, and politics so confused that they could be unraveled only in the unrealistic thinking of those who think in terms of the geometrical simplicities of the eighteenth century.

It was inaccurate, though the liberals charged it at the time, to accuse Southerners in doing what they did in 1928 of violating religious freedom. Few were interested in denying a Roman Catholic the right to run for office or the right to worship God as he pleased. Moreover, it is feasible to believe that Southerners voted against Al Smith because of the political rather than the doctrinal implications of Catholicism. They have often been willing to vote for high-church Episcopalians who are doctrinally akin to Catholics, but who, unlike Catholics, do not owe allegiance to a foreign potentate.

The South today holds to denominational differences to a greater degree than it did in the frontier days when because of inadequate housing different denominations shared the same church buildings. The Community or United Church Movement of the North and of Canada has made little progress in the South because of social reasons and because a pious people interpret narrowly the teachings of Jesus.

Southerners adhere firmly to the Christian dogma that there is but a single road by which a person can be saved. Because each denomination believes that it has the right road to the Heavenly Kingdom, there is no room for compromise with those who claim other roads. The devout Southerner thinks that to meet other Christians on common grounds of belief might leave only a residue of vague affirmations closely kin to Unitarianism or Universalism. His dogmas are too exclusive for that. It might also create something beyond his understanding, a religion that is not a religion, an ethical culture that has not thrived in the South since the time of Jefferson. The Southerner believes that it is hardly possible to lead an exemplary life unless that life stems from faith in the Resurrected Lord. The thought has never entered his mind in the past one hundred and fifty years that it is possible to follow Christ's teachings without a precise affirmation of His divinity such as given in the creeds of the different denominations.

Despite loud denials by the official keepers of the Southern conscience, the region below the Potomac accepts strong social distinctions. Its proclamations of democracy so far as group relations are concerned are largely a pose. It therefore follows that the churches, in order to accommodate themselves to the regional realities, must accept these social distinctions with grace. In fact there is no conscious problem of adjusting the all sorts and conditions of men to the separate religious denominations that conform to their several humors and dispositions. Everyone is satisfied with these divisions; he seeks naturally in church, as in other aspects of social relations, his own level.

The Southerner of all classes has never been willing to kowtow to his betters. He therefore does not want to be thrown in church with those who do not wish to associate with him in a free and easy fashion. The propaganda for social democracy in which all churches indulge is no fit substitute, in the thinking of the proud Southerner, for the informal comradeship he is able to give and get from members of his own class. So, without formal decree to that effect, certain social types become members of the Episcopal church; other types join the Presbyterian, Methodist, Baptist, and Primitivist church bodies. What are the social distinctions that bring about these denominational differences is hard to say, but everyone who knows the South knows that these differences exist.

These separations are not only interdenominational but exist within the denominations. In the typical Virginia town in which I live are three Methodist churches. One is for Negroes; another is dominated by the artisan and laboring classes among the whites; a third is dominated by the professional and merchant classes. These church divisions along social lines just happened without any thought on the part of anyone that they were not meet and right.

That the separation of the churches along social lines is as immutable as the procession of the seasons is illustrated by what happened in the little town in South Carolina in which I was born. It had three Baptist churches—one for Negroes, another for the white cotton mill operatives, and a third for those who were prosperous or given to aristocratic conceits. Our ambitious politician—one who now holds high office—had learned in his sociology classes at college that social distinction (within the white race) before the throne of God should be abolished. He implemented his belief by having the church in the mill village discontinued in hope that all white Baptists could worship in the same sanctuary. This attempted revolution proved abortive. The more modest among the mill operatives organized a Holy Roller church, and when the bolder spirits out of the destroyed church entered the church of the prosperous and the family-conscious, the snobs in the latter church—those who had been to college and had learned to drink cocktails, or belonged to the highest ranking families—withdrew from the church of their ancestors and joined the Episcopal church.

The segregation of races in the churches often provokes bitter attacks on Southern denominations. Condemnatory resolutions are passed by assemblies of churchmen both within and without the South. The separation of the races in church is said to be a mockery of the Christian ideal of the Fatherhood of God and the Brotherhood of Man. The exclusion of the colored race from the white man's house of God is as rigid as in any other aspects of the color line. Today—except in the case of deliberate experiments carried on by a few progressive clergymen—a visitor never sees a Negro in a white church. It would take more courage than most Negroes have for one to crash the gates.

It was not thus in slavery days, and I can remember almost a half century ago in my home church in South Carolina half the congregation was composed of Negroes. They sat in the back of the sanctuary and took the Holy Communion after the whites; but after the acts of worship they lingered in the church yard to participate in the small talk with the white parishioners.

I regret that this type of interracial familiarity has vanished. If I were to tell the younger members of my old congregation that our church once had a large Negro membership they would suspect me of playing on my imagination.

The separation of the races in church started with the abolition of slavery. A little historical investigation will prove that it was more on the initiative of the Negro than the white man. The whites were reluctant to surrender the rigid control they had over their Negro members under slavery. The Negroes, on the other hand, felt that their accustomed habit of religious subordination to the master race was incompatible with their status as freedmen. They demanded the elementary American constitutional right of religious freedom, including separate church organizations and congregations, and ministers and church officials of their own race and choosing.

Realizing the separation was inevitable, the whites of most denominations allowed the blacks to withdraw in peace, often helping them financially in the building of separate churches. Typical of what happened is the experience of the First Baptist Church at Montgomery, which came out of the Civil War with three hundred white members and six hundred colored members. When it was felt wise to separate, the two races co-operated in the erection of a new church for the Negro members, who continued to use the old church while theirs was being built. When all was ready, the colored congregation was launched with the blessings of the whites. The whites of Montgomery, as elsewhere in the South, were confident that structural independence would not be accompanied by doctrinal innovations abhorrent to Southern tradition. It is a tribute to Christian tolerance that this parting of the ways took place without the acrimony that characterized the political estrangements of the Reconstruction period. The South fortunately has no heritage of racial hatred along religious lines.

The largest number of blacks joined the Negro Baptist church where they were allowed the maximum independence from white control. The white Baptists were prompter than other denominations in granting the Negroes church autonomy. They facilitated the ordination of Negro ministers by not demanding as high educational standards as Presbyterians and Episcopalians. Soon the white Baptists learned to be almost indifferent to the religious behaviour of the blacks; this made it possible for Negro Baptists to do as they pleased.

The Methodists lost heavily in their Negro membership because, in the crucial years immediately after the war, they did not grant the blacks the right to have independent congregations. Because the Episcopal church has down to the present failed to give its Negroes an independent church organization, it has lost almost all of its colored members, except a few among the elite. Negro Episcopalians are forced to submit to the authority of a white episcopate.

"Does Dr. Addleman love you?" I asked a Negro professor of a Negro college of the college's sponsoring bishop. "Yes, he does," was the reply; "he has spent much time and energy collecting money among the white people to make our college prosperous." I then asked the Negro professor, "Do you love Dr. Addleman?" The reluctant reply was, "I ought to love him but I don't. He has done so much for us. But he demands and receives more kow towing from his Negro beneficiaries than he could ever get from white persons. Unconsciously this Southern gentleman is a snob."

Then my informer, as a member of a race that understands the white man better than the white man understands the Negro, made this generalization. "The white man in the United States," said this professor, "whether he is a liberal or a conservative, a Democrat, a Republican, or a Communist, demands the right to dominate in social relations with Negroes. This is especially true when the white man has benevolent intentions. Most of us Negroes have the privilege of avoiding contacts with whites in our church relations, and we intend to exercise this privilege even to the extent of depriving ourselves of gifts that might come our way."

The right to have an independent church is the greatest liberty the Negro won as the result of his Reconstruction experience. It is a privilege all white Southerners, with the exception of a few philanthropists, are willing for him to have. The white man's respect for religion gives the Negro church a freedom from intrusion that is not enjoyed in the Negro home. The Negro church, says Gunnar Myrdal, the most complete student of American race relations, "is such a good community center that it might almost be said that anyone who does not belong to the church in the rural South does not belong to the community." As Richard Wright, the Negro novelist, puts it, "Our churches are where we dip our tired bodies in cool springs of hope, where we retain our wholeness and humanity despite the blow of death from the Bosses. . . ."

The same could be said of Southerners in the middle of the twentieth century that Richard M. Weaver said of them when they embarked on the Civil War: They were "one of the few religious people left in the Western World." The conversion of some of the clergy of the recent South to modernism is counterbalanced by a much larger proportion of the Southern people in the Christian fold at present than in ante-bellum days. The masses of both races are feeling with greater intensity than ever before the influence of the Christian affirmations. Those who twenty-five years ago were compromising before the secular and materialistic influences that came from the North are now being influenced by the neo-orthodoxy coming from Europe and the

North. There is today a Solid South based on faith more uniting than the Solid South based on politics. The Holy Rollers and the members of the upper class churches are divided more by social distinctions than by distinctions of doctrines. Both are dominated by natural piety and hostility to rationalism and free inquiry in Biblical matters. Conservatism in faith did not rank far behind racial attitudes as a significant cause of the South's retention of its regional distinctiveness.

Much criticism is still hurled at the South because of its peculiar customs. In politics, in social relations, and in schools its racial attitudes have been challenged in Congress and by the Supreme Court because of their supposed violation of restrictions imposed on the States by the United States Constitution. Time alone will tell how effective these challenges will be. But the Constitution proclaims absolute religious freedom and gives no pretext for outside interference in the ways Southerners conduct their churches. The region therefore bids fair to retain indefinitely its freedom of action in this field, and through the dynamic influence of religion maintain the regional identity.

ROBERT D. JACOBS
Woods and Water

*A tall hunter shifts his position silently in the undergrowth near
the watering place. Dawn is breaking. He sees the large dimple in
the water as a bass rises to take an insect. Then the buck comes whis-
persoft to drink from the Elkhorn. The tall hunter sights and squeezes
the trigger. The buck falls, flounders in the reddening water. "We'll
shore God eat tonight!" the hunter thinks as he draws his knife and
moves to cut the buck's throat.*

*1957—one hundred and fifty-seven years later. The old watering
place is gone. Bulldozers have been rooting up the bank, shorn of most
of its trees, for the gravel needed for a county road. Up the Elkhorn a
hundred yards in a clearing, a family picnic is underway. There are
ten of them, who came crowded in an old pickup truck. A fire is going; hot dogs are being roasted. Three teenagers are splashing furiously in the shallow water (it's not really deep enough to swim). A
boy of six is a little way upstream skipping rocks across the water to
the intense disgust of a fly fisherman who whips his graceful line
through the air in an S-curve and lets his dry fly down gently in the
ripples where smallmouth bass lurk. Within the next hundred and
fifty yards are six more fishermen, one a novice from Frankfort, slip-
ping awkwardly on the wet rocks, raising enough rumpus to scare
every bass from there to the Kentucky River. He is using a casting
outfit, with a heavy jitterbug surface plug almost as big as the fish he
hopes to catch.*

*Back where the picnickers are having their fun, the testimony of
delight burgeons: paper napkins, sandwich bags, empty Coke bottles,*

a few beer cans; for this is not a public park, where people are required to clean up their litter. This is just a clearing on the banks of the Elkhorn, and if anyone objects it is the fly fisherman and the ghosts of the tall hunter and his ten-point buck—and these are silent ghosts.

WHEN OSCAR HUBBARD, one of the more repellent characters in Miss Lillian Hellman's mordant drama, "The Little Foxes," goes hunting, he shoots for the pleasure of killing. Birdie, his ineffectual wife, objects on the moral ground that he never lets anyone else hunt on the land and "It's wicked to shoot food just because you like to shoot, when poor people need it so——." Birdie has tried, and failed, to preserve the concept of *noblesse oblige.* When Lionnet, the plantation now owned by the Hubbards, was still in the possession of her family, the master apparently had distributed the spoils of the chase among the slaves and allowed them to supplement their rations with what they could kill for themselves. However, when Oscar is approached by his Negro servant Cal, who tells him that the field hands "ain't had no meat since cotton picking was over" and that he (Oscar) had killed "enough bobwhite and squirrel to give every nigger in town a Jesus-party," Oscar warns him that if "any nigger in the town" goes shooting, "you know what's going to happen."

Although it's unlikely that anyone will take obnoxious Oscar as a typical representative of the new hunting class in the South, Miss Hellman does point up a change in the *reason* for hunting, a change that many Southerners alive today have been able to observe. In the long, dark days of reconstruction many people in the South were obliged to resort to field and stream to get meat for their tables; and even in the 1930's game and fish furnished many a depression-lean larder. Although Miss Hellman's play is set in 1900, when the poor in the South were very poor indeed, Oscar Hubbard does not need to hunt for meat. He is a member of the new privileged class, a commercial class to whom the tradition of *gentilesse* (fondly ascribed to the old system) was as foreign as the notion of lending money without security or interest. No longer needing the game they kill for food and feeling no particular burden of obligation to the underprivileged, the new overprivileged class presumably hunted and fished for sport.

Whether the sportsman of today takes game primarily for the love of killing or for self-aggrandizement or for the pleasure of pitting his skill and knowledge of the forest against the trickiness of the animals must be left to the psychologist to determine, but one element of the motivation is obvious. Because we no longer need to hunt for meat, an urge for ego-building must be one of the great impulses we take to the field. Contests sponsored by newspapers, Chambers of Commerce and clubs, all of them awarding prizes and publicity for the biggest fish or buck taken during the season, foster on a grand scale the feeling of achievement of the new sportsmen. And we start them off early: In Louisville, Kentucky, a fishing "rodeo" is held for the children, with prizes for the "biggest bass, the biggest fish, and the most fish."

In William Faulkner's magnificent hunting story, "The Bear," Old Ben, the great legendary bear of a certain Mississippi Delta region, is hunted annually by a small group of skilled huntsmen in a kind of ritualistic ceremony. "They were not going into the Big Bottom to hunt bear and deer, but to keep yearly rendezvous with the bear which they did not even intend to kill. Two weeks later they would return, with no trophy, no head and skin." It was "the yearly pageant of the old bear's furious immortality."

The boy, Ike McCaslin, who after he was ten was allowed to go on the hunt, felt an almost compulsive urge to see Old Ben, not to shoot but simply to look at the great bear. Look at him he did, after he had discarded compass, watch and gun and pitted his knowledge of the wilderness against the instinctive cunning of the animal. Twice later he had an opportunity to shoot Old Ben, but his respect for one of the old gods of the woods was greater than his desire to kill the biggest bear in the Mississippi Delta. When the old bear is finally killed, his time, the old time having gone and his continued survival impossible in the diminished wilderness, he is killed, not by the automatic rifles of trophy seeking sportsmen but by the knife of the half-savage Boon Hogganbeck furiously trying to save the life of the great dog Lion who is being disembowelled while his jaws are locked on the throat of the bear.

This is only a story, of course, but the contrast of the motivation of these hunters to that of the gentleman who told in one of our sports magazines how he killed the biggest bear in the East is something for moralists of the chase to ponder. Our Eastern hunter set out to hunt deer and quite by accident came across a tremendous bear, who turned and looked at him. Thinking that the bear might possibly have in mind doing him some damage, the hunter, wishing that he had his automatic rifle instead of the unique experimental three barrel gun he was carrying, fired a .32/40 bullet into the bear's head. The creature collapsed and then the sportsman fired the other two barrels (12 gauge shotgun) into the dead bear's skull. The carcass, 540 pounds, was too big for him to move alone, and when he finally got help the flesh was beginning to putrefy. The hide was spoiled, but the measurements—important to the ego of the hunter—proved that this bear was the largest ever killed in New York State, possibly the largest in the East. The hunter was pleased, because he has the front paws, the head is being mounted, and after all, one doesn't shoot a record bear every day. And so the Old Ben of the East dies an inglorious, almost an accidental death, from a chance encounter with a deer hunter with a three-barrel gun.

Later perhaps in the South than in other sections of the U.S., gunning and fishing for trophies has largely replaced meat on the table as the primary motivation of the man in the field. Techniques have changed as well as attitude. With the relatively tremendous increase in the general prosperity of the South since the beginning of World War II, people no longer need to hunt and fish for food, and the new wealth permits the accumulation of equipment unthought of a few years ago.

When the old rural fishermen in the South went out for food, they were likely to use trotlines, which are inexpensive, especially when constructed by the fishermen, seines, often a group purchase, or homemade traps. The trotline was simply a heavy cord, frequently stretched from one side of a stream to the other or perhaps cutting off the corner of a bend. Many short lengths of line with baited hooks attached depended at regular intervals from the long line into the water. The trotlines were "run" every few hours, and the riverbank dweller could count on a fairly steady supply of fish for his table. People who owned seines, when they were close enough to the Mississippi, used them in the quarter-moon shaped lakes caused when the river cut a new channel across a bend, leaving a shallow pond where the river bed used to be. A dozen or fifteen families could expect fish from such a seining expedition—buffalo carp, spoon-billed catfish, drum—mostly "rough" fish, rarely any bass or crappie.

Even the more sophisticated fishermen in the country did not often use the casting or fly techniques. The equipment cost too much. A cane pole, cut from the cane brake on the creek, sufficed. To catch the wilier denizens of the inland waters with this close-range armament, stealth and skill were required. One old fisherman on the Big Topisaw creek in South Mississippi came in regularly with a long string of largemouth bass ("trout," he called them). Others failed. Old Dan Gunnels succeeded because of his infinite skill in approaching through the undergrowth on the stream banks. Never a shadow fell across the water, and he could drop his minnow or "soft craw" (a crawfish that has just shed his hard outer skin) over the nose of a lazy bass without raising a ripple. His was consummate woodcraft, the knowledge of exactly where the fish were feeding at a given time of the day and the ability to place his live bait directly on the fishing ground with a sixteen-foot pole and a ten-foot line.

But there were more primitive methods still. One was "muddying." Very poor people, usually Negroes, went fishing equipped only with their field hoes. Finding a shallow slough or pond or barrow pit along a railroad embankment, they would muddy the water with their hoes until the fish, mostly mudcats, came to the top to breathe. Then the fish were deftly scooped up and deposited in in tow sacks for the big catfish fry that evening.

Strangest of all was the system in which man pitted his knowledge and dexterity—and courage—directly against the fish without the adventitious aids of civilized ingenuity. This was called "grabbling." The fisherman, submerged to the neck in a shallow stream or lake, moved silently through the water, feeling with his hands in sunken hollow logs and stumps and sinkholes for the fish, risking severe punctures from the fins of large catfish as well as the sometimes fatal fangs of the water moccasin that might be lying almost invisible on the very drift that the fisherman was exploring. Not the least risk was the chance of losing a finger to the ironhard jaws of the great snapping turtles.

Now, not many years later, the trotline must be abandoned or its use modified in any stream that can accommodate a boat. Roaring up

the river at fifteen or twenty miles an hour the motorboatman can't
stop to investigate the possibility of a heavy cord a few inches under
the water, so the trotline fisherman must stretch his line close to the
bank or across small streams too tangled with undergrowth for the
speedboats.

Not long ago an old Negro was fishing with his cane poles from the
banks of the Kentucky, at the ideal fishing ground where a small
stream emptied itself into the river. He was oblivious to the speeding
motorboat towing a water skier along dangerously close to the bank,
until the bow wave from the Chriscraft washed up the shoreline and
over his feet, upsetting his bait can and his lunch sack. Shaking his
head the old Negro gathered up what was left of his equipment and
climbed back up the steep bank. Fishing was over for him that day;
and perhaps fishing is over for most of those like him, except in the
most inaccessible streams and ponds, far up in the hills and down in
the swamps. There, where not even a jeep can travel, the cane pole
fisherman can still sit, like Pogo in the Okefenokee, perhaps with his
hat over his eyes, waiting for the big catfish to bend his pole tip to the
surface of the water.

The old methods were the expedients of meat hungry men to whom
Shakespeare was not even the name of a writer, much less the trade
name of a line of fishing equipment. And these meat fishermen, *sans*
improvements of deep freezers and refrigerators, perforce took only
what they could eat in one, or at most two sittings. Game laws, "limits"
to sizes and catches, were almost unknown or at least ignored in the
deep South. Less than twenty years ago the overall-clad fishermen in
a certain swampy neighborhood on the Pearl River in South Mississippi welcomed the first game warden's boat with a fusillade of bird
shot. He, like the revenue agent, was a source of danger to their way
of life, their food on the table.

Now, the sons and grandsons of the meat fishermen are sportsmen.
They course the streams in their motorboats, casting the banks, discoursing learnedly on the relative merits of River Runts, Lazy Ikes
and Bass Orenos. A "limit" catch is a source of enormous pride, to be
photographed, to be talked about, perhaps even to be publicized on
the sports page of the State newspaper. But the limit catches are increasingly seldom. For every fisherman who thinks like a fish, who

knows where and how the fish are feeding, a hundred amateurs are beating paths to the water, and the noise of their gabbling frightens even the lazy catfish, lurking in his hollow stump deep beneath the surface of some quiet bend.

Yet even without skill, the myriad amateurs take some fish. There are not enough game wardens to police the fishing grounds. "Fished out" is the label more and more frequently applied to once prolific waters in the South. But the fishermen are not to be denied. Such artificial impoundments as the great Cumberland, Dale Hollow and Kentucky lakes in Kentucky and Tennessee have become the Eldorado of the sport fishermen of the South. Here the successful ones are those with enough money to bring or rent a motor boat, hire a guide and stay long enough at an expensive camp to be certain of good fishing weather. The catch, perhaps several eight-to-ten-pound largemouth or maybe even a thirteen-pound walleye, will be pictured in the hometown papers and might even win the sportsman a "valuable prize of tackle" or a certificate to be framed and hung on the wall of his den.

All fishermen, though aided by guides and hundreds of dollars worth of tackle, do not catch fish in the large artificial lakes, where some skill and luck is still necessary; so methods for easy fishing have been devised. Small private lakes, stocked yearly with bass and bluegill, have become the fishing ground for clubs with stiff membership fees and a limited number of members. In such lakes the fish are plentiful. Natural food is scientifically maintained at the level to keep the bass hungry, and the club member can come to the lake after a hard day at the office and get several bass before he has finished his first cigar. The meat fishermen, those that are left, are kept out by watchful caretakers, and only an occasional small boy manages to slip over the fence and try his luck with a cane pole.

In Caroline Gordon's fine story, "Old Red," Alec Maury, a retired professor, likes to go fishing with an old Negro who can "smell fish." Mr. Maury's family disapproves. Such a companion is not dignified; but Mr. Maury keeps his companion because he respects him for his knowledge. The Negro was one of the last of the old meat fishermen. He had to know how to find fish—or go sometimes without meat on the table.

Annually, the sale of fishing equipment runs into millions of dollars, more money than is spent on equipment for any other sport. All over the South, from Lake Herrington, near Lexington, Kentucky, to Okeechobee in Florida, from Aransas Pass in Texas to the Outer Banks on the Carolina coast, motors are roaring and plugs are cutting the water. The sportsmen are searching naïvely but desperately for the thrill that once could be had by a small boy with a hand pole, sitting on the bank of a quiet, unpolluted stream. A clerk in a Lexington hardware store admitted having a thousand dollars worth of tackle and lures; but he hadn't caught a fish on his last three expeditions to Lake Herrington. One wonders: We search for the lost thrill, the big bass taken from the silent pool, but we search like civilized men, at the sporting goods counter, hoping that we can buy with money our lost heritage, that we can find our way back to instinctual living in the woods and the satisfactions that even silent-flush commodes cannot replace. But we insist on taking our gadgets to the woods with us. Recently *Popular Mechanics* published an article displaying new equipment for the "outdoorsman." Now, if one has the money, he can go camping and live as comfortably in the woods as in his glass and steel apartment. He can even take a clockwork mechanical shaver, so that the fish and deer—and the ladies of the party—won't be startled by a week-old beard.

No longer having the knowledge, we depend upon the experts to supply us with lures designed to attract—or scare—the fish into striking; and the biologists of our Fish and Wildlife Departments experiment endlessly, striving to produce bass that will reach spawning size in one season and still retain enough of their hatchery stupidity to become the catch of the fish-ignorant taxpayer as he throws his red and yellow Krazy Killer over to the shallows where the bass had just been frightened away by the speed boat now far up the lake.

Of course we no longer need to go hunting, either. In Mississippi thirty years ago a country boy began his hunting with his dog and a "rabbit stick," usually a light throwing stick, walking cane length, weighted at the end with an iron nut. When his dog "jumped" the rabbit from a briar patch or tall grass, the boy had one throw. If he missed it was up to the dog. Surprisingly often the boy hit the rabbit.

He had to know things: How to place himself just where the rabbit was likely to emerge, and of course, how to throw. If he hit the rabbit, he gutted him then and there, because the rabbit was meat for the table, and it kept better if the entrails were removed promptly. Also it was lighter to carry.

When he was twelve or thirteen, if he were lucky, the boy got a single barrel shotgun, obtainable then from Sears, Roebuck for less than ten dollars. Next, buying his shells two or three, or maybe even five at a time, he went hunting. He couldn't afford to miss, at least not many times; and whatever he shot he ate. At first he might bring home blackbirds, doves, or robins; but he always ate them. The memory of lean times was probably a family tradition, with tales handed down of "possum-meat" and "rabbit stew" in the winter and "poke-sallet" and catfish in the summer. So the boy, though he enjoyed his "sport," didn't believe in shooting anything he couldn't eat. Surprisingly, he knew it was bad to shoot sitting rabbits, quail on the ground, doves on the wheatfield. Sometimes he yielded to temptation, but he was not likely to tell anyone. He also knew it was bad form to go around shooting into squirrel nests; besides it was wasteful of ammunition. More times than not the nest was empty. The best plan was to go hunting squirrels early in the morning, before the break of dawn, and wait silently till they started playing in the tree tops. If you were good, you carried a rifle and shot the squirrel through the head. Then the meat was better. If you were very good, sometimes you could "bark" a squirrel by shooting the edge of the limb beside the squirrel's head, momentarily stunning him. But you didn't shoot him with a shotgun if you could help it, because pellets in the guts do not improve the flavor of the meat.

Not long ago some Kentucky sportsmen were arrested for shooting doves on baited fields. These men were prosperous; they were not hungry for meat. They wanted the cheap thrill of shooting without the effort of hunting for the game. Their only deterrent was the law. Now, hunters *must* be restrained by laws. One must not shoot a doe, except where specifically authorized by statute. One stag or bear per season is allowed. There are limits on squirrels, quail, and even rabbits. A certain highly publicized hunter in Tennessee shoots woodchucks; there is no limit on woodchucks, and with his high powered, scope-equipped .22 he can shoot as many as he likes.

In the society of only a few years back, the rural hunter didn't worry much about limits. He killed what his family and maybe his friends could eat. He didn't shoot any extra because it was a waste of effort and ammunition. He was reluctant to shoot a doe because he knew from his agrarian experience that one bull and ten cows will maintain a herd but when there were ten bulls and one cow, all you had was too much meat. You left the does, because then you would have deer when you were hungry again. As personal prestige takes the place of necessity, however, the strings of fish, the kills of game, become larger to attest the prowess of the hunter, and only legal restraints serve to protect the game.

It is scarcely necessary to mention the commercial hunter. When dollars replace both food and prestige as the object, female animals, the young—all go. We know what happened to the carrier pigeon and the buffalo. Surely, however, it is self-aggrandizement that threatens the whooping crane and the bear. Perhaps in the not distant future we shall read an article, "I Killed the Last Whooping Crane," and the great bird, stuffed by an expert taxidermist, will be on display in the proud hunter's club cellar. Shooting for sport is less a threat to the game than commercial hunting, perhaps, but the combination of the two present a danger that only the law can control, whereas when we hunted for meat, the game had a chance for survival on natural terms. Predators were hunted and trapped because they threatened the farmer's way of life as well as the wild food animals; but the farmer was a part of nature and did not upset the balance. When man behaves like the weasel and kills purely for the joy of killing, the efficiency of his weapons and the disappearance of natural hiding places ensures the final destruction of the game. Only the law remains as the agent of preservation.

Recognition of the law as a proper agent for the control of hunting and fishing has come slow to the South. The old idea that God put the critters here for man's use, that they were free to all who could take them, still persists. Southern hunters, particularly rural ones, are likely to become impatient with the signs, "Posted: Trespassers will be prosecuted to the full extent of the law," and either shoot them full of holes or tear them down. Yet these signs are becoming numerous. As the small farmer is being wiped out, as the large farms get larger, the big landowner, considering himself as lord of the manor, is likely to take as cold a view of poachers as the British nobility of old. While it is unlikely that any farm boy will ever be hanged in America for something equivalent to "slaying the King's deer," it is certainly obvious that hunting grounds are fast disappearing. William Faulkner, an old hunter himself, lets Ike McCaslin express the regret that should be every man's who loved the old wilderness: "This land which man has deswamped and denuded and derivered in two generations so that white men can own plantations and commute every night to Memphis. . . . No wonder the ruined woods I used to know don't cry for retribution! he thought: The people who have destroyed it will accomplish its revenge."

We can, perhaps, forecast the nature of the revenge. Perhaps it will be the final vanishing of the hunting grounds, with shooting left only for the large landowners, who will pot at doves over baited fields, using the living creatures like clay pigeons, seeing how many they can bring down without a miss. And the few meat hunters who are left will content themselves with frozen fish-sticks and neatly packaged, predressed, commercially raised rabbit from the corner delicatessen. This will be revenge enough.

But the picture is not totally dark. Though the woods are dwindling in the South and there are few streams left both large enough to support good fish and remote enough to escape the weekend hordes of fishermen, there are dedicated woods and water men who do their utmost to keep their sport as pure as possible. New codes have arisen, unwritten for the most part but based on the desire to make skill and a sense of accomplishment the primary satisfaction of the hunter and fisher. Among those who can now be called purists are the dry fly fishermen who scorn the unwary "tame" fish of the hatcheries, who penetrate the most inaccessible water courses—the rocky streams of the Blue Ridge or the Cumberlands—with all the stealth of the primal forest dwellers. These men have mastered the difficult art of laying a dry fly within inches of the nose of a feeding trout, as lightly as a live insect would drift to the water. Such men are zealous conservationists. They fight the politicians who occasionally make an effort to turn over our forests and hills to the greedy lumbermen and strip-miners. One sees their letters in newspapers and sports magazines protesting the grabs. They are contemptuous of the methods of the meat fishermen. Live bait is for the amateur, the Saturday afternoon novice who leaves his desk or factory bench to go roaring down to the most convenient parking area near a stream, armed with worms (bought by the hundred from a "live bait house"), minnows, or gaudy plugs guaranteed by the manufacturer to bring in bigger fish. He is even more contemptuous of the modernized meat fishermen who bring their iceboxes to store the fish in and ignore size and string limits. The new purists go out for pride of achievement, and they regard their sport as an art.

Even among the hunters there are those who are making an effort to repeal the law of progress and return the sport to the condition in which woodscraft was a prerequisite to success. Archery clubs are becoming fairly common. The latter day aborigines of the archery clubs hunt small game, even deer, Indian fashion, stalking their game until they are close enough for an effective shot. These men are attempting to recover what has been almost lost. The wilderness nearly gone, they hope to save what is left and recapture knowledge of the ways of the wild.

A sense of the pure aesthetics of the chase has never been quite absent from the South. A foxhunting method used rather widely in the hills of Tennessee, Alabama, Mississippi, and Georgia brings the sport as close as possible to the condition of a fine art. The hunters, not wearing pink coats, not mounted on thoroughbreds, *sans* photographs and social page accounts, loose their dogs on the hunting ground on a chill Autumn night and sit quietly around the campfire, perhaps drinking from a jug now and then, waiting for the music of the hounds, none sweeter to their ears. They can distinguish each dog by his voice. The object of the chase is to listen to the dogs in full tongue, not to capture the fox and exhibit his brush as a trophy.

The future of field sports in the South lies with the purists. The danger is in the swarming amateurs, the millions who do anything to feed their egos, not their stomachs, who are restrained only by the poorly enforced laws of our wildlife departments. Our progress, of course, cannot be halted. The factories will continue to belch their poisoned wastes into the once clear inland streams. Politicians will continue to allow the greedy to cut down the trees and tear up the hillsides for surface minerals. The maw of the industrial giant is insatiable. The ranks of the purists are all too few, and the fisherman who will release a ten-inch bass because it is unworthy of his skill is only one to the thousands who will pick the bones of fish almost too small to dress.

Yet industrialization has come late to the South. There is still a chance for the idealistic few, those who prefer knowledge carried to the heart to that coffined in the head. And in the South, as Faulkner has told us many times, there are those who can still make the old times live in the actual of today: "Those old times would cease to be old times and would become part of the present, not only as if they had happened yesterday but as if they were still happening, the men who walked through them actually walking in breath and air and casting an actual shadow on the earth they had not quitted."

The old traditions of the wild have not yet quite died out in the South, and as long as each new generation learns of what used to be, an effort will be made to preserve some of our streams and woods for the men of skill, the purists.

And the silent ghosts of the tall hunter and his ten-point buck will still haunt the remote reaches of the Elkhorn, though sandwich bags and beer cans litter the shallows at the old watering place.

WALTER SULLIVAN

The City and the Old Vision

THE URBANIZATION of the South, if not indeed a *fait accompli,* is at least a certainty of the future. It is no longer necessary to quote from the latest census figures—or from the latest Chamber of Commerce brochure—to prove that Richmond and New Orleans and Memphis are larger than they used to be. Recently, I heard a book salesman who had been born and raised in Pittsburgh complain of the difficulty he had encountered in finding his directions in Atlanta; the traffic on the new expressway there made him nervous. New roads and new buildings are everywhere. The South is covered with housing developments and expanding schools, and every day boys and girls leave the farm by the hundreds. If one needs them, however, statistics and percentages exist to support personal observation. For example, in 1930, 31 percent of the South's population lived in urban areas. Twenty years later, this percentage had jumped to 43, and by now, city dwellers are perhaps a Southern majority. In the single decade between 1940 and 1950, the population of the Birmingham area increased 21.5 percent to a total of 559,000. In Miami, the percentage of increase during the same period was 84.9, in Norfolk-Portsmouth, 72.3, in San Antonio, 48, and in Memphis, 34.7.

This increase in the size of Southern cities has been accompanied by and is to a large measure the result of industrialization, factories and plants that have been founded in the Southern region or brought into it from the North. But whatever the cause of urbanization, the growth of the Southern city is a fact, and there is slight chance, indeed, that metropolitan areas will suddenly begin to atrophy or that the process of dynamic growth will be reversed. If, as some sociologists believe will occur, the growth process should level off, the cities which are already created will remain, and in their region they will exert a cultural and economic hegemony. One can go even further than this, and point out that industrialization—which spawned the cities—is a Malthusian necessity of life. We rest ourselves upon the ledgers of Lion Oil and clothe our children in the earnings of General Motors. The South, no less than other regions, recognizes these realities.

We may even believe that urbanization is a desirable trend from a spiritual or artistic or religious point of view. And in the end, such a view might prove to be completely justified. But there is another facet to the problem: The advent of the city threatens to vitiate or to destroy entirely some of the traditional Southern standards of judgment and decorum, and this threat to most Southerners is a matter for concern. As they see it, the problem is not to turn back the clock, or even to resist change, for change of some sort is irresistible. Rather, the problem is to control the alteration, to retain for the future, some of the principles and attitudes that Southerners have cherished in the past.

I speak of retaining principles and attitudes rather than of preserving a "way of life," for in any technologically oriented society, the way of life is bound to change. A culture, like an individual, seeks its own comfort, and it is quick to adapt itself to inventions that make the mechanics of life a little less wearing on the flesh. In his book, *Not So Long Ago,* Lloyd Morris has pointed out, graphically and amusingly, the tremendous impact that the invention of the automobile had on American civilization; and certainly this impact was no less on the South than on the North. It is ridiculous to think that one section can isolate itself from the great change and flux that goes on around it, or that anyone in his right mind would recommend such a course. Even the dumb animals know that the conditions of life are not constant, and the 'possum and the 'coon adapt themselves to life in the suburbs and survive, though whether happily or not, I cannot say. And there is the unfortunate example of the passenger pigeon, which, according to Roger Tory Peterson, could not alter its gregarious habits and therefore went down to extinction in a changing world. If on this point I sound rudely insistent, it is because too many fools have tried to define the Southern tradition as a matter of simple choice between

an outhouse and an indoor, tile bath. This sort of argument is completely beside the point.

If I may be permitted the use of an old-fashioned word, I should
say that what must be preserved is not the *way* of life, but the *tone*
of it. This is a term that our grandfathers were fond of using, and
they employed it sometimes to refer to society as a whole and sometimes to refer to a specific individual and its meaning was larger on
some occasions than on others. But it was a word with a great facility
for aggregating its meaning, for adjusting itself to particular applica-
tions without modifying the basic principle that it expressed. In the
study of literature, we are told that tone is a reflection of the poet's attitude toward his material. Yet tone is not the attitude itself, but something almost separate, an adjunct, an epiphenomenon, a result. So in
the life of the South, tone was flexible and tone varied, for the basic
attitude might be reflected in different ways. But the tone was the
fashion, the manner of living, and alter though it did through the
long years, the tone would serve and it was right, as long as the attitude
remained uncorrupted. For that is how the South is always described
by capable observers who know it best—by Allen Tate, for example,
and Richard Weaver. It is described in terms of its view of itself and of
its larger more general view of the world and its attitude toward life.

When one comes to examine the basic belief of the South, he sees
that a significant threat is posed to the Southern tone by urbanization.
For what the South believes in fundamentally is the sure and certain
imperfectibility of people and things. Undoubtedly, as Richard
Weaver has pointed out, the South has profited spiritually by losing a
war. For one thing, it knows as a people that the worst can happen—
that you can hope and pray and try with all your might, but you do
not always win. But the Southern attitude and the Southern philosophy are too personal to be accounted for solely in terms of a group
experience. They are something felt immediately and individually,
they are something learned as well as something inherited; and they
are learned most easily in a rural environment.

For those of us who live in the city, especially in a period of prosperity such as we now enjoy, life is relatively stable. Of course, one is
beset by certain dangers. People are killed in automobile accidents
and little boys fall and break their arms, and teeth still ache and we

catch colds and wear glasses. But the city, as everyone knows, is well organized to deal with these annoying weaknesses of the body. If we are broken we can likely be fixed; otherwise our families can collect our insurance. And for the healthy and the careful, life is more routine and safer yet. From an economic point of view, we are told, nothing bad can happen. There is social security augmented in most cases by a pension plan, and there is unemployment compensation, and there are a score of other devices and programs to make life easier. There are few who would have things any other way. As populations increase and cities begin to grow, there is a deterioration of the individual sense of family and community responsibility, and a vacuum is created which a government agency then must fill. And the danger to the Southern philosophy is not so much in what the government does, but in the attitude that the government creates among its people. Under pressure from advertising agencies and automobile salesmen, from stock brokers with optimistic analyses and charts and clergymen with a new and more progressive eschatology, we are seduced by the philosophy that the future holds nothing for us to fear, that whatever can happen is bound to happen for the good.

Now, of course, the traditional Southerner does not believe this. He has no logical arguments with which to refute his more economically sophisticated friends who tell him that we can never have another real depression. He is simply pessimistic by tradition, and by upbringing; he has been taught that the worst can happen and that its advent is often unforeseen. But this is an argument we do not have to settle. Whether or not we have another depression, or another war, or another epidemic of poliomyelitis is not the essential question here. The problem is rather, whether or not we believe we can get appreciably closer to the millenium simply by devising ways to prevent economic fluctuations, or by discovering a vaccine or a specific for this or that disease. Before he gives you his solution to this puzzler, the Southerner, especially the rural Southerner, will ponder the alternatives for a long, long time. He is slow to praise change, for his tradition and his experience have educated him in the spurious quality of the world's alteration. He knows there is always something, and that for every old ill he can remedy, there is a new one—or two, or three— to take its place. We have penicillin and an increase in lung cancer;

we have the United Nations and a good deal more juvenile delin-
quency than we used to be bothered with; and if wages and profits are
very high now, so is the divorce rate. He observes the mixed blessings,
too—television and the drive-in movie.

Once again, let me emphasize that no one in my acquaintance advocates that we stop using modern drugs or that we abandon efforts to
attain world peace, or that the Federal Reserve Board be abolished
in favor of a freer economy. We find ourselves, like Alice in Wonder-
land, constrained to run twice as fast as we can simply to stay abreast of
where we were. It is our doom to "change the place, but keep the pain."

This is what every Southerner of fifty years ago understood and
what the rural Southerner comprehends today. But in the cities, one
is likely to lose sight of the old principle that proclaims the imperfect
nature of human existence. Somehow, in an urban environment, the
essential reality of things is hard to grasp. For one thing, since the
great depression of the 1930's, the problems that city people have
faced have been more or less individual matters, to be faced alone.
When domestic or personal reverses overtake a man who lives in the
country, they are the concern of and therefore a lesson to the community. But the concern must come first, or one can learn nothing
from another's misfortune. In the city, the accident that happens to
the other fellow is a statistic; the other man's bereavement is his own
secret, and the other man's legal entanglement, a sociological fact. As
city dwellers, we fail to identify ourselves with each other, we fail to
recognize a broadly common fate. (I refer, of course, only to this
nation. What I say here would not apply to European cities during the
last war.) In a word, year after year, the city man lulls himself into
believing that throughout the future things are going to happen for
the best. We have trouble, he thinks, but it can be remedied. A law
passed here, a court decision there, a little more research on heart disease, and then, the urbanite is likely to think, general happiness will
have been achieved.

On the other hand, life in rural areas is different, because where
there are fewer people, those few are apt to take a greater interest in
each other. A personal tragedy is a blow and a warning not to a single
person or family, but to the countryside at large. The weather is important in the country, and the weather is unpredictable, and there is

not yet much hope that we can do anything to control it. Those whose comfort—and in some cases, whose existence—depend on rainfall or the lack of it, are not inclined to believe that the world's problems can be solved by a joint committee or by executive order or by judges on a bench. And it is not only a matter of weather; it is living close to nature, and dealing with living things. One watches the seasons and the cycle of birth and death, the sowing and the reaping, the planting and the pulling, and understanding comes. A man gets a sense of his own frailty and the brevity of his own time, when he considers the large world and how long it has been turning from day back to night and following its own course from spring to winter. The man who is conscious of his frailty is the man who knows best his own individual worth.

The question arises here why, if a rural orientation is so important to the Southern tradition, that tradition is not shared by all rural communities. Properly to answer this question, we must go almost full circle and return, almost, to the place where we began. We must go back to the peculiarity of Southern history, and to the South's peculiar status in the nation, if not in the world. As everyone knows, the South has been conscious of itself as a section at odds with other parts of the Union since the early abolitionist attacks of the 1830's. Since that time, the South's awareness of its sectional identity has been confirmed by defeat and political and social reconstruction, by freight rate differentials, and absentee landlords and a new generation of abolitionists and by the Supreme Court. Decade after decade, the South remains embattled; and through the years, battle after battle is lost. Pragmatically incompetent by nature, and forced by her more clever adversaries into fighting her battles almost solely in terms of issues on which her position is weakest—for example, the race question, as C. Vann Woodward has pointed out—the South comes again and again to discomfort if not to grief. Thus the public, sectional experience confirms the private experience of the individual citizen. The personal philosophy bears extension until it is applicable to the region as a whole. The result is a spiritually integrated, philosophically homogeneous society in which public and private feeling, public and private duty coincide.

So much then for the attitude, the state of mind which describes the South, and which motivates what I have referred to as the Southern tone. The tone, itself, varies superficially from generation to generation, but it is characterized by a general individual and community effort to make as easy and pleasant as possible our human passage through an uncertain and often cruel world. Recognizing the inevitability of grief, the Southerner takes some comfort in good breeding. Manners are rules which impose form on life, and form is requisite to beauty. In a world where trouble enough is expected, good manners help people to avoid misunderstandings and unnecessary and unintended slights. Thus the Southern world is seriously concerned with the task of palliating the difficulty, of making a sometimes hard life a little easier.

The Southerner, faced with a questionable future, turns his eyes to the past. For the past, though often painful to recollect, is at least static and sure. It exists in a climate of certainty in which the worst is known, and from which, because the worst is over, the honor and the glory can be leisurely cherished by the heart. It is perhaps because the Southerner is so prone to consider the past that he is so preoccupied with questions of decorum. Like a character from one of Ernest Hemingway's novels, his hope is not for ultimate earthly victory, but for the dignity that is inherent in the bravery with which the inevitable defeat is faced.

The Southerner is a religious conservative who is unwilling to modify his fundamentalist concepts of original sin, the necessity of God's grace to individual salvation, the divinity of Christ, and the last judgment. Indeed, religion in the South furnishes an excellent example of what I mean when I speak of preserving not the specific way of life, but the tone of it. The recent great growth of the Roman Catholic Church and the Churches of Christ in the Baptist-Methodist South is evidence not of a modification of the Southerner's religious point of view, but rather of a change in the practices and beliefs of certain religious institutions. Sometimes it is necessary to change the way, to abandon the house of one's father, in order to maintain the old angle of vision and the old tone.

But, as we have seen, this view of life is not likely to survive for long in an urbanized society similar to that of New York or California. Far removed from nature, and deceived by the city's promise of a perfect tomorrow, an urban South will be in danger of losing its identity. And yet, in this time of falling farm prices and increased mechanization, the hope of a Southern agrarian society for the future is little more than an idle, visionary dream.

The South will be urbanized. But there are circumstances which mitigate the process; the South will not be urbanized in the image of the North. Now that adequate transportation is available to industry almost anywhere in the United States, business men who are looking for plant sites are not limited in their search to coastal and river ports and to rail centers. Proximity to raw materials is not so important a factor in a manufacturing operation as it once was. Today, the major considerations in plant location are the consumer market, the labor supply, the local tax rate, and in some cases, the availability and price of electric power. Given a choice between locating in an already heavily industrialized area or in a small town where no industry exists, most concerns will choose the rural area where they can exercise a monopoly control over the supply of labor, even though certain other previously important advantages—for example, a transportation complex—must be sacrificed. Therefore, principally because of the invention of the motor truck and the automobile, the South will probably have a great number of small cities and not a smaller number of very big ones.

Also, a number of Southern factory workers live in rural areas and commute from farms to work in the small town plants, and return at night to milk the cows and feed the chickens. These people retain much of the rural Southern point of view, but the influence that they exert on the culture of the urban South is easily exaggerated. Some sociologists point out that Southern cities are being peopled by immigrants from Southern farms, and they reason that as a result of this, the cities will assume something of the rural tone and outlook. I do not think this is true. I do not know how one would go about measuring the cultural impact of rural immigrants on the cities in which they settle, but it would appear from personal observation that the height of a country boy's ambition is to have his neighbors believe that he was born in town. This happens, I think, because city people are rude enough to make jokes about their country cousins, and country people are polite enough to want to please.

Let us admit readily, then, that the urban pattern of the South will not be exactly similar to that of the North. Birmingham will never be as large as Pittsburgh, and not even Houston will grow as big as New York. But this is cold comfort when one considers what has already happened, when he looks at the present size of Southern cities and sees how in these cities the old traditional view of life has begun to change. Certainly, the more slow the growth of cities, the better the chance that the cities will remain Southern, but any growth is a distinct threat. The only thing that will keep the South the South and keep it from becoming a paperback edition of the rest of the nation is some series of events, some concatenation of circumstances that will be of almost universal public consequence and that will prove that the urban promise of perpetual happiness and tranquillity is a lie. And we have these circumstances, of course, in the Supreme Court segregation decision and in the painful division of the South and of the Union that has followed.

History, as everyone knows, is fraught with irony, but there is no irony more striking than that which has always attended relations between the Northern and Southern parts of the United States. To put it as charitably as possible, for more than a hundred years the Yankees have spent their energy in a continuous and undeviating effort to keep the South somewhat subordinate to the rest of the Union, but otherwise to rebuild it in the image of the North. This process began before the Civil War; it has been going on ever since. Through the War and Reconstruction, through feast and famine, prosperity and panic, other wars and other readjustments, the North has insisted that the South stop being different, and the more vigorously the North has insisted, the more tenaciously the South has clung to the status quo. Whatever the issues involved have been, whatever the ultimate motives on either side, the American sectional argument has always been couched in terms of race. Because of this tendency of the conflict to refine itself to a question of the Negro's welfare, Professor Woodward believes that the South has argued always from a point of disadvantage and the North has held the throne of righteousness in the eyes of the world. This undoubtedly is true. But as Kierkegaard pointed out, on this earth the quality of irony is seldom final. This ability of the North always ironically to make the contention turn on the Negro question, has been a major factor in the perpetuation of the sectional identity of the South. For time after time, as the South has been defeated physically, as Southern institutions and the Southern way of life have been forcibly altered, the Southern philosophy and the Southern tone have been refreshed. Disappointed often by the painful realities of the world, time and again the South has turned more determinedly to the cult of good manners and to a study of the past and to a rejuvenated belief in the old virtues of honor and courage. Despite the superficial changes that the North has been able to induce, the South remains about as much the South as ever. If, as her enemies sometimes assert, this be a result of sectional paranoia, or of a simpler kind of regional insecurity, it is still preferable to the widespread notion that men live by bread alone and need not feed the spirit, and to the material ethics of a city oriented civilization.

So for good or bad it is conflict that has preserved the South in the past; if the North had been shrewd enough or restrained enough to deny itself the moral indulgence of the Civil War, there would be no South now except in so far as people speak of going South when they are heading for Miami. It is generally conceded that by 1860 slavery was doomed. The increases in population and the rise of an industrial economy adumbrated the end of an agrarian civilization. Change was in the air throughout the world and particularly in the United States, and Southern men were lured away from home by the cities of the North and East and in Southern towns the talk was all of factories and railroads. Then, as now, bankers, who had survived the panic of 1827, looked to the future with some confidence, and businessmen, gentlemen of affairs, spoke of a golden time to come, when under the spell of trade and the industrial machine, the millenium would all but be upon us. To win the South, the Yankees need only have left well enough alone. But they did not do this. They won a war, thereby confirmed the South in her old ways, and prolonged the conflict.

Since the ante-bellum days, seldom has the South been nearer the rest of the nation in spirit than it was in the years immediately following World War II. Cities were mushrooming. Industry, some of it lured from other sections, was settling throughout the area. Young men, just out of the service, were restless, and many of them gravitated to the growing urban centers where in their restlessness they felt at home. Traditional ceremonies and customs were being abandoned; traditional loyalties were being forgotten; and most important, the traditional attitude toward life itself was losing its hold on the Southern mind. Whatever the North or the West wanted in the way of a Southern resettlement, they needed once more only to bide their time. Chamber of Commerce presidents, politicians, union leaders and school teachers worshipped the god of progress throughout the South. And things were changing, for better or worse, depending on how one looks at it, but changing in such an unmistakable direction that many historians had already written off as archaic any concept of the South as a separate and different national section. In this more or less natural course of change there was a certain unevenness, and there were those who would hurry the process, particularly among Negroes, though according to many of his own evaluations, in the last ten years, the Negro had made great strides.

Now, in the mid-fifties, the situation is different. Under the impact of the greatest and most tragic domestic tensions that the South has experienced in this century, the myth of human perfectibility, the philosophy of the city, has been sternly questioned and found to be spurious. The population of the South, particularly the urban population, is in the process of being disabused. It is true, certainly, that many people approve of, or are at least generally in sympathy with, the social and economic changes that are being made at the insistence of our national government. Many, indeed, think change has come tardily and proceeds now at too slow a pace. But many others, and these are a majority, oppose any change at all that they themselves have not initiated; they resent Northern interference as hypocritical and officious and in many cases downright dishonest, in view of contemporary race relations in the North. But this is all common knowledge, and such argument obscures the significant point.

The important fact is that once more the South is going to lose. She is going to lose as she lost the Civil War a century ago, and the North is going to win a very similar victory. To the great distaste of most Southern white people, there will be some kind of real or ideal racial integration in public conveyances, in schools, in parks. It will be delayed longer in some places than in others. But it will come. As in every conflict with the North, the white South is doomed to defeat.

But will the Negro win? It is his doom to think so. Because for a hundred years his Northern white neighbors have been telling him, and he has been telling himself, that his only source of discomfort and failure in the world was his black flesh. Or as he put it in a song, "My only sin is in my skin." But he is wrong there. Like the white man, he is the son of Adam. And on the morning when he wakes up to find himself completely integrated—if indeed such a morning ever comes, even in Chicago or New York—he will find the world still cold, still hard to get along in, even with unemployment compensation and social security, even with socialized medicine and FEPC.

So for all of us the disillusionment is here or it is coming. For the white and the black, the good and the bad, the wise and the well meaning and the foolish. And the promise of the city, which almost had us convinced for a little while, has been exposed once more by the course of history with an assist from the liberals in the North. Maybe later, the philosophy of the city will get another chance. In fifty years or seventy-five or a hundred, maybe once more we will be lured into believing that all that glitters is the twenty-four carat reality, and that all men love each other and are born good and pure, and that we will all have an atomic dishwasher by and by, which will be the best possible happiness insurance to carry into a very certain and well fed tomorrow.

But in the meantime, we are not very comfortable down here. And this in spite of big payrolls, of price supports and TVA lakes and new highways and GI loans—this in spite of industrial development and urbanization. For the moment, and at least for a few moments to come, the Supreme Court has made it possible for the South to retain its old view of the world, to keep the tone, and bear the suffering and to remain, for better or worse, a little bit different from the rest of the nation—possible, beneath superficial, visible alterations, to remain the South.

ROBERT RAYMOND BROWN

Southern Religion, Mid-Century

IN HIS ESSAY on Southern Religion which appeared in *I'll Take My Stand,* Allen Tate wrote that there was no longer any respect offered the professional man of religion and no credence given to his ability to speak convincingly on high things. Probably he was right. Mr. Tate, who frankly confessed his own irreligion, seems to have been a product of his times. The 1920's to 30's rather fancied themselves for their spirit of agnosticism. Mistaking crudeness and assertiveness for reality, they strutted boldly down the avenue of months, completely satisfied with their self-estimates. Then they ran directly into something called a depression.

In that day I was a Southern college boy, complete with corduroy balloon trousers, a yellow slicker adorned with names, slogans and doubtful art, and a felt hat turned up jauntily at both ends. My cigarette hung from the corner of my mouth with studied nonchalance and the inevitable copy of *College Humor* peeked carelessly from my pocket; all this to proclaim me an up-to-date student of life. I was a junior grade example of the times; a representative of twenty in the roaring twenties. Humanism was still in the saddle for me, too. Religion wore plus-fours. Man was the master of things. I could not permit myself to be fettered by any false pretensions to personal modesty, for the world required only the talents of my college class to bring it to its golden age.

Looking back now, I must confess that whatever respect my colleagues and I had for cassock and collar was mostly on the order of indulgent courtesy. It was the kind of esteem one pays a very old gentleman as a reward for past usefulness and in spite of present in-effectualness. Oh, we attended church in that day; but usually for one of three reasons. We went because of family insistence, or to watch the pretty girl who sang from the front pew in the choir, or in order to remain eligible for the church basketball team. Perhaps religion *per se* held its moments of inspiration for us, but for the life of me I cannot remember any of them. In fact, I cannot recall being really enthusiastic about any religious-related enterprise at that time nor more than coldly courteous to any professional man of prayer. Yes, I suppose I was just as representative of the youth of the twenties as Mr. Tate was of adulthood. And my own sophomoric thinking veri-fied to the letter his contention that religion was the anachronism of the age.

However, that era is dead in the South. The Depression killed it. And now, a new age has been born. With this new age, a new light has dawned concerning the things of the spirit.

Who, or what, creates the character of an age? Who, or what, moulds it? Does it result from a mass movement of little people all advancing unconsciously in the same direction? Is it brought into being by a few giants who have thrust themselves above mediocrity to do the thinking and leading of those who will not think or lead themselves? Or does Deity, like a loving earthly parent, offer His own affectionate, behind the scene, guidance? Modern historians, and even theologians, vary in their opinions.

They vary as to who or what creates an era's character and the how of it; but they vary almost not at all on the fact that it *is* created. His-tory itself makes denial impossible. Look at the 1920's and compare them, religiously, to the 1950's. There was a supreme confidence in man's ability to lift himself by his own bootstraps thirty years ago. Now, there is general admission of a need for, and a dependence upon, what is outside oneself. In the 1920's, to use Mr. Tate's words, "Reli-gion was not properly a discussion of anything." Now, a rediscovery of the answers it offers to the burning issues of life is making it the center of intelligent man's thought and practice. In the 1920's, reality was defined in terms of human sensory experience and judged by the tests of taste, touch, smell, sight, and sound. Today, even the most avowed pragmatist admits to the reality of the spiritual and eternal

verities. In the 1920's, H. G. Wells' battery of scientists were not only
going to save the world from invasion, but also lead it to its bright,
new Shangri-La. These thirty years later, men of science are bidding
the world to repentance and to prayer. A remarkable number of them
are quitting their laboratories in favor of the sacred ministry. Those
who do not, are nonetheless putting the church first in their lives. This
could not have happened in the age just past.

Again, the family is rediscovering God today. The world's needs
and the church's answers have combined to re-establish a program of
family worship which was practically non-existent two or three decades ago. This revitalization of the religion of the home is strong
throughout the South. One sees in the last quarter of a century, as
never before, a return to breakfast table prayer, to a grace at mealtime
tradition and to an established habit of Sunday worship as a family
unit. And the best part of it all is that it seems to be motivated, not by
a sense of cold duty, nor enforced discipline, nor yet from a hold-over
habit which has lost its meaning. It appears, rather, to be a simple,
natural and warm desire to praise God with a sense of family together-
ness and home solidarity.

Young people have changed today. The youth of the twenties really
were indifferent. They just didn't care. Granting a few exceptions, the
rest were caught up in a postwar triumph and a Wall Street prosperity
which gave the self-assurance false security always provides. It is not
so now. I never cease to be impressed by the difference of, say, the
fraternity house of today and the fraternity house of the twenties. A
lot remains unchanged, of course; you have no difficulty understanding you are in a fraternity house. But at the same time, you can find
books on religion. You can listen to religious discussions based on
information and not conjecture. You can see an easy acceptance of
religious responsibility and a marked consciousness of the moral law.

Perhaps the most remarkable thing of all is the transition which
has taken place in the man on the street. The indifference he manifested in the twenties has given place to a present willingness, indeed
a desire, to talk of things of the spirit openly and without embarrassment. Take any bus, any stop for coffee in a cafe, listen to any conversation in a country club locker room; the chances are you will hear
religion and church being discussed as naturally and normally as any

other important aspect of life. This was assuredly not the case thirty years ago. The norm then was for a man to protest the demands of church and worship. As regularly as possible he would take out his religion in his wife's name. And while he might tip his hat to God, he would hasten his steps to get past Him as quickly as possible.

Truly the pendulum has swung from its secular position all the way over to the religious conviction that God, not man, is the Master of things. It is a new age indeed!

Naturally, there has been a lot of catching up to do. Having confessed their need, sincere, thinking people of the South have also had to confess their ignorance of that which opens for them all the inevitable resources of God. Lacking a firsthand knowledge of Biblical theology and personal experience in a personal religion, they are flocking to the church for public worship, and, more especially, for the small study groups and prayer cells which the church sponsors. The movement is not completely and solely characteristic of the South but there never has been such a general rush for information and experience in the things of God as there is today. Especially popular are the informal discussion groups and prayer groups.

"I have attended Sunday school all my life but I still don't know how to make my religion effective in my life." "My work is important. It demands everything I have. I cannot meet my opportunities and responsibilities alone and without God." "For the first time I am beginning to see a meaning to life and my own relation to it. That meaning is God." These are a few of the fairly representative remarks which lay men and women are making today.

In a certain Virginia parish, a professional writer, a corporation lawyer, the dean of a medical school, a public relations executive and the president of a large trucking concern met regularly for a discussion of Christian theology. Similar meetings were also held with a second group composed of graduate students, junior executives and young professional men. In Little Rock, Arkansas, another body of leading citizens meets periodically for the same purpose. A number of such groups gather in Washington, D. C., in Houston and Dallas, in Birmingham and Atlanta. Such informal sessions seem to be mushrooming up everywhere in the South. People are coming together, worshipping together, discussing the great church doctrines together, and then going out as individuals to apply their knowledge and experience in their everyday lives. They are thoroughly sincere in this and their influence is being felt in homes and communities as well as in the church all over the South.

And lest it be thought that this "catching-up process" is confined only to the intelligentsia of the larger communities, let it be hastily stated that there is no such social and metropolitan discrimination. Starting from a different premise, people in the towns and country are doing the same thing. The very lack of fellowship and of adequate library facilities on religion in some rural areas is making the clergy and the local church the natural focal point for much of the moral education in the area. People are meeting in hamlet and village, too. Their theme now is, "Let us know the Christ." The metropolitan group system is being duplicated over and over again in less populated districts.

It is interesting to note that men entering the ministry come from certain specific backgrounds. They come first of all from families where the father is a clergyman. They come next from the farm. Then, in diminishing order, they come from the professions, the arts and sciences and trades. Aside from the families where there is a clergyman, more young men are entering the ministry today from rural areas than from any other source. Not only is this because they live close to nature and have a firsthand experience of the reverent awe which inevitably comes with close association to God's natural law; it is also because the life and teaching of the rural church has sharpened their awareness of Him. And never forget that the South is still essentially an agrarian society.

Thus, while the metropolitan population is beginning its quest with a search for knowledge which leads to experience, the town and country citizen is starting from experience and searching for a confirming knowledge. Whichever the way, they both end at the same place, with a quenched thirst for a knowledge and experience of God and of eternal life.

Of course there are those who explain the whole movement away as a kind of "fox-hole religion." They insist that the crises of the times and the countless burning issues which face the South are prompting the fearful to dig into their little superstitious burrows of hoped-for security. They contend, with some truth, that the contemporary rush for popular literature which portrays religion as the granter of personal rewards and the open door to secular success, is basically a selfish one. They even infer that the changes which are occurring in the South, despite the Southerner's wishes, are forcing him to return to religion as a nostalgic escape to "the good old days." In a word, they question the motives and the consequences of this religious action. They point out that apples come from apple trees and persimmons come from persimmon trees. You cannot get an apple from a persimmon tree and you cannot get a persimmon from an apple tree. The fruit of the tree is the inevitable result of the seed which is planted. Even so, the end result of an action is always the consequence of the means taken to reach it. For these reasons, there are those who discount this increased interest in the South concerning things religious. They think it is only temporary and prophesy that its results will be little more than negative.

Possibly they are right but there is another side. The subject of pure motives would demand still another essay on the Christian doctrine of man. There is no space for it here. But a reminder should be given that to date there has been only one historic person, a carpenter from Nazareth, who has shown complete purity of motive and perfect virtue. No mortal man has yet approached the throne of heaven with an unadulterated mind and heart. Nevertheless, God has still had a way of transforming motives, of directing minds and of purifying hearts. What is often begun in selfishness is directed into selflessness from above. Perhaps this is what is happening in the South right now. Whatever the primary reasons men may have for approaching the church's door in our times, as they enter through it and take a permanent place within the environment of God's house, the miracle of God's transforming grace can begin to take place. Persimmons can become apples and I cannot refrain from mentioning it!

To explain, specifically, in what ways this miracle is occurring in the South is, however, a more difficult matter. There is not one South. There are three. There is the Old South of Virginia and the Carolinas; the Deep South of Georgia, Alabama and Mississippi; and the Southwest of Arkansas, Oklahoma and Texas. Besides, there are the border States which are composite of all three. The Southern States have their common denominator in history and the "Southern way of life." Yet, each has a distinctive mark which separates it from its neighbor. And again, without invading the field of another essayist, it is important to understand that these distinctive characteristics give color to Southern religion even as they tincture every other aspect of its life.

Look first, then, to the Old South. How is the religion of this section to be characterized? Perhaps with the word "gentleman," or "gentle-man." This characteristic of the Old South has been smiled at as a carry-over from a long dead plantation aristocracy. It has been contemptuously called the consolation prize of a defeated Confederacy. It has been discounted as the poverty-stricken recompense of a poverty-stricken people. Yet all such estimates have failed to make it any less real. Thoughtful little courtesies, extravagant but well turned praise, charm of manner and warmth of hospitality, are considered as fruits of the spirit in the Old South. One must not only be a gentleman, he must be a gentle-man.

Occasionally outsiders become impatient with the seeming casualness and unhurried approach to so-called progress which such gentleness assumes. But Virginians and Carolinians make a courteous response to impatience, too. They explain it isn't that they are lacking in spiritual adventure or religious vision; it is simply that their three hundred and fifty years of history have taught them to make haste slowly. They have their own traditional way of doing things and it has served them well. As it was in the beginning, is now, and ever shall be—Old South Religion!

Virginians have canonized their own company of saints and proceeded without fanfare to cut the cloth of their lives according to such historic virtues as those saints manifested. They begin with Thomas Jefferson. Recognizing his philosophy of humanism, they refuse to emphasize it. They prefer, rather, to point out the worth-whileness of human dignity and the accent on academic freedom which he practiced and preached. Lesser saints include George Washington, John Marshall, Stonewall Jackson and Woodrow Wilson. But the chief apostle of Old South morality and religion is, of course, Robert Edward Lee. His own sweet courtesy, his deep personal humility and his untarnished loyalty to duty, have removed all abstractions from Southern religion and offered a personal example which Southerners everywhere strive to emulate.

This approach of gentleness, history and Southern sainthood have resulted in a morality and religion which is very deep and altogether fine. It has created a faith which is completely unified with every other aspect of life; economic, academic, historic, and social. It has made religion a kind of broad river flowing easily between two high banks. The individual worshipper is permitted to swim where he will within that river, but he is always restricted by the banks of its tradition. And the river itself can never flood with the tides of license. The banks are too high.

Furthermore, the Old South's approach has established a deep loyalty in the individual church-goer which will not permit him to question any responsibilities the church might lay upon him. More often than not, the layman and not the clergyman, is taking leadership in ecclesiastical affairs. When he holds a church office or stands in any other position of influence, he plays his full part and exerts his greatest energies to bring about the desired result. This sense of duty and responsibility is deeply felt by the Southerner and it does not occur to him to protest when he is called upon.

Again, gentleness plus history have fashioned an easy way of incorporating religion into the home life. Clergymen are regularly considered as members of the family. They are called upon to engage in occasions of family joy as often as they are asked to preside over family sorrow. It is expected that they will be on hand for family reunions, graduation exercises, debutante parties and every other type of family gathering. And they are not treated as visitors or strangers; they are accepted as any other member of the family, without trace of formality or self-consciousness. The children, meanwhile, are being raised in the traditions of their grandparents to the third and fourth generation. They are taught that, "There are certain things our family doesn't do." They are trained in a natural approach to religion. It is understood by each of them that the family pew is to be fully occupied on Sunday, that worship is a family matter, that lack of courtesy and refinement and responsibility is a mark, not only against the individual, but against the family of which he is a member.

Of course there are always exceptions to the rule. There is a mild rebellion here and there against such characteristic "gentlemanly" religion. One occasionally finds a reaching out for progress and an almost ludicrous pride in modernization. Witness the advertisement of the Virginia church which invites its readers: "Come and worship in the beauty of holiness, the warmth of Christian fellowship and the comfort of air conditioning." Newcomers have also had some small effect with their insistence upon a modern, streamlined church polity. The great rush of government employees from Washington into Northern Virginia has completely changed the character of that section of the State. But, then, Virginians no longer accept it as a part of the Old South. And from Fredericksburg, Virginia, to Charleston, South Carolina, the traditional character remains. The people are resisting the encroachments of "Yankee philosophy," whenever and wherever possible. Freedom of the individual, a studied humility, loyalty to duty, and gracious courtesy are still the hallmarks of Old South religion. The words "Christian" and "gentleman" are synonymous.

This emphasis on a "traditional" religion may seem to deny what has been said concerning the casual religion of the 1920's. The paradox is more apparent than real. Virginia and the Carolinas were as caught up in the irresponsible humanism of the twenties as any other Southern State. Theirs was the same indifference, the same lack of warmth for spiritual matters and the same belief in the ability of man to work out his own salvation. But, in the intervening years, a new pride has been aroused in the life and customs of the Old South. The bankruptcy of humanism sent the people back to the "old time religion" of their ancestors. The many excellent fiction and non-fiction works on Colonial and Confederate history assisted in creating this new interest. Thus, a very real renaissance has taken place in the past thirty years which has revived the customs of ante-bellum days and applied them, as far as possible, to the practical problems of modern life. In no small degree, the religion of the Old South today is not the religion of its fathers—but of its grandfathers and great-grandfathers.

The Deep South of Georgia, Alabama and Mississippi portrays many of the same religious characteristics. There is a similar respect for freedom and for duty; the same regard for gentleness and responsibility. This is especially true of the more liturgical church bodies. Still, there is a difference. This section, with its higher percentage of Negroes, its greater dependence upon the land and its more sparsely populated rural areas, has a character of its own. It is reflected in the uniquely personal and individualistic quality of feeling and emotion which its religion possesses. There is a certain reserve in the worship of the Virginian and the Carolinian. Even those church bodies which are normally characterized by their zealous appeals to the heart are more restrained. But in the Deep South religion is uninhibited. The fruits of the spirit are not so much gentleness of nature and a dependence upon history as they are an elation born from the knowledge of salvation, and a tenacity in holding onto the spiritual freedom which has been rescued from moral sadness.

The Deep South carries Martin Luther's Justification by Faith and the Priesthood of All Believers to its highest power. God speaks personally to the individual, grants him the gift of faith as proof of his salvation, then opens the wicket gate to the presence of Jesus for him. But the Devil also exercises his powers. He whispers cunningly into the believer's ear and tears away at everything which God has wrought. The people believe strongly in an anthropomorphic Satan. One gets the impression they believe more in the reality of Satan than in the reality of God.

This is the "Bible Belt" country and the stronghold of verbal inspiration. The emphasis is upon the "Thou shalt nots" of moral restriction and the Books of Daniel and Revelation provide the proof-text of its teaching. Its adversary, the Devil, does indeed walk the earth as a roaring lion, seeking whom he may devour. And the righteous man must continually be on guard lest he fail in his responsibility to heaven and thereby become the slave of hell.

In some ways this approach to religion is reflected by a stern Puritanism and a rigid legalism. It is filled with warnings and threats of things to come. A traveler driving through these States cannot but notice with what regularity road signs will call him to repentance and warn him of the coming of Christ. A revival of some sort is always under way in communities of over five thousand population. The most popular ones are held under canvas and the sawdust trail is everywhere evident. The Deep South is serious about these revivals. It does not look upon them as mere entertainment, or an easy means of granting fellowship to the isolated. Neither is its evangelical approach an artificial thing. Granting the power of Satan, it is the responsibility of the Christian, and an act of friendship, to assist his fellowman toward salvation. It is most energetic, therefore, in its concern for the unchurched.

But there is also great stress upon the comfortableness of the Gospel and the security provided by the presence of Jesus. The economic insecurity of so many people naturally tends in this direction. "Jesus, Lover of my soul, let me to Thy bosom fly," expresses a deep longing for many of them. Other such hymns and camp songs as "Throw Out the Lifeline," "Harbored in Jesus," and "Revive Us Again," stand high on the hit parade of their revival music. And, in the conviction of possessing the sought-after security, there comes the climaxing hymn of praise: "Joy, Joy, Joy, Joy, Down in My Heart." The religion of the Deep South is quite sentimental and nostalgic. Its desire for security does not find solace in *Peace of Mind,* or *The Power of Positive Thinking,* so much as it does "In the Little Brown Church in the Wild Wood." It wants its worship to be tinged with emotion and feeling. It wants to be aroused and purified and cleansed. It believes in the power of faith healing and in the drama of instantaneous conversion. Above all else, it believes in spiritual joy—the joy which comes to an individual when he realizes he has been saved from the clutches of Satan by the power of his faith in Jesus.

Obviously, the liturgical churches and the other more firmly established denominations of the Deep South will find much to criticize in this characterization. It is not fair to them. They are indeed of the Old South pattern in their gentleness and history. But this exaggerated Protestantism with its joy and its sadness, its Puritanism and its nostalgia, its escapism and its salvation, is in the majority and more characteristic of the land.

The question again arises whether this Deep South religion has continued uninterrupted over the years or is the result of a recent revival born out of the insolvency of the humanistic 1920's. In this case it seems to be both. During the twenties the Bible Belt remained constant to its beliefs. It did not succumb to the carefree deification of man in any-

thing like the degree of the rest of the South. In fact, it resisted this
heresy with the same determination it fought the "new thought" of
J. T. Scopes and the arguments of Clarence S. Darrow at the Scopes
Trial. But at the same time, the attacks of the "new thought" forced
it back upon itself until it had practically to withdraw from the arena
and isolate itself. Its insistence upon verbal inspiration found few converts in those days. The sneers of the age gave it an inferiority complex.
It became, as a consequence, a little island of puritanical, legalistic, joy
in a vast ocean of indifference. It was there, but it was not very effective.

In the next thirty years conditions changed. A new revival began
to take place. The Deep South became increasingly vocal, more evangelical. Today it crowds the air waves with its radio broadcasts, calls
constant attention to itself with its loudspeaker trucks and reaches even
into the North for converts to its beliefs and practices. There is no inferiority complex now, nor any hesitancy in making prophecies, insisting upon Biblical infallibility and calling for repentance. This is a
convinced faith. It stands unresilient before the criticism of others even
while it offers its special rewards of faith, health, salvation and joy.

If anything, the religion of the Southwest is evangelical in the
Chamber of Commerce sense of the word. As people have moved
from the Old South and the Deep South to settle in Arkansas, Oklahoma and Texas, they have brought with them the religious characteristics of their ancestors. One has little difficulty in finding the gentle,
cultural religion and tradition of ante-bellum days along the Mississippi delta in Arkansas. There is a plantation type civilization and a
traditional approach to church and worship which possesses a definite
Old South character. At the same time, the Deep South has its influence. Moving further West and South, you will find a new "Bible
Belt" with the same religious traits found in Georgia, Alabama and
Mississippi. Added to this, is the large influx of Northerners during the
past thirty years. They have brought their energetic, production-line
traditions, too. These people, from whatever part of the nation, have
come to the Southwest as a new country. They have come with the
vision and faith that their new life will offer a new security, a new
culture. Pour them into the crucible together, add the well known
resources of their new land, and there comes out—progress. It is obvi-

ous that all this would be carried over into the religion of the section.

Perhaps its most apparent feature is the leadership offered by its laity. Businessmen are bringing into their churches the same enthusiasm they employ in commerce. They are concerned with building and with growing. And they are employing the methods of the secular world in order to reach these desired ends. Sometimes this is a little shocking to the old-line worshipper. He is not accustomed to the type of church advertising encountered in the Southwest nor to the boldness with which he is solicited for church membership and support. It is amusing to note the farsighted planning which begins to think of "branch offices" almost before a new congregation is formed. In the matter of fund raising, it is amazing to see how expeditiously church people turn to the experts for assistance in reaching their goals. The friendly partnership which exists between clergy and laity and the way the clergy trust their congregations in church planning is unusual, too. Laymen head up the local committees on evangelism. Laymen conduct many of the public worship services. Laymen show the vision and confidence when sometimes the more conservatively trained clergy do not. The results are readily seen in the size of the building campaigns, in the support of local church budgets and in the founding of new churches. Religion in the Southwest is building monuments to God in the form of new, impressive, physical construction and with rapid advances in the establishment of more congregations. This is due, in no small part, to the part played by the people in the pews.

In accordance with its Chamber of Commerce philosophy, this area of the South is also emphasizing numerical growth as a sign of prosperity, and numerical involvement as a proof of spiritual health. For instance, a certain Texas community with a population of 3,500 had a "Go to Church Sunday" recently and worked to get 4,000 people to their churches on that date. Inasmuch as their goal was 500 more than the entire population of the town, their efforts might be considered as slightly over-optimistic, but they came close to achieving it nevertheless. It is even so throughout the Southwest. How many members? How many "additions" per year? How many in church and Sunday school each week? The answers to these questions are vital. For the health of the local church, the denomination and the church as a whole, is judged accordingly.

Another aspect of this "newness" and Southwestern pioneering is seen in the architecture of its churches. There is a very real effort to build its dreams into its construction. Traditional Gothic and Greek Revival buildings are no longer satisfying. Their conservatism is accepted with resignation when it must be. But given the opportunity, congregations will vote for the new transitional or contemporary or "characteristic" architecture. They want color and lines and a practical efficiency in their churches as well as their homes. They are not impressed by the tried and true, nor yet by their historical buildings. They will take visitors to the Alamo and the Spanish missions in San Antonio, or to the territorial capitol in Little Rock, but they, themselves, are far more impressed by the great edifices which have gone up where only vacant lots stood several years ago.

Of course, as all this shows, religion in the Southwest is more inclined to be activity-centered than subjectively experienced. The experience is there, but it is not personal in the sense of Old South tradition and Deep South joyfulness. This is a "learning by doing" approach. It is the employment of individual energy and talent for the mutual spiritual satisfaction of completed spiritual goals. In countless small congregations men form their own "labor parties," and give their Saturdays to the erection of their buildings. Young people cut the church yards and trim the hedges. Women give benefits for carpets and draperies and make large contributions to the annual church budgets. It is rare indeed not to find elevations of proposed construction hanging on church walls as reminders to the congregations of their future.

Undoubtedly there is more money available in the Southwest than in either of the other two sections of the South. This is a fast growing area with a rapid industrial expansion. This is not a one-crop economy. There is a diversification of cotton, cattle and oil plus the security of industry's regular salaries. This fact contributes greatly to the optimism of the land which in turn expresses itself in continued expansion and a studied indifference to costs. Arkansas, Oklahoma and Texas have their conservatives. They know they are not as wealthy as the East believes, nor as many of their own people would like to believe. In some areas there is a distinct poverty complex. But on the whole, optimism rules and it is carried over into religious thinking even as it is into secular pursuits.

In the 1920's, "religion was not properly a discussion of anything," in the Southwest. What there was of it was habitual and uninspiring. This is not to imply that men of God were not doing their energetic best to bring their people alive to the things of the spirit, nor that there were not a conscientious few who took their real place in preserving the faith and instilling it in the minds and hearts of their off-spring. It is only that they had such poor success in overcoming the indifference of a humanistic age which was far more concerned with eating, drinking and being merry. The change began to take place when religion grabbed hold of the coattails of secular prosperity and growth. It took the Depression to bring men to heel. But when they began to climb back up the ladder of success again, religion was ready to go with them.

In spite of this Chamber of Commerce approach to religion, there is still a deeply entrenched understanding of the things which belong to the faith. It is difficult to determine which came first, the faith or the building. Probably they had an equal effect upon each other. Certainly faith gave the impetus which set the building in motion. Yet in literally thousands of instances, it was "progress" which captured the flagging interests of previously unexcited people and brought them back into the church's life and showed them how to expend every effort in developing that life. Now, God is worshipped, not only at a Sunday service, but in the erection of lasting monuments, in a program of personal evangelism and in the optimism of individual trust.

The South finds itself today in the midst of a religious revival where each of its separate parts is relating itself to the whole. There is, of course, a great deal that is amiss in the temper and disposition of its religion. One could wish that the Old South would reach out beyond courtesy to evangelism, that the Deep South would have an equal place for the mind along with the heart, and that the Southwest would dress up its shirt-sleeve religion a little with a spiritual coat and tie. Still, when you look back to the lifeless, emaciated and misdirected thing which passed for religion a quarter of a century ago, you cannot but agree that today's Southern religion is a living, breathing, growing reality which has become unbound.

Now, religion is a discussion of everything. People in the South are recognizing the reality of the supernatural world. With thirsty minds and zealous hearts, with calloused hands and bended knees, they are approaching the church as an eternal home. It all may be a "fox-hole" religion; the normal "escapism" of insecure times. In the final analysis only history can make the judgment. Meanwhile, I prefer to think that the spirit of the 1920's will never return, that God is truly alive, that the day of the humanist is past; and that the South will continue to go "from strength to strength in the life of perfect service."

RONALD F. HOWELL

Education for the
Uncommon Man

THE UNCOMMON MAN is the *gentleman*.

Around the turn of the century, kindly but impoverished old South-ern ladies, whose singular mission was to maintain the genteel tradi-tion of ante-bellum days, were wont to ask aspiring youths, returning from summer vacation in the North, if they had perchance met a gentleman among the Yankees. Those who replied that they had were certain to encounter stares of pained incredulity from the *grandes dames*. Discounting the practice of the very wealthy in dispatching their sons to Princeton, all decent Southern folk of course knew that the kindred of Sherman, Sumner, and Stevens, whatever their mate-rial fortune, could hardly vaunt that most exalted of titles. The pro-duction of the gentleman, the prime enterprise of university experi-ence, could be fully guaranteed only on a Southern campus, preferably one of pre-Civil War vintage like Mr. Jefferson's Charlottesville. And the old ladies, many of them widows of Confederate soldiers, who now earned a paltry livelihood as matrons of Southern dormitories, held fast to their creed and subtly helped indoctrinate a generation of South-ern youths. For if the purpose of the university was to make the gentleman, then the most worthy byproduct of that achievement was to have taught the romantic message of the Old South and to have inspired a reminiscent longing for its ways. Hence a typical sentiment of the alumnus who years later returns to his wooded alma mater is that somehow Southern education has always been infused with nostalgia for the tradition.

When Thomas Wolfe returned to Chapel Hill shortly after his graduation, he experienced pangs of nostalgia characteristic of all who hold sentimental affection for the universities of the South. Of Eugene Gant he wrote in *Look Homeward, Angel:* "He went back to Pulpit Hill for two or three days of delightful loneliness in the deserted college. He prowled through the empty campus at midnight under the great moons of the late rich spring; he breathed the thousand rich odors of tree and grass and flower, of the opulent and seductive South; and he felt a delicious sadness when he thought of his departure, and saw there in the moon the thousand phantom shapes of the boys he had known who would come no more." In *Lanterns on the Levee* William Alexander Percy, decades after leaving Sewanee, reflected on that happy Arcadia: "It's a long way away, even from Chattanooga, in the middle of the woods, on the top of a bastion of mountains crenelated with blue coves. It is so beautiful that people who have been there always, one way or another, come back. For such as can detect apple green in an evening sky, it is Arcadia—not the one that never used to be, but the one that many people always live in; only this one can be shared."

Legions of other old grads besides men of letters have expressed similar emotions, though usually in less poetic words. For Southerners, with their strong yet probably subconscious sense of history and community, feel an identity with the old (perhaps wistfully with the Old South that preceded and thus knew not defeat); and they enjoy, however sadly, their own collegiate memories of youthful comradeship, of shared experiences, of well-being, of belonging. The feeling itself is as innate in the Southern way as are its objects: Regional, local, and family attachments, legal order, balanced social life, good manners, leisure, organic growth within the tradition. The Southern campus remains one of the essential symbols of the Southern way, and the Southern gentleman is at once its child and protector.

It is commonplace to hear the misunderstood ideal of the Southern gentleman parodied in derision. Even eulogies of the ideal, this continuation of the chivalric tradition, are apt to sound like enraptured orations to the Kappa Alpha Order on Founder's Day. Yet, as is equally true of "gracious living" in the South, the ideal is neither hollow nor untenable. It emphatically does not refer to the narrow sophisticate, the superficial dilettante, or the callous snob. Instead, sympathetically portrayed, the Southern gentleman is tolerant, kindly, broad-minded, non-puritan, moderate, hospitable, and courteous. His ethics are Aristotelian and religiously oriented (frequently though not essentially cast in an Anglican mold), and his politics, a subject that enlists his earnest participation, non-doctrinaire. Laying claim to what the Renaissance called *virtù*, he is a man of parts, catholic interests, and large compassion. A totally integrated personality, he is also supremely gregarious and sees himself as rightly assimilated into an organic familial and social order that has a sense of purpose and continuity. More concerned with *being* and *thinking* than *doing,* he has a critical though genial view of life. His character is well-balanced and honorable. The Southern gentleman boasts the spiritual lineage of the English Cavalier transplanted to these shores centuries ago.

As the vestige of a status, hierarchical society, he encourages the doubt that his kind of gentleman is possible in any other society. Nevertheless, his status society, while properly aristocratic and conservative, does not reject the democratic principle of equality of opportunity. Translating "aristocracy" literally as the "rule of the best" and understanding by "conservatism" the philosophy of "preserving" the best, it restricts the highest offices not to the "rich and well born" but to the most qualified and deserving, wherever they are found. In his *Idea of a University* Cardinal Newman, speaking of just this kind of gentleman and his society, concluded that "it is almost a definition of a gentleman to say that he is one who never inflicts pain." The Southern ideal contains the manifold implications of that definition and adds to it the classical Greek concept of the gentleman as the man of virtue whose natural function is social and political participation. One has only to recall Hugh Swinton Legaré's dream of establishing an Athenian democracy in Old Charleston to admit that Southerners once took this ideal seriously.

To commend the ideal of Southern education as it was espoused in the Old South is not to assert that it was invariably or ever completely realized, even when the South most fervently thought it was. *Ideals* seldom are. But it did serve as the standard and, Greek democracy and status society aside, so should it serve in Southern education today. How wide the South is of the mark, or how nigh to, is the subject here for later speculation and impression. Education in the Old South, not initially but at least in late colonial days and until the Civil War, approached the goal, and Southern education today has a clearer opportunity to approximate it than had that of the period from 1865 to 1920.

Now, education in the Old South was pre-eminently education for the planter aristocracy. "Tobacco planters, eagerly creating a privileged aristocracy," explains Merton Coulter in his *College Life in the Old South,* "sought to transplant from England the Renaissance education for an ideal gentleman. . . ." And although much later Thomas Jefferson castigated William and Mary, the South's oldest college (chartered in 1693) and his alma mater, for not producing scholars, "it did train gentlemen who rendered vital public service in the hour of need." Few of its students remained in residence long enough to obtain a degree—this was not their intent. College days at William and Mary in the eighteenth century were a pleasing interlude for the wealthy, preceding the regimen of agrarian life to which they were committed. The college curriculum consisted of Latin and Greek, sacred theology, logic, rhetoric, ethics, metaphysics, and mathematics; how profound the professors' scholarship in these studies and how thorough the instruction of their charges are conjectural. Students were there primarily to refine the social graces befitting their elite station, already introduced to them by their plantation tutors, and to become moderately adept at rational discourse. They learned to adorn their letters with Latin or Greek phrases and to converse with apparent intelligence on the fundamentals of Christianity and the currently fashionable metaphysics. A few of the more diligent and gifted Southerners even proceeded to England's Oxford and Cambridge, though fewer received degrees abroad.

Jefferson, disturbed about the financial and curricular plight of William and Mary after the American Revolution, sought first to amend the college program, and eventually to propose the establishment of a completely new university as a logical and historical extension of William and Mary. Designating educational improvement as the "earliest and latest public concern" of his life, the Monticello sage tried at session after session of the Virginia General Assembly to entice sufficient funds for the founding of the University of Virginia. Further, he proposed the introduction of more intensive courses in the physical sciences, in modern languages, and in economics and politics—studies that he thought had been unduly neglected in the old college, thereby hindering its preparation of good citizens and competent scholars alike. He also favored the elective system, the honor system, and active student self-government. Leaving aside the minor influence on the South of German academicians after 1815 and Northern-published textbooks, the new directions that Jefferson gave for the University of Virginia were in large measure followed by other Southern colleges.

Before the Civil War dealt as destructively with the academic as with all other facets of Southern life, the State universities of Georgia, Alabama, North Carolina, South Carolina, and Tennessee had already been established and were operating successfully with the help of tuition charges, endowments, gifts, and State funds. Both Georgia and North Carolina claim the first State university in the nation. Creditable private universities—no distinction is being made between "universities" and "colleges"—founded prior to the holocaust include the College of Charleston, Emory, Furman, Hampden-Sydney, Mercer, Davidson, the University of the South, and Tulane. Advanced military colleges, notably V. M. I. and the Citadel, flourished. In fact, before the firing on Fort Sumter, higher education was at least as advanced in the South as in the North, despite the large and non-reciprocal migration of Southern youth to Northern schools. The pedestrian task of comparing a few statistics from the *Census of 1860* is necessary to underscore the point. By that date, Georgia had thirty-two institutions of higher learning with a faculty of 181 and a student body of 3,300, Tennessee thirty-five colleges with a faculty of 149 and a student body of 2,900, and Virginia twenty-three colleges with a faculty of 163 and students numbering 2,800. These figures compare favorably with the seventeen colleges, 126 professors, and 2,900 students of New York, the twenty-four colleges, 156 professors, and 3,300 students of Pennsylvania, and the eight colleges, ninety-six professors, and 1,700 students of Massachusetts. College men in the South exceeded by one-third in number their counterparts in the North. The University of Virginia had more students than Harvard, and Virginia annually spent more money on higher education than did any other State in the Union.

The immediate post-Civil War period understandably told a far different story. During the war, many college buildings were used for hospitals and barracks, and many, like those at the University of Alabama, were razed by Federal troops. Although most Southern universities bravely re-opened their doors not long after peace came, they did so with such stunted facilities and such meager funds that full-fledged operations along the old lines were impossible. Meanwhile, university income in the North skyrocketed, and in 1870 the total college income (from all sources) in New York was $2,260,000 as contrasted with a feeble $222,000 in Georgia. To some degree, appreciably by the founding of Vanderbilt in 1872, Northern capital came to the aid of education in the South; Congress made needed appropriations for land-grant colleges as specified by the Morrill Act; and an English banker named George Peabody earned the gratitude of the South till this day for the magnanimity of his generous donations. But all these were far from enough.

Not only financial distress but the multiplicity of small, substandard, and impecunious colleges and the deficient preparation of youngsters beginning university work deterred Southern education after 1865. "The thirteen Southern States . . . stand in the tables [*Education Report, 1889-1890*] as possessing 114 [colleges], but no one of these, except the University of Virginia, attains the first rank; and the great majority are undermanned and hampered by the imperfect preparation of the students whom they receive." So observed James Bryce in *The American Commonwealth* in the 1890's. Almost the same evaluation was made by a native Southerner in the May, 1893, issue of the *Sewanee Review*: "It is notorious, that apart from cities, centres of wealth and population, there are few schools in the Southern States, at least south of Virginia, which prepare boys adequately for the freshman class in any reputable or self-respecting college. The burden of collegiate labor is increased immensely by the amount of purely mechanical teaching which is needed during the freshman year." This problem, still grave today, had its origin partly in the decline of the Southern academies, whose counterparts across the Atlantic were the English public schools, the German *gymnasia,* and the French *lycées,* and partly in the attendant introduction into the South of public education along the urban and standardized patterns of Horace Mann. Although the days of the academies and the plantation tutors were gone, the Southern student perhaps now had reason—in an epoch of laissez-faire economics and "survival-of-the-fittest" social theory—to feel less sanguine about the opportunities afforded the gentleman and scholar. Yet by and large Southern education continued to be culturally associated with the leisure class and pretended to be non-materialistic. To produce the gentleman according to the old model was still, *in theory,* its objective, and the Southern campus his natural habitat.

Another factor that militated against Southern higher education at the end of the nineteenth century and the beginning of the twentieth was the isolation of the Southern college from effective contact outside the South and its purblind opposition to new scientific and social ideas and to industrial advancement. With regard to industrial advancement, moreover, the opposition curiously persisted even when Southern intellectuals as well as Southern businessmen and politicians were eager (unconfessedly) for the South to emulate Northern methods. Some, however, like Henry Grady of Georgia and General Daniel Harvey Hill of North Carolina, did not conceal their true convictions. As early as 1866, in *The Land We Love,* Hill argued: "The old education in the palmy days of the South gave us orators and statesmen, but did nothing to enrich us, nothing to promote material greatness"; therefore the South "must abandon the aesthetic and the ornamental for the practical and useful." But in the main Southern professors were busy lauding the "Southern way," which was no longer so pure as the old ladies in the dormitories would have one think. The tragedies of Appomattox and Reconstruction left it severely adulterated with what W. J. Cash has aptly called the "savage ideal." In his controversial *Mind of the South* he defines the savage ideal as "the patriotic will to hold rigidly to the ancient pattern, to repudiate innovation and novelty in thought and behavior, whatever came from outside and was felt as belonging to Yankeedom or alien parts." The "savage ideal" bore little resemblance to the university's avowed objective, implicit in so many founders' statements, of producing the gentleman, the mature individual who pursued truth, welcomed diversity, encouraged freedom of thought and expression, and desired the stimulation of minds disagreeing with his. Most Southern educators, however, refused to admit there might be a conflict between the two.

Even when the remembrance of the culture of the Old South was affirmative and sincere, even when some in the post-Reconstruction South honestly recognized that though times had changed it was still possible to accept the new while preserving the best of the old, as did General Lee at Washington College, general hatreds had become too firmly fixed for the university's purpose always to square with its practice. The "savage ideal" was a new and insidious Southern conceit that harkened not to the long, constructive maturity of the Old South but to the awful moment of its defeat and the aftermath. It was born with the appearance of the Yankee as someone different and separate and horrid, a phenomenon that had not existed for too many years before Secession. Sometimes comically chauvinistic, the "savage ideal" was no less than an obsessive struggle to preserve, in a very negative and self-defeating manner, the altered image the South now had of its tradition. The price that the South and Southern education paid, morally and intellectually, for forsaking a balanced and realistic memory of the Old South and substituting that which never was, and for stressing a discrete and superficial part over the noble totality of the old, was almost as great as the price it had paid at Northern hands.

Usually the struggle was silent, passive, quiescent, and it was always defensive. At times, however, the deep, corroding, inward bitterness of a people whose morale had broken manifested itself outwardly and aggressively in the furtive masks of the Ku Klux Klan and cognate organizations on the campus. To seal off the South as a vacuum package, to reject all that seemed "alien" or "subversive," to despise and fear "efficiency" and "newness" and "industrialism" and "progress" as diseased imports from the North—these were the sentiments that then permeated the Southern campus, no less than the Southern home, church, courthouse, and marketplace. (To repeat, all this was true despite hidden, unexpressed hopes of imitating Northern inventiveness for the South's benefit.) In this light one can understand how stintingly radical economic and biological concepts were to fare below the Maryland border (the thriving young Johns Hopkins University being unaffected by the malaise), and how Darwin and Marx and Veblen now rivaled Garrison and Stowe as anathemas to the hidebound reactionary philosophy of most Southern academicians. But this would not have been the attitude of the cosmopolitan Old South, so sure of its local roots; and complacently to assume and teach this new chauvinism was damningly to corrupt the tradition and pervert the truth. If the university's vocation was to make the gentleman and to pursue truth, and the two had once meant the same thing, rather than to perpetuate the "savage ideal," then the nourishment of such sentiments on the campus was more dangerous than anywhere else. Because the South's future leaders would be the college-trained, it made a great deal of difference what they believed and how they had come to believe it during their formative years.

A brief but important demurrer must enter here. What has been said refers to Southern higher education *generally* in the late nineteenth and early twentieth centuries. Obviously, and providentially, there were exceptions, for not all Southern universities were alike, degrees of "academic freedom" varied, professors differed in their views, and student receptivity fluctuated. Edwin Mims in *The Advancing South* (and Cash after him) documented numerous instances of teachers who survived their own lectures when they strayed from the norm and who actually made an impress on the plastic minds of their auditors. It was indeed a happy circumstance for the South that these subterranean currents, always present however frequently suppressed, managed a little at a time to find outlets, to plunge against the confining walls, and eventually to break through. But defensive convictions die hard and the process was necessarily a slow and arduous one, abetted at last by the forced contact of the South with the outside occasioned by two world wars, an intervening depression, and the tardy arrival of industry on a large scale. It was not until after the First World War, and more authentically after the Second, that something resembling an intellectual renascence became apparent in the South. Yet in the long interim Southern education had lost much, its standards of scholarship had been low, and too many of its best and enlightened minds had taken refuge in the more prosperous and secure North.

Today the notion of a renascence in Southern higher education is more than a pleasant anodyne to soothe a long-wounded Southern pride. Material conditions in the South now favor it. A few figures (as of 1954 and thus altered somewhat since) compiled by the United States Office of Education might be laid bare for inspection. They are

encouraging. Of the 1,832 universities, liberal arts colleges, independent professional schools, and junior colleges in the continental United
States, the South claims 509. The category "South" here excludes
Delaware, Maryland, Oklahoma, and the District of Columbia. Of
the 509, the public institutions account for 184 and the private 325, of
641 public and 1,191 private in the United States as a whole. Perhaps
the South still has too many small colleges that refuse to die. This is
an old complaint. Interestingly enough, the percentage of public to
private schools is about the same in the South as outside, somewhat
over 35 percent public in the South, and somewhat under in the
rest of the country. Of some 2,500,000 students enrolled in colleges
and universities throughout the country (again including junior colleges and professional schools), roughly 540,000 are to be found on
Southern campuses. Steadily increasing stocks of outlanders are invading Southern universities, and more and more professors from outside
are finding teaching palatable below the Mason and Dixon line. Evi-
dently the mid-nineteenth century attitude typified by the caustic remark, "Who in the North reads a Southern book?" has been modified.
As for staff, including faculty and administrative personnel working
on a full time basis, there are about 46,500 employed in the South,
leaving some 152,000 of the nation's total of 198,000 employed in other
regions. Hence, there is a staff member for slightly under every twelve
students in the South, and for slightly over that number in the rest of
the country. The conclusion is that the capacity, on an average, of
Southern colleges today to give individualized attention to the needs
of their students is a fraction superior to that of other sections.

The physical plant and financial resources of Southern universities,
while still surpassed on a per university basis in other parts of the
country, are yearly improving as a consequence of general prosperity,
the increase in the number of students seeking college education, and
generous donations for endowment, construction, and special projects
from national foundations, government, and alumni. Scholarships and
fellowships on a scale and in an amount unheard of even ten years
ago are being dispensed. Since the war, Southern college campuses
have expanded through the addition of impressive new classroom
buildings and dormitories, and faculty salaries are rising. Although,
financially, Southern (and national) academic life is still inexcusably

depressed when contrasted with that of other professions, improvements are evident in terms of gross income if not of purchasing power. All these material advances form part of the overall picture of the growing health of the Southern economy as the South undertakes imposing commercial and industrial ventures that it earlier scorned or was denied.

Still, in significance for the renascence these facts are secondary. To reckon primarily in terms of them would give an undecipherable blueprint of what Southern education hopes to accomplish. Vastly more important are the spiritual and intellectual values which may be sustained by material assistance while overwhelmingly transcending it. If there is not a spiritual and intellectual renascence in Southern education, then there is to be no renascence at all. Assuming there is, the caveat must here be asserted that in the material, which paradoxically has aided the cause of the spiritual and intellectual, there also lurks a grave danger. That danger is that Southern education might succumb to the material if Southern colleges betray their initial ideal, the Southern ideal, of turning out the gentleman who pursues truth in an environment that will not smother, in Adlai Stevenson's words, "the lonely, defiant spirit of the free intelligence." If the Southern ideal is being revived, though necessarily adjusted to the demands of the New South, then there is indeed the beginning of a renascence and a valid criterion for the development of Southern education in the future. However, what has been implied about the desirability of maintaining the right tradition refers to the objectives and the spirit of that tradition rather than to its surface expressions. Surface expressions and symbolic rituals undeniably are important, but that they will survive in any case long after their underpinnings are destroyed is a lesson that history amply demonstrates.

Thus the Southern ideal, the production of the gentleman who is concerned with truth, whenever and however he may discover it, does not call for the singing of "Dixie" at college convocations or the placing of Southern history and Southern literature as required courses in the curriculum. Southerners stand up loyally when "Dixie" is played in any case, and optional courses in the South's history and literature draw their share of students. Southern students will read Faulkner on their own, if they will read anything. Likewise, one can be reasonably sure that a Southern football team will not board a bus for a game in the North without first decking the mechanism with Confederate flags, that the soft, lazy Southern accent will continue to be defended, that Lee's birthday will be remembered, that Old South balls will be the costume event of the year, and that Southern fried chicken and biscuits will remain among the epicurean favorites of the college dining hall. Southerners born and bred take these things for granted, while, amusingly, it is often the converted who insist that the ritual be observed and who mistake it for the tradition. The Southern tradition, that is, willingly permits diversity, encourages local loyalties yet is not narrowly provincial, and fights against an imposed uniformity and conformity, even from one university to the next. Thus, the outraged protest a few years back of students at the University of Virginia against the authorities' "high-handed interruption of the old custom of drinking mint juleps in chairs on the Lawn" would hardly issue from the inmates of Bob Jones University.

Education for the uncommon man, for the gentleman or potential gentleman, the province of the Southern college, is non-specialized liberal arts education, principally on the undergraduate level. Although graduate, vocational, and professional training are as important in Southern education as in any other, and indeed the training of able technicians and specialists in all fields is becoming essential in a modernized South, such training is not a facet of the Southern educational ideal. And Southern universities that give disproportionate emphasis to their graduate, vocational, and professional divisions, with as yet inadequate facilities for so doing, stand in danger of defeating the original purposes of their more significant undergraduate programs. In large part the leadership of the South for many years will come from those holding the Bachelor of Arts degree only. A reliable observation is that the average graduate student of most Southern universities is intellectually inferior to the best of Southern undergraduates. Usually he is at most no more than the mediocre senior one year older.

Non-specialized education does not rule out specialized education by any means, but merely says that a broad liberal arts foundation is imperative for the later education of the expert. In these anxious days the two must be complementary, not exclusive. There is no more ra-

tional ground for finding a dichotomy between them than between
the spiritual and the material, or the beautiful and useful. The question is simply, Which comes first? Traditionally it has been the theory
of Southern education, as of the ancient English universities, that the
man who has followed through a varied curriculum and who has read
widely in a number of subject-matter areas will be better equipped to
engage intelligently in one profession in which he will *then* become
an expert than will the less versatile man who has dedicated himself to
that one only.

The mind of the former is liberated and expanded rather than con-
stricted. He has developed his taste, enlarged his outlook, clarified his
opinions, and refined his critical judgment. He is proficient in general
knowledge. He knows that real knowledge, which has an intrinsic as
well as a utilitarian worth, emerges from the interstices of overlapping
disciplines. Having acquired or extended a philosophical habit of
mind, he can envisage his own specialty in the realistic context of
other specialities of which his is only a part. Furthermore, he understands himself and finds his own niche in an integrated society. Assuredly Milton had all these qualities in mind when he said succinctly,
"I call therefore a complete and generous education that which fits a
man to perform justly, skillfully, and magnanimously all the offices,
both private and public, of peace and war." Newman was even more
explicit: "The man who has learned to think and to reason and to
compare and to discriminate and to analyse, who has refined his
taste, and formed his judgment, and sharpened his mental vision, will
not indeed at once be a lawyer, or a pleader, or an orator, or a states-
man, or a good landlord, or a man of business, or a soldier, or an
engineer, or a chemist, or a geologist, or an antiquarian, but he will be
placed in that state of intellect in which he can take up any one of the
sciences and callings . . . , or any other for which he has a taste or
special talent, with an ease, a grace, a versatility, and a success, to
which another is a stranger." In short, he exhibits many of the attributes of the gentleman.

Of what should this Southern liberal arts education consist in order
to produce the gentleman whose constant search after truth prepares
him to discharge the complex obligations of modern living? To entertain seriously the possibility of reviving the Seven Liberal Arts of the

Middle Ages—grammar, rhetoric, logic, arithmetic, geometry, astronomy, and music—is as much an anachronism as to advocate restoring the medieval religious and political community. The early curriculum of William and Mary, even with Jefferson's proposed changes, is insufficient. Thorough absorption in the classics on the older model of Southern universities, almost to the exclusion of equally important studies, seems not quite appropriate in the middle of the twentieth century. Yet something of the spirit and intent of each of these earlier forms must guide the contemporary Southern college if a truly intellectual renascence is to be more than an empty phrase. The liberal arts surely include philosophy and the pure sciences, logic and mathematics, literature and languages, political and economic theory, history, theology, and the fine arts. Southern education is thus duty-bound to demand more of its students than that they be exposed only to abbreviated elements of philosophy, to instrumental English composition with mere snippets of literature appended, to oversimplified mathematics and "general" science, to the classics in translation, to meaningless catch-all courses speciously labeled "social science," to outline instruction in world history, and to only one foreign language. This is true of any system of higher learning, but the subject here is *Southern*.

This is not painting the picture in too somber shades: It is fortunate when current students get as much as this foundation before the idle move on to the more appealing electives and the industrious to their pre-professional majors. Although these defects are far from peculiar to the South, it is submitted that it is within the framework of the Southern educational tradition that they can be best corrected. Possibly as a result of the pernicious intrusion of "progressive education" in public elementary schools (and neither "progressive education" nor the public school system as presently structured is indigenous to the South), students have grown accustomed, in selecting their courses, to decidedly too much freedom for their own intellectual good. One solution to the problem is to modify the elective system. Southern colleges that whine that for financial reasons they cannot make changes most beneficial to their students, lest the students (especially the pre-professional) desert to a more liberal campus, might well do without the students and close down. On the bright side, more and more medical and law schools are stating a preference for college graduates with a liberal arts, rather than a strictly pre-medical or pre-legal education. Again on the bright side, in Southern colleges since the Second World War there has been noticeably revived enthusiasm about theology, philosophy, and political theory to parallel a continuing interest in economics and the physical sciences. A symptom of the age nationally and a characteristic of the aspired renascence, the enthusiasm is also indicative of Southern awareness of and reaction to the world crisis. For these subjects tell, together with the humanities, what values are worth preserving, and, together with the physical sciences, how they might be preserved.

It is in some measure because of the poor preparation of students entering Southern colleges today, as it was when Bryce wrote in the 1890's, that the goal of a liberal arts education for the gentleman falls short of realization. Southern educators are well aware of the problem. Freshmen who literally cannot read, write, spell, and do simple mathematical equations *must* spend their first college year learning "tool" courses, memorizing when they should be digesting, acquiring basic disciplines that should have been theirs before they were graduated from high school. Southern educators who discuss the problem invariably must debate the larger issue of *democratic* education. Is every youngster entitled to a college education simply because he wants it? Will he necessarily be happier and his society better off if he gets it? A more germane question is: Will the educational experience of the really promising and qualified, whatever their economic condition, be marred as a result of an inevitable lowering of standards if everyone *must* have a college education? Sensible people will say that the question is rhetorical. If the issue be joined whether to reduce academic standards or to stiffen entrance requirements, then the Southern tradition demands the latter with, however, two qualifications. The first is that at the present time, when there is no dearth of students clamoring for entrance into university gates, entrance requirements in private institutions, and in public institutions with respect to out-of-state applicants, *are* being bolstered. The second is that some better way must be found to gauge the intellectual potentialities of worthy students whose only fault is that those potentialities have not been recognized and developed in their high schools. It is frequently these students who, lacking mastery of tool disciplines in their freshman and sophomore years, give an academic performance in their junior and senior years superior to that of their more affluent classmates who enjoyed the advantage of private preparatory education. Jefferson addressed himself similarly to the problem as early as 1779.

In thus making its position clear, the South would violate no democratic precept. In every society, and the South is still a diverse and particularist society, if it is to stay or become free, if it is to advance, if it is to *be* democratic, indeed if it is to survive, there must be present, tolerated, and encouraged what Carlyle called an "aristocracy of talent," Matthew Arnold "the saving remnant," John Stuart Mill and Arnold Toynbee "the creative minority." Arnold averred in *Culture and Anarchy* that in every community "there are born a certain number of natures with a curiosity about their best self, with a bent for seeing things as they are, for disentangling themselves from machinery, for simply concerning themselves with reason and the will of God, and doing their best to make these prevail—for the pursuit, in a word, of perfection." Any understanding exponent of the Old South tradition would agree.

The Southern professor has a crucial responsibility in maintaining the Southern ideal of the university as "an Alma Mater, knowing her children one by one, not a foundry, or a mint, or a treadmill." He is not in a factory fabricating on a mass scale identical mechanical units and cannot think of his profession as a punch-the-clock proposition. Moreover, his primary job is teaching, not research, however important research may be today and however necessary it is that universities try to make plentiful provision for it. But it is at least an argument that teaching and research actually constitute distinct professions and that only the rare scholar can perform both with excellence and commitment. In the past twenty or thirty years the curious pattern that the two are of a cloth has been needled into Southern education from the outside, and the outcome has often been a travesty on respectable educational procedures. Amenable students are frequently handed impersonal "multiple-choice" and "true-false" examinations by an impersonal graduate assistant (who has composed them and will grade them) while the professor "seeks truth" (and more money and repute) by writing a mediocre textbook. New professors are often hired, for graduate school purposes particularly, on the basis of the amount of published research they can claim, and promotion is too often dependent on publication alone. The intense pressure to publish can drive even the willing professor from his classroom duties. Happily, though this may tread on sensitive toes, the dilemma is still not so critical in the South as in certain other regions of the country, and there is still time and inclination in the South to find an acceptable solution. For if the Southern professor does not intend to give his paramount attention to the business of training youthful and pliable minds, then despite his scholarly reputation, he is inferior to those gentle old white-bearded teachers of an un-Ph.D. era who strolled leisurely with their pupils along isolated campus walks and discoursed sympathetically on the beauties of Virgilian poetry and the Battle of Marston Moor. It is they whom Wolfe and Percy and other old grads hold in affectionate memory.

Close personal relationships of professors and students, as in seminars, small classes, tutorials, and office discussions, seem imperative for the individualization of education, upon which the Southern ideal insists. As increased financial assistance becomes available in Southern colleges for the expansion of their faculties—it is hoped for undergraduate as well as for graduate—the process of individualization *can* be intensified, not only in the small, secluded college but also in the large State university. In varying degrees of emphasis, such Southern universities as Emory, Sewanee, and Virginia are utilizing the tutorial system for brighter seniors, and colloquia, preceptorials, and honors programs have been found to work successfully. Their larger purpose, in the words of the Presbyterian founders of Davidson, is "not to teach the student how to make a living, but to teach him how to live more abundantly."

The South, which historical, economic, and geographical necessity has made less materialistic than certain other sections of the nation, may yet tap unusually felicitous spiritual and intellectual resources, embedded in its tradition, for the building of non-materialistic education in the machine and atom age. That education must be capable of fitting industrialism and commercialism into the context of Southern history and community. Industrialism must adapt itself to the South, not the South to it. Southern colleges of the post-Reconstruction era often talked piously about the tradition but seldom followed it. Southern colleges of the New South must find anchorage in the Old—not to surrender the benefits of materialism but to enjoy them more intelligently, "to live more abundantly." The function of integrating the spiritual and the material, the beautiful and the useful, is the peculiar task of Southern education today. The South cannot expect to make its own rich contribution to the culture of the nation if, in accepting the new, the urban, and the industrial, it abandons the old, the rural, the agrarian. Wantonly to discard the old would quickly make the South a second-rate North at best, with all moorings gone. Other regions of the country may not need a sense of history. The South cannot escape it.

ELLINGTON WHITE

The View from the Window

THE SOUTH is too much with us late and soon, the more so perhaps because it will so soon be gone. The factories have long since settled on the meadows, some of the recent ones without even bothering to remove the cattle, and where yesterday stood a house with moss on the doorstep, today we find a service station—tomorrow a supermarket; for technology, that smoking instrument of overnight change, has arrived like Sherman and swept to the sea.

I admit that the comparison is not altogether just: Where Sherman destroyed, technology improves. And who can doubt that the South has not benefited from having technology in the house? Certainly not the Chambers of Commerce. Certainly not the man in the street. "Why, it was only the other day," he will tell you, "that I was talking to this guy from Ohio, and what did he say? 'Why, hell, fellow, what's so different between this place and where I come from back home!' " And the guy from Ohio, of course, is right. He knows it's the same house all over again, only newer. Here stand the factories, the used car lots, the neon signs, the shopping centers, the developments "designed for modern living." True, the Ohioan probably found the highways a lane narrower than the ideal realized on the Ohio Turnpike, but the same advertisers have visited both places and advertisers the world over speak the language of hope: Friends, wait until tomorrow.

The point is that when technology arrives, it does not arrive alone, any more than Sherman did. Sherman brought despair. Our great-grandfathers, faced with a distorted society, found the cause of that distortion in themselves, in the human condition. So out of defeat came understanding. But out of the North came technology, fuel necessary to keep the factories running. Optimism forecast the millennium, heaven on earth. It displaced despair, dispersed gloom, and shone forth upon North and South alike with the same merry brilliance. Happy days were here again.

But technology has still another companion, blood kin to the first. This is change, the yearly—nay, daily—mutations technology needs in order to make room for the new. This is different from natural flux. Natural flux at least spares us an illusion of permanence—the moss on the doorstep; it is kinder to us, less hurried. But technology has another word for permanence. That word is "static." A thing is static when it abides, when it maintains a permanent form. A thing is dynamic when it moves, when it changes its form. And technology, like a top-heavy load, must keep moving; otherwise it would collapse under its own weight.

Were dynamism confined to the merely material, it would be what the South would like it to be—a bringer of comfortable tidings only: Highways, jobs, factories, automobiles, television. But such, unfortunately for the South, is not the case. Dynamism effects the ideas and manners of a people as well as their things. It works upon behavior with no less energy than upon highways. Highways the South wants to change; its behavior—no. Consequently, we have the paradox that is inherent in the South today. The same voices which have been for a good many years proclaiming the arrival of technology (and how often have we heard the throbbing vitality of these voices busily putting down the "reactionaries")—these same voices are today being raised in angry defense of those institutions which dynamism must displace because by technological standards these institutions are static. I mean in particular the institution of the Negro and the white Southerner's relation to him. Our first impulse is to say, "Well, you asked for it; now bellow." But we know this isn't quite the truth. We know that technology is an idea and that any idea powerful enough to move people eventually will have its own way over the minority, especially if the minority has the double disadvantage of being itself without power, as the South discovered after the Civil War. Technology was accepted by the South because actually there was no other alternative. But accepting it was one thing, welcoming it another. And if there is anything false within the South today, it lies here. For the South has welcomed technology with one hand while holding within the other sufficient cause, it believes, for disregarding the most painful (for the South) of technology's consequences, namely that the South's racial institution is static. Also it might be argued that in the eyes of the machine all men are equal, a point of view which leaves out the embarrassing issue of God altogether, which may be just as well, as there appears to be some doubt about the correctness of His vision.

Dynamism, then, and its consequences—these seem to me to be the causes underlying the South's current dilemma. In this case, however, knowing the cause in no way removes us from the dilemma itself. Would that it did. But causes are abstract. Can we say that they belong in such a place as this but the dilemma belongs in the novel of the poem, in the dramatic situation? I think so, if for no other reason than because the dilemma is concrete, because we feel it all around us, because it makes up our everyday life. Today one goes to town for groceries. On the way he picks up a Negro man who is hitchhiking. They talk about the weather, about a river where the fishing is good, about a man they both know. It's an ordinary, uneventful ride. Then the Negro who is out of work because of a bad leg—this comes out as the ride nears its end—wants the price of a pack of cigarettes. He gets it, after which there is an awkward silence and these words, "My people are like a pail full of crabs. One gets to the top and the rest pull him down." Here is the dilemma. How is one to take these words? How is one to feel? Ashamed of himself? Angry at a situation which made the Negro feel his little speech was expected of him? Or is his speech no more than a plainly spoken sentiment brought on, not by the white man, but by something which happened—an argument maybe or an unpaid debt—before even the white man came into the picture? Not long ago there would have been no question. The speech would have gone immediately into the writer's notebook shortly to issue forth from the mouth of some "silverhaired old darky" who would have been—can we guess?—a combination of wisdom and charm and limber-hipped graciousness, one of "the old kind." Sambo we call him. And his wife? She is a good ole black mammy with the misery in her head. One sees them still in the foreground of quaint Charleston and New Orleans watercolors and in the pages of even quainter little regional tales. But do they live in our everyday life? This is the question the writer must decide on when he hears the above speech. It is nothing new to him. All his life he has heard similar ones. He has heard them from his playmates, small boys who wore his cast off clothes and rolled rubber tires with him down a clay road. He has heard them from the mothers of these boys. He has heard them from his own mother and father, from aunts, uncles and cousins. If experience is any test of truth, then the writer must decide that, yes, Sambo does live in his everyday life. Sambo is real. But the alternative suggests itself with force. Is Sambo a mask put on by the Negro when he comes out into a white world? Are these speeches no more than that, speeches prepared for and recited before a white audience, made up camouflage necessary for survival? If so, aunts, uncles, cousins, himself—all have played the fool, have been taken in by words and actions designed solely to please them. And that faint noise he has heard behind him so often, is this no more than the delight of the players now chuckling to themselves over the cunning of their fiction? The "old darky" may indeed be wise, but wise in a way much wiser than the Southerner has dreamed.

Such a view of the Negro, while exaggerated (but no more so than the view of him as an irresponsible child), nevertheless confronts the writer with an honest problem. It demands a reappraisal. He has to hear again those speeches and live again the days he spent rolling tires on a clay road. Only this time he will have to bring to them no quick and easy acceptance of what they appear to be, but rather respect for the complex human beings they involve.

If the Southerner has been at fault in simplifying the Negro, and this much is granted, then also we can say that the North has been equally at fault in simplifying the relation between the Negro and the Southern white. Like all things human that have been around for a long time, this relation, like the Negro, has taken on a complex character, and when the Southerner says it will never be entirely understood by the outsider, he is not merely avoiding the issue. He knows that the spoken word, apart from experience, takes one to the portals only of understanding. Yet the outsider has repeatedly assumed an authority in this matter beyond his knowledge, and in so doing has as repeatedly forced the Southerner's hand. I need not mention the most obvious case where this has been true. Let me instead mention another which applies to the writer alone.

It wasn't long ago that I talked with a teacher at a mid-western university who told me in all seriousness that one could fairly well determine the racial attitudes of a writer by whether or not he capitalized Negro. Of course this is nonsense, but it does bear on the question of language. Take the word "nigger" for instance. Here is a word whose power of ugly suggestion is larger than the person it denotes. If the writer puts this word in the mouth of a character, already that character's attitude toward the Negro is decided. His actions mean nothing. The character in question may have spent the energies of his life in the Negro's behalf, but let him use the word "nigger" and that energy—as well as the writer's—is wasted in the eyes of an outside audience. However hard it may be for this audience to believe though, there are Southerners with nothing but respect and admiration for the Negro who nevertheless use "nigger" in their daily conversation because for them the word is strictly denotative. If the writer wishes to use such a person, however, "nigger" had better be left out of that person's vocabulary: It involves a value judgment contrary to his character. Removing it may take away from the character something which the writer will have to make up elsewhere, but such is the nature of the Southern writer's problem when language assumes a larger significance than action.

Nor does the problem stop here. Suppose the writer has in mind a situation which involves an act of kindness on the part of a Southerner toward a Negro. Hitherto, perhaps, the writer has gone on the assumption that any pure act of kindness anywhere elevates the stature of anybody, but such he finds not to be the case when applied to the foregoing situation. The Northern reader, who more often than not distrusts any motive on the part of a Southerner, will say, "Oh, well, what's this but somebody indulging himself in the prerogatives of the master-slave relation," in which case kindness becomes either the uncleanest of vanities or patronage or both. One might argue that this will depend entirely on how successfully the writer renders the situation, and to a degree this is true, but likewise it is true that in dealing with such a situation the writer works under a disadvantage that would not be there if the situation were reversed so that the kindness were coming from the Negro. Then the action would entirely determine the effect, as it does not in the first situation.

The problem outlined so far is the property of Southern writers alone. Other complexities—I think in particular of industrial change and optimism—belong to any writer in a technological world. The only difference is that the Southern writer is facing them now for the first time. The view from his window is so unlike the view he knew as a child that he wonders whether he's in the same house. Trees have come down to make room for modern "multi-levels" that crawl over the sub-divided hillside like so many squatty little beetles moving in on him, and the recently split open earth bleeds red water into the river where yesterday he swam. The families of his childhood have either gone in pursuit of the factory or the factory, having come in pursuit of them, is camped in their place. The strangers who have moved in he won't bother to meet because the chances are that next year they will be replaced by others. So it goes, and improvising as usual, he will make his adjustments. But the question persists: What abides?

Keats found permanence on the face of a Grecian urn and was led thereby to believe in the superiority of art to nature. Can we see in the recent flowering of Southern literature a similar discovery? Southerners confronted with the dismantling of their society felt all the more sharply a need for permanence and found it, like Keats, in art. Also they found it in their past. One thinks of Faulkner and Robert Penn Warren, both of whom locate their subjects in the past; of Eudora Welty whose characters belong to the pastoral tradition, which is always backward looking; and of Thomas Wolfe who harkened back to the town in order to orientate himself in the flux of the city. John Crowe Ransom and the Fugitives took refuge in the classical fixtures of art in order to preserve it against the vulgar liberties of the new order, and in instances where art was felt to be deficient as a solitary bulwark against change, it was supported by the religion that comes closest to it, Catholicism, to which other Southern writers most un-Southernly have been drawn. The ends may differ, but the quest is always the same: What abides?

Southerners have been brought up aware of the fact that there was a period in the history of their region when, due primarily to its agrarian character, their ancestors enjoyed a moment of comparative social stability that enabled them to build up around them a tradition of some eloquence. Few would claim that as a way of life this tradition was sound from the basement up. Like all things man made, it had its distortions. But also it had certain characteristics which have been found good, namely an intense concern for family and place and—this especially—a capacity to accept the possibility of heroic action. The South does have its heroes, as well as organizations whose primary function is to keep the temple of their names. Lee, Jackson, Stuart—they have become almost mythical in size. But because ours is a debunking age, one in which truth is curiously equated with whatever can be spaded up to explode the hero, almost daily one expects a book the purpose of which is to make a fraud out of Lee or a religious masochist out of Jackson. Admittedly there is a good deal of Don Quixote in the South, but at least Quixote had the happy faculty of making a knight-errant out of a lackey, not vice versa.

The family has transcended all other interests and affections in the South. It acts as a bridge linking the Southerner to his past. By means of it he is in immediate and concrete touch with both ages, and this contact provides him with a vision that does not begin and end with himself. Thus he is spared the horrors of solipsism. He feels himself as belonging to history, by means of which he is better able to measure the accomplishments and deficiencies of his own time. Let him lose interest in the family, however, and he has at the same time lost his contact with the past.

The family's closest rival for the Southerner's affections is his place. Should the two clash, his larger allegiance would belong to the family, but he is as proud of the one as he is of the other. Largely this pride in place is aesthetic, having to do with the pleasure it gives the senses, but also it carries with it the idea of the place as a sustaining force imparted by nature, and as such it has tended to replace other sustaining forces in the Southerner's life. The nation is one of these. With the advent of the welfare state, however, a new concept came into being, and from this time forward one sees a steady falling away in the Southerner's dependence on the powers of his place. Aesthetically, too, his place has declined; perhaps one day it will dawn upon him that unclean rivers eventually find their source in the mind.

Likewise our region is witnessing the deterioration both of the family and of the capacity it (the region) once had for heroic action. Here are the nomads camped in trailers. Here is the idea of the world as everybody's pot. Here is the morality of "I got mine, now you get yours." And here, most dangerous of all, is prosperity's smiling countenance, that healthy bemused face we sometimes see plastered above us on billboards, set there in all of its rosy splendor with a cut of greed in one glittering eye. The effect of the spell cast over America by this eye we find everywhere, from the advertisements to the pages of *Life* magazine in which American writers have been urged to assert the well-fed condition of their country. I say this face is the most dangerous of all because its charms are so many. Who is not beguiled by health and vitality and cheeks glowing with "fun"? Who is not beguiled by innocence? And who does not rather despise the father who makes a point of telling his son there is no Santa Claus? Yet without that father's truth-telling, the son would eventually become unbearable, and a nation of such sons, not only unbearable but dangerous.

For this reason it seems to me that now more than ever before it is part of the Southern writer's job to reassert those values inherent in the history of his region which are in keeping with heroic behavior because heroic behavior assumes an intelligence which goes beyond its own interests, which subordinates personal happiness to nobility of conduct. The South is rightfully proud of its aristocratic heritage, but all too often we forget that aristocracy is a state of mind, a morality, the conditions of which are sacrifice and obligation and a concern for the welfare of others. The aristocratic mind is the mind least of all conscious of class because it is least of all afraid of losing its place in society. That fear belongs to bourgeois morality, by which I mean that morality which views life in terms of rights rather than obligations, and difficult as we find it to admit, Southern behavior surrounding the Negro question has been inescapably bourgeois. (Much is said about States' rights but little about State obligations.) If this morality is allowed to maintain its control over the South, the South is doomed. To prevent this from happening, the South will have to relearn the aristocratic principles of its past, and if the writer, no matter how humbly, presumes to the teaching role, his main concern will likewise have to be a restoration of those principles; for only on the basis of them will the South be able to maintain itself with a measure of dignity in a technological world.

ROBERT HAZEL

The Southern Writer
and His Region

SOUTHERN WRITING has achieved an excellence above that of other regions of this country. It has been the presiding influence in poetry, fiction and criticism during the modern period. Distinguishable by its passion, moral depth, irony and lyricism, this body of writing would seem to have grown out of materials as different from those of other regions as the culture of Athens was from Rome. Such is not the case. Time and circumstance, which reduced the South in nearly all its areas of existence, gave paradoxical and fortuitous birth to brilliance in that single area which concerns us here: The imaginative construction of the human condition. For the history of the South bestowed upon a region not substantially unique an essential difference of mental cast, a regional complexion dark with time, a brooding countenance (from Poe to Wolfe) which naturally searches selfhood and otherness for those concretions of emotion and action that compose a high literature. Prior to any use of the physical substances of the region, attitudes in formation since the Civil War had to cool and solidify in those areas of the regional mind, for from this peculiar mental state were derived that structure and rhetoric which made possible a Southern renascence to resuscitate our letters where no other such phenomenon existed in America. The wonder is not that the writers of the South should have assumed that leadership; rather, who could have explained their failure to do so?

There is finally not much to distinguish the Southern region—particularly the upper South of Atlanta and farther north—from, say, the Ohio and Indiana country. The traveler from Raleigh to Indianapolis finds much the same clay hills and limestone crags, creek bottoms bounded by ill-kept county roads, quiet public squares, and barnlots where mules stand motionless. Steam engines and cowbells and trace chains sound the same in the fields west of Atlanta and east of Vincennes. The ordinary people, too, for whom history has no meaning which cannot be immediately objectified in the loss of a son at Anzio or Pusan, or a drop in the price of hogs at Birmingham, pursue the same objects enveloped in tedium, greed, and the details of fundamentalist Protestant religion. Sycamore trees, redbirds, dogs, honeysuckle, stacks of crossties, lumber sheds, roadhouses—these are all the same between Asheville, N. C., and Columbus, Ohio. (Sherwood Anderson had very nearly the same objects of sense and contemplation as Faulkner, his acknowledged pupil.) Yet in the only sense which concerns writer and reader of fiction, these landscapes have been made different by the triumphant use which the Southern writer has made of his region's substance: That region has, by its tragic history of defeat, compelled a serious attitude toward and close observation of regional materials.

This history has achieved also a fit method for registry of its effects: A highly symbolized mode of writing to accommodate depth and a rhetoric capable of sufficient lyric intensity to make its contents memorable. As compulsive observation penetrated the region, the abstractions of symbolism became not merely convenient but necessary if any sort of detachment was to be preserved. That aesthetic detachment (estrangement even) from slavish involvement with the actual objects of the landscape in turn permitted the writer to separate the common substance and the unique essence of those materials, and freed Southern writing to its contemporary greatness. This aesthetic condition is paradoxical: If there is any critical notion tenaciously held in common by Southern writers it is precisely that writing *must* be concrete, not abstract; yet the nature and solution of the paradox is easily seen. In Southern writing, materials are urgently immediate, sensory, intimately scrutinized, yet symbolically removed, transformed and elevated; at the heart of this paradox lies the secret of a dimension and stature that has made the Southern renascence the envy of other regions where relatively shallow, oversimplified, rootless work continues on the dated models of social realism. The actual landscape remains most faithfully sensed in gorgeous particularity during the very process of its being abstracted to the level of a real scene where that powerful distortion occurs which so easily differentiates Southern writing. While the house in Ohio settles into an earth unhaunted by anything more portentous than the failure of a national administration to hold farm price supports, the house in South Carolina holds echoes of voices that incriminate, terrify and purge.

Inevitably the fact that the South remained agrarian longer than other regions gave birth to the condition in which the fictional terms of that curious isolation and estrangement were realized. Separateness, relative solidarity and homogeneity of the white community, dispirited enterprise—all conspired to make the region seem stable, to make change almost imperceptible and to urge the cherishing of local myths of permanence. (Synonyms for or approximations of permanence are common to Southern writers; for example, *timeless* in Wolfe, *unalterable* in Faulkner.) More subtly, the semblance of an inscrutable and changeless reality engendered in Southern writers a compassion for what exists at the moment, in the historical present, and a cautious suspicion of or outright contempt for those elements spawned by progress: Man in the mass, worship of the future, equalitarianism, utopianism. (Here, through no consciously acquired virtue of their own, Southern writers largely escaped the swift fading temporality of "social" themes, and have constructed their poems and stories on the firmer bedrock of fundamental human values shown in terribly clear relief of dramatic conflict.)

A stronger sense of the continuity and relative permanence of the appearances and attributes of things in the South has led to the fictionally fruitful illusion of retention (augmented and sustained by a psychological factor which reaches beyond the scope of this essay), and the comfortable embrace of a system of values, however erroneously held, has enabled Southern writing more nearly to arrest time and permit images to reside in our sense. As one instance, the image of guilt for having lost a war for independence—not for consenting to a war and fighting it, but for losing it in a continent where every venture is supposed to terminate in unqualified success—has been exploited by the writers of Wolfe's and Faulkner's generation particularly. Theirs has been the ironically successful attempt (in print where victories do not count) to retain during certain fictional moments an idealized, untarnished image of passion, valor, sacrifice. These images have, however, that dark complexion of irony and can be sustained without serious embarassment because the modern Southern writer knows and records the rebellious deed also as spendthrift in nature, an emotional extravagance in excess of the historic occasion, vainglorious and wrong. That this sense of permanence is certainly illusory, that the Nashville agrarians succumbed to it with very unheroic lack of intellectual resistance (holding their thumbs in the dike to save a way of life that had already vanished effectively before they were born), and that it has also tricked William Faulkner to embrace irrational, and at times amusing, absolutisms and archaisms is rather an extra-literary concern. Most Southern writers have at one time or another confused the forms of something that in many ways resembled a culture with values supposedly inherent in these forms.

The most crucial factor in the use of regional materials in Southern writing is that sober coloring taken from eyes that have kept watch on folly, injustice, bravery, tenacity and defeat—all seen intensely and refracted through the lens of a tragic history: The unique possession of a region and the cause of fictional attitudes and constructs wherein the fictive nature of those materials is transformed and determined by their use. It has fallen to the lot of the Southern writer to exercise more than usually the faculties of recall and introspection, to carry forward the most notable experiments of French and Irish writers (alike citizens of lands where defeat has demonstrated its very sobering possibility and decay is president of cultures) and to make memorable the quality of sensory and imaginative data: Train whistles in mountains, public squares at dawn, the odd brief gestures of farmer and townsman, to bare the bones of disease and strength that in varying degree enfeeble and sustain us all. To that region of America where the human condition was most exaggerated one had to go in search of whatever momentary truths (in this case the moment has lasted more than 2000 years) could be insighted by imaginative labor aided by the erosions of time.

The elements which made the South a region have not, by their nature, demanded qualities of aggressiveness and trail-blazing energy in most areas of activity. After the Civil War the South was trod down and let lie smoldering beside the rest of a country which was

restlessly shaping and attuning itself to the competitions and exploita-
tions of a great industrial nation. The South has since been conspicuously stubborn, sullen, irrational, lethargic, oar-resting. Yet it
was precisely these slow-moving, cud-chewing, history-cherishing
tendencies which made possible a remarkable pioneering ingenuity in
shaping the materials that lie at hand into fictional analogies and
equivalents of experience. The intelligent Southerner still retained
interest in those rather leisurely arts of reading and writing. Language
as art did not break down there so rapidly as it did in other regions
where expression suffered successive painful condensations under the
tyrannies of efficiency and communication. (No newspaper editor
demanded of Wolfe or Faulkner that he must say all he knew in one
paragraph.) In the South language remained relatively full, complex
and malleable, capable of both power and nuance. Southerners have
naturally taken the lead in our period's development of modes and
techniques for the simulation of the rich vagaries of mental action
and the analysis of character. Since the decline and death of wit and
imagination in New England, there was no other group possessed of
a language and a material and a *necessity* to reconstruct and demon-
strate dramatically the estranged and loving and grief-stricken and
guilty actions of modern mentality reflected in the world of immediate
objects. Forced by a calamitous history to an artificially arrested and
stunted condition, to the curious state of a living anachronism, the
South has blessed and cursed its writers with a view of the human condition in its extremes: Not simply piety, but fundamentalist wrath;
not poverty alone, but squalor; and not merely the consciousness of
history, but the crushing weight of a personal past. The Southern
writer is born in sort of a rectory of a pigpen of a wax museum.

A Southerner living in New York City wrote to his wife describing
his sense of the movement of time down the slope of the Eastern
seaboard

"... slowly southward from Harlem past the barricaded-against-
Negro-vandalism east side of the Columbia University campus,
past Columbus Circle and Times Square in one second's exposure
of blurred incandescence, then flickers with image-scything rap-
idity, gathering speed past a tall gothic clock-tower standing over
winking beer and bread advertisements at Philadelphia, through
the narrow street where U.S. 40 trickles into the stagnant pool of

Baltimore, losing itself among bricks and cobbles, tortuously
emerging southwest in an instant to sweep up the thimbled Capitol Dome in Washington, D.C., where an ancient warrior probed
by white floodlights stands beside his stone shield and Ulysses S.
Grant gestures to plunging bronze horses and men on the western
slope of the lawn, curving down the Mall, illuminating Washington's monolith, and further west discovering Lincoln in a forest
of stone pillars, hands on knees, regarding time, then gathering
history like a bundle of rags under some hoboing Whitmanian
arm, makes the prodigious leap, crosses Memorial Bridge over
the Potomac, finds the going easier, then, in Virginia, in the
South, in another country where clocks are fewer and time a
little more real and comprehensible, and the night sky less disturbed with arrogant fitful commerce, a province more of stars,
pines, red-winged blackbirds clinging to cattail reeds in marshes,
moves swifter now past time's dead stumps and hollows, nearing
Richmond, seen in one instantaneous illumination of clarity and
fury, Richmond where on the continent once, and only once, men
had tried to conceive something truly indignant and brave, the
protest that is not finally boyish and awkward, the courage that
does not mean suicide alone, the freedom, the virility of defiance
that cannot be laughed at but finally makes sense—and had failed
to conceive those things but at least had tried, the failure not because of self-deception; they had known all along that the structure of their world was false, rotten in the core; and that was why
they had to fail but not why they had tried; the effort itself had
been outrageous pride—and departing Richmond, the focus holds
no further clarity; large abstract things cannot be seen, only near
fenceposts and telegraph poles filing stately past, leading deeper
into that land where toothpicks and sulphur matches look large,
where hand-mirrors look as bright as the moon and multiply the
cold fires that lick a desolate landscape. . . .

    ". . . to drink cokes and smoke cigarets past all the ham-greasy
diners from Richmond to Rockingham, to see drifting by the car
window, like tattered fragments of futile human promptings, the
crude-lettered highway signs: Ice Water, Fireworks, Virginia
Hams; the radio unctuous with cures for asthma, ringworm,
eczema, and with advice from the State agricultural experimental
station about how to raise broiler chickens whose feet never touch
the ground; and a sermon by a Greensboro Baptist preacher
condemning daylight saving time: not Gawd's own time; and the
flatchested, leatherhocked poorwhite woman, unafraid because
paralysed; then scrawled upon the sunset-bloodied windshield the
sudden image of a Negro in a red hat plowing, trailing pow-

dered soil in the acrid uplands that climb down from Rockingham, Cheraw and Columbia to Augusta; and to see the slanting
trucks girt with logchains hauling clean-scented pine lumber. . . .

  ". . . it was strange to see at twilight grown men, farmers in over-
alls—your father, my father—riding kids' bicycles toward the water
tower of some little town, or maybe just wobbling in circles on
the weedy yards. But that childishness, that emotional fatuous-
ness is as much a part of the South as every non-tubercular, non-
jaundiced adult in Rockingham donating a pint of blood to the
Marine Corps to save my life in 1942, and in the same day the
blood donors hauling their tobacco up to Henderson and trying
to kill themselves with whiskey and tent-show religion. . . .

  ". . . evening has come to North Carolina. The fat Negro women
sit sloven, colored knees cocked to air cotton undergarments, beside huts surrounded by stifling odors of poverty's pone and sow-
belly. The car radio plays Spiritual airs sung by the Greensboro
Group at the big professional Gospel Sing in the Rockingham
ball park. The moon is up full, so bright that I could drive without
headlights . . . Chancellorsville with its stone wall is far behind,
was yesterday. Now it's Cheraw, solemn under the Chinaberry
trees. Always night there, the melons and peaches coming through
under the black tarpaulins of trucks. . . . Inside the Carolina Cafe
in Cheraw the ceiling fans whirr listlessly after the flies. There
are a stainless steel coffee urn, a black wrinkle-painted cash reg-
ister, a red cigaret vending machine. A neon Budweiser sign
trails its script across the bluish mirror behind the lunch counter,
and a jukebox squats near the screen door. Outside in the moon-
blanched street—U.S. 1 to Raleigh and Richmond north, to Columbia and Augusta south—loom the Chevrolet Sales Agency
and the O.K. Used Car Lot. . . . The bread rolls in the Carolina
Cafe taste doughy, flat, Southern. . . .

  ". . . it is easy to go south from New York until you reach the
outskirts of Richmond, the grassed-over breastworks of another
strange fortress of the soul. Beside the James River that slimes its
gray rocks the gods of history overtake you, sit beside you in the
car, bum your cigarets, drink your beer, then curse your flawed
humanness, your paralysing ignorance which you would weep to
shed, but cannot. South of Richmond the highway begins to obscure itself, spilling in dilatory streams southward, so that you
blunder by word-of-mouth to the Y with an Amoco Service Station ten miles north of the town of Rockingham that bakes on
the side of a sunburnt hill thirty-two miles from Cheraw. And
no matter what time of day you may think it is when you reach
Cheraw, you will never see the sun, only the fantastical everpres-

ence of light paled and filtered and dashed like whitewash on the used car lot and the window of the Carolina Cafe. An overweening desire for sleep seizes you. The somber talk of men and women like dream-voices rises and falls, sinking into profound stupefaction that denies intelligibility and obliterates even regret. When you wake in an old-fashioned folding bed, the headboard garlanded with carved leaves and walnut-stained flowers in a tourist home which in 1847 was a mansion that hangs even now the portraits of six generations of men and women on the walls above peeling mirrors ascending from mouse-holed baseboard to cobwebbed ceiling, when you see a huge china pitcher and washbowl on the marble stand, and hear dawn birds in rotten dew-crusted eaves chatter, then you remember the nightbugs that had cheed and chirred in the clumped verbena at the foundations of scaling columns, under the entire cave of earth, seeming, and there in Cheraw in the milky dawn you twist suddenly in your hired bed, mystified by an incomprehensible but inescapable sorrow. . . .

". . . tomorrow Augusta beside the flat yellow river lined with a solid red-brown mile of boxcars, the marshland of the Savannah dizzy with yellow-and-black butterflies. They have to be scraped off the radiator grill or the water will boil. Then I'm going to cut across to Savannah to see the old slave market. I don't know whether it is still standing or if it has been taken down by whites who have grown self-conscious and ashamed under decades of constant ridicule from the North. . . . In Cheraw I had a breakfast of Florida orange juice, ham, grits—for the first time in two years—hot rolls, cherry marmalade and coffee that would knock a New Yorker down at 6 a.m. . . .

". . . I'm saying all this because we Southerners have to think about what we saw and heard and did, and try to tell each other who we are and what it was that shaped us. . . ."

These are some of the materials that bear upon the consciousness of the Southerner. A heritage is bred into him, so that whether the young writer proceeds to tell a story in the guise of ingenuousness (like *Other Voices, Other Rooms* or *The Heart is a Lonely Hunter*) or quite contrivedly "conscious," (like *Shiloh* or *Lie Down in Darkness*) he has an initial advantage over the young writers from other regions: The Southerner writes about something of weight and density to which a sense of importance adheres. The material he works with (and this writer has never heard of a Southerner who had to go out "looking for material"—even Warren's and Foote's studies of regional history are only for adjustment and refinement of materials ardently and priorly conceived) has been produced by a more nearly whole and consistent scheme of values than exists in other regions. (That the easy availability of a weighty matter makes the faking of profundity also easier for the Southern writer than for others is beside the point here; that would mean taking up the subject of inferior works, which the South probably has produced more of than any other region also.) And regardless of the quality of that heritage or its lack, it *exists* as an entity for rich observation and contemplation. The comparative intactness of the South has been of inestimable value to writers born and raised there. Even in hating it and fleeing it (as many have) the Southern writer carries with him the cogent presence of something highly organized and related and available. And the phenomenon of the Southern writer's alienation from the actual materials of his parent region is not strikingly different from that incapacity of certain writers of the Irish Renaissance to abide the paralysis of their land; rather than lessening the value of those materials, that estrangement quite probably supplies a valuable part of the motive force spent in their transformation to literature.

The materials of the Southern region once composed almost a culture. New England and the South have been those parts of America where sufficient coherence of belief, public involvement in custom and ritual, and community persistence in tragic error and guilt succeeded in giving tone and meaning to existence. New England blessed us first with the fruit of Calvinism's decline—her great writers, most of them born near the turn of the nineteenth century. We have had to wait almost another hundred years for the second flowering, in the South.

Since 1900 the materials of that region have been in preparation through several necessary stages of transformation. We had to wait until that system of materials entered its concluding dissolute phase just prior to extinction (in another fifty years there will be no South as we have known it) and for that history to fall into decay not from disuse but from misuse. We have seen the Joyners, Pentlands and Snopeses who misused all things. We have stood with Tate beside the cemetery wall and sensed the loss of relation between the individual self and the history which had provided that relation. We waited for three generations of men and women to be confronted by the shock-

ing disparity between the once active history of that region and its
intolerable wreckage in present time, to perceive the unbridgeable gap
between what was and what is, thus to develop that moral consciousness which is so prominent in Southern writing—an achievement that
rescued American fiction from the ephemeral proletarian excitement
of the 1920's.

A powerful aspect of Southern writing is its comprehensiveness and
cohesion as a body of work, covering the whole expanse of an under-
standable regional experience. That experience extends from the his-
tory-ridden eulogies and obituaries of dead grandeur to sober, ironic
documentation of something else that has usurped its house. Fortunately that experience was shaped by an intelligible and workable
aesthetics, incorporated to a large extent in what has been called the
New Criticism, its views derived from a value system based organ-
ically on the nature of a correct relation between writer and materials,
this relation being quasi-religious in character and drawn from theological ideas of just relationships. A high degree of integration is the
result: Southern writers and critics easily converted the energies of
lost religion to the realm of aesthetics. The salvagable objects of a
decayed Protestantism and its attendant evils supply a fair portion of
the sense of loss of full, reasonable dignity and its ironic import in
figures ranging from Hightower to Sister Bessie and Jesus Fever and
the psychotic young man of *Good Country People*. In all the defeated
alcoholic men and cold indrawn women of Wolfe, Faulkner, Tennessee Williams and Warren, we have observed human nature goaded
and obsessed, and have witnessed the last flickers of a faded grace in
Ransom. Under the breakdown of community and family, decay of
religion and the encroachment of industrialism, we have observed the
poorwhite, the cabin, the Model-A, the juke, the mill—and a humanity
corroded and transfigured by struggle. It has been an experience of
painful and powerful recognition to revisit imaginatively ourselves
divested of superfluous trappings and evasions of meaning, called to
the Wolfian Odyssey, consigned to Faulkner's holocaust. Yet here
again, one cannot be surprised or chagrined: Such is the potent nature
of the regional matter and urgent its promptings to the imagination.
Those are the most fortunate and ruthlessly driven of writers who do
not choose their material but are chosen by it.

K. V. HOFFMAN

A Yankee in Dixie

I HAD BEEN long in love with the North country when I came to Dixie just after World War II. I still am. There is something about the austerity of northern New England that appeals to the contemplative mind—the rocky coast and wilderness lakes of Maine, the granite ledges and juniper of upland pastures in New Hampshire, the Green Mountains of Vermont "endlessly rolling." The moods and meanings these evoke had become part of me.

I was, and am, what Robert Frost called himself, an "environmentalist," sensitive to the natural harmonies of a region, and inversely, to off-key incongruities. I was not quite as provincial as the lady who, with her husband, for the first time in her life had ventured outside the border of her native Massachusetts—all the way to Los Angeles, as a matter of fact. And by car. As so many New Englanders do, when in Florida or California, this middle-aged couple gravitated to a Yankee colony. After the long and strenuous trip, it was very pleasant to relax in the inevitable cocktail lounge of the hotel, where they found themselves chatting with a couple of other Bay Staters.

"How did you drive to the coast?" the lady was asked.

She turned to her husband.

"By way of Dedham, wasn't it, John?"

This is one of my favorite Yankee stories. What it illustrates applies equally to the provincial Southerner, the *petit bourgeois* of France or the *Buerger* of Hannover. In varying degrees it is true of us all. Our understanding is circumscribed, more or less, by the horizon of the workaday world-we-live-in.

We can learn about regions outside that sphere, by reading books or the National Geographic, or watching cinema travelogues. We can go to new places on winter or summer vacations, but we cannot hope fully to understand a region and its people until we have lived there for some years.

I found it so 25 years ago, when, after years in the New York-New Jersey metropolitan area, I pulled up stakes to settle down in the most northerly part of Vermont, where there are only two seasons—"winter and late in the fall." In the 1930's the middle-aged generation then living there was about as genuinely Yankee as you would find anywhere. Every little town had its Civil War monument, near the depot, a granite base topped by the stereotyped "Boy in Blue" gazing southward into the past of Shiloh and Chancellorsville.

Now that generation, which preceded my own by some 20 years, was still very conscious of the part its fathers had played in that war. Many of the veterans were still around and kept memories green. Even as a school boy in Connecticut, the visit of some ruddy-faced, blue-clad veteran, tasseled campaign hat and all, had been a high spot of the school year for me. This annual treat occurred a few days before "Decoration Day." The windows of the classroom would be open and in my mind the memory of fragrant schoolyard lilacs is mingled with the annual Memorial Day parade of GAR veterans, most of them still in the prime of life, and firmly ensconced as heroes. Not until World War I was their glory dimmed by the whiter glare of a war in which the North-South dividing line became for the moment indistinct and almost obliterated.

Regional prejudice posing as history had been accepted unquestioningly by my school generation. "The War" had been fought to free the slaves. *Uncle Tom's Cabin* was historically accurate. General Lee had betrayed his soldier's oath to the Union. Grant was the greatest military genius since Alexander. And the descendants of Johnny Rebs were either filthy rich and decadent, or shiftless and illiterate.

Where did we get those ideas? From overhearing conversations, smoldering contemptuous remarks, perhaps in families whose kin had fallen on battlefields of that war. It was a distorted picture, perhaps not quite as much distorted as my brief summation, but still definitely a hangover of war's aftermath. Over all was The Great Tragedy—the assassination of Abraham Lincoln—whose figure, on the dais of divinity, was only one step below the radiant image of Christ.

I mention, in brief, these highlights of a Yankee boyhood to emphasize that in the growth of my affection for the South, a preconceived bias played no part.

One recollection of my school years comes to mind. It marked a turning point in my regional thinking. As a high school freshman wandering idly through the school library, I came upon a red-backed volume, lettered in gold *The War Between the States*. What made me pluck the book from the ranks? It was the title. War between *what* States, I asked myself. A glance at the opening chapter made me realize that what the author was writing about was the War of the *Rebellion!* Not until I had read that book did I realize that there had been a Southern side to that conflict, that it had not been, as we had been taught to take for granted, a simple case of treason against the Union, but essentially a showdown over the constitutional right of any State to withdraw from a federation it had voluntarily entered.

Not until much later in my high school years were we informed that "The War" was fought not to free the slaves primarily, but to preserve the Union, and that the slave traffic which had originally supplied the South, had been engaged in, not by Southerners, but by Yankees. This altered the ideal, black-and-white "moral picture," and somewhat painfully led to an understanding of the self-sacrificing determination of sovereign Southern States to resist compulsion.

Whether most of my classmates saw the War Between the States in that realistic light, I do not know. In families whose grandfathers and great-uncles had died on the battlefield, or of wounds, or survived as community heroes to lend prestige to the family, the illusion that Appomattox represented a complete moral victory remained unimpaired.

Who, after all, North or South, would relinquish, without an inner struggle, the conviction that a beloved member of the family was killed in the defense of an immaculate ideal? Such illusions are the household gods, man's most precious possessions. To question them is heresy. To retain such illusions, by either side in any struggle, between any countries or within a nation, would be a harmless self-delusion, were it not for the fact that false pride breeds bias, misunder-

standing and automatic hatred in any future controversy. None knows
this blind, automatic reflex as well as the politician, and no one appeals
to it so unscrupulously. The almost solid alignment of Northern editorial and political opinion on the side of the Supreme Court desegre-
gation decision may be attributed to this inherited bias, completely
unreasoning and therefore firm as a rock in what it believes to be
conviction based upon moral grounds.

Woodrow Wilson, alone of the topflight statesmen who assembled
at Versailles in 1919, recognized the peril to peace inherent in ancestral
memories. He realized that the imposition of a foreign government
upon a territory predominantly of a different ethnic group would
lead to future enmity, not because of the intensity of feeling over new
grievances, real or imagined, but because of the ineradicable memory
of old feuds.

I was, in a minor way, involved in Mr. Wilson's effort to reduce
that "cause of war" to a minimum. Under the guidance of Professor
Charles Seymour, the historian, later President of Yale, I made a large
wall map showing, by diagonal colored bands of varying width the
derivative nationalities of populations in Styria, Istria, the Sudeten,
Croatia and Dalmatia. This was the map Mr. Wilson took with him
to Versailles, a prop in his campaign to "sell" his plan for eliminating
such inflammable fuses to the powderkeg of intra-European tensions.
But the politicians to whom victorious peoples looked to bring back
from Versailles something more substantial than victory, could not
be swayed. They were not interested in Wilson's dream of making
the world "safe" for democracy; they were concerned with the safety
of their own position.

For the same reason Northern politicians reject as unrealistic any
suggestion proposing a sympathetic discernment of the Southern side
in the school controversy. They may realize the grave dangers to
national unity inherent in their refusal to do so, but only the most
unselfish statesmanship can be expected to look that far ahead. Most
of them are interested only in the next election, and with how what
they say will affect the outcome. I believe their timidity and fears of
reprisals at the polls to be greatly exaggerated. The intermingling of
servicemen of many regions during the second World War, and the

steady northward migration of the Southern Negro have, I believe, made the average Northerner, and surely those of above average intelligence, receptive to a reasonable exposition of the Southern case. There are other hopeful signs, I believe, that many Northerners no longer will be swayed by blind prejudice in their appraisal of the Southern problem.

Affection is the catalyst to bring about that mutual respect for differences in culture and tradition. For while we may preen ourselves on taking the intellectual view, and may be doing so to the best of our ability, the vista is tinctured by our emotions, suspicion, fear, self-righteousness. The most "educated" are sometimes prone to these emotional influences, which cause them to accept the most absurd preconceptions as fact.

I am thinking at the moment of a Yankee municipal judge, middle-aged, staunchly Republican, a lanky, lantern-jawed gentleman of Mayflower stock. I used to visit his office in the colonial court house on the elm shaded street to swap yarns and smoke a friendly pipe. He was a dour, hardbitten individual, with a wry sense of humor, and utterly provincial. During either the Harding or Hoover administration he had been for four years a United States Attorney in one of the Southern States.

When I informed him that I was preparing to leave the North and settle down South for keeps, he shook his head disapprovingly.

"You won't like it," he said. "The people are too different. They hate Yankees. But if you must go through with it, remember that you'll always be a stranger in a strange land. I know. I've been through it. And whatever you do, don't make any passes at their women. There are more men packing guns in the South than you can shake a stick at."

I could not restrain a laugh at what sounded like lines from a Broadway farce.

"Ah," he said sourly, "you can laugh. But I'm telling you that if, you, a married man, make sheep's eyes at another man's girl he'd just as soon shoot you as look at you."

Now here we seem to have a demonstration of the possibility of a man's having lived a fairly substantial time in a region without losing the ludicrous preconceptions he had before he did so. This, too, is something to keep in mind when blithely waving away the problem of regional differences of the "in-group" and the "out-group," as Sumner called them.

A college professor's wife's reaction to the news of my going South was quite different.

"So you're going to live in Virginia," she said. "How I envy you. You will love the country and the people. I wish I were going back."

It turned out that she was born in the Old Dominion, and of an old Shenandoah Valley family. Inter-regional marriage, of course, is a powerful corrective of misunderstandings.

I remember, some weeks after V-J Day, being present at a dinner meeting addressed by Ernest Gibson. He had been in Military Intelligence, and even then was slated by his party to become governor of Vermont. He had married a Southern girl, and thereby had come not only to learn, but to understand a people whom his fellow Vermonters of a generation ago would have classed as "furriners" with the same mild contempt implicit in the Southerner's "damyankee." One sentence of Gibson's stuck in my mind; I have since been able to confirm it.

"There is very little difference," he said, "between a Virginia Democrat and a Vermont Republican. Both are essentially conservative and at the same time tolerant."

To that snapshot-of-insight I would add, that they also share a quality which has endeared Southerners to me, perhaps because I am, by temperament, a "country boy." Like the New Englander outside industrial cities, your Southerner, be he Carolinian, Georgian or Virginian, is blessed with the same countryman's kindness and common sense which, in this highly industrialized age, are actually holdovers from the more agrarian period of our national culture.

I believe this quality of the Southerner to be of benefit to the spiritual and political well-being of the nation. What it lacks in urbanity and sophistication (of which cities have a surfeit) is balanced by a lack of cynicism.

When cynicism attains the point where it asks itself the price of everything without considering the value, it opens the door to a loss of principles, the very principles which must be conserved to preserve the identity of the American people as a hopeful, peaceful, energetic breed. Take away the capacity for adhering to principles and substitute the cynicism that calls them naïve and unrealistic, and you are well on the way to the acceptance of centralization as a guarantee of Utopia.

The Southerner, still close enough to nature to know better, is, like the New Englanders, a skeptic when it comes to political panaceas. Because his land is not overpopulated, and still has ample elbow room, he is not subject to the claustrophobia, the dread of insecurity that, in times of stress, threatens to paralyze native common sense of city dwellers jammed together in complex economic areas subject to disruption by the slightest shocks.

Perhaps the most apt measure of comparison is offered by the subways of New York City. There, twice a day during the rush hours, human beings allow themselves to be pushed and shoved into cars in a manner that would not be tolerated in shipping cattle. The human being is then reduced to a unit to be transported. Year after year treatment of this kind finally dims the individual feeling of identity, and the magnitude and complexity of the underground system itself overpowers what, in a less cynical age, men considered as their souls.

The Southerner may never have looked upon himself as different in that respect; yet I have met over the years Southerners who resisted the lure of bigger salaries "up north" because they were wise enough to know that a bigger salary would never compensate for the loss of identity.

There are undoubtedly some reformers who would like to see such differences wiped out; would like, via centralization of government, to see us all equalized. That would be a tragedy. I do not think it can be done, so long as the older and less urbanized regions of the nation, rich in tradition, refuse to be seduced by the socialist will-o'-the-wisps of the egalitarians.

In that will to resist what others blindly accept lies the greatest strength of the South. We shall continue to be besieged by the Marxian doctrinaires whose blueprint of heaven on earth would make us all as alike as peas in a pod. It is my hope and my conviction that they will not succeed.

JAMES JACKSON KILPATRICK

Conservatism and the South

"By and large," wrote Russell Kirk in *The Conservative Mind,* "radical thinkers have won the day. For a century and a half, conservatives have yielded ground in a manner which, except for occasionally successful rear-guard actions, must be described as a rout."

The Southern States, at mid-century, find themselves very nearly alone in fighting this rear-guard action against the legions of Change, the armies of a supposed Enlightenment. They represent, collectively, the last and best hope of conservatism in the American Republic. If the conservative cause is to survive at all in the United States, as a political philosophy, as an approach to the perplexing problems of our restless and edgy civilization, it will be largely because a body of tradition exists within the South and will not lie down.

It is useful to consider this hypothesis, whether it is so; and if it is so, why it is so. What is it about the South that has made the South, historically and presently, a bastion of conservatism? It is profitable to think upon the value of a conservative force, if it has value; to search out the meaning of "conservatism," its Southern roots and branches; and to examine the function of the Southern conservative in a society both antagonistic to the South and hostile to the conservative spirit.

One may begin, and there is splendidly pessimistic tradition for doing so, by observing that the Southern conservative's lot, these days, is not a happy one. This is not because of the "race issue" alone: It is no more proper to assert that every Southern States' righter of the mid-twentieth century is "pro-segregation" than it was proper, a hundred years ago, to charge that every States' righter of that day was "pro-slavery" or even "pro-secession." Alexander Stephens, in the Georgia of 1860, struggled to keep Georgia in the Union but defended to his death her right to secede from it; similarly, a number of Southern conservatives today entertain, privately or publicly, strong doubts of the wisdom of a rigid racial segregation, but they will assert vigorously the right of a State to exercise its reserved police powers in this regard.

There is more to the defensive posture of the Southern conservative than this. Conservatism generally is unpopular, and the antipathy rubs off on the South. Two factors, one instinctive, the other semantic, are in part responsible for the conservative's repeated setbacks.

Instinctively, it seems to me, the American is a dissatisfied, critical person. Curiosity, rebellion, experimentation—these are built into his gene string; and from many standpoints, it is well that this is so. A great republic has arisen from the conviction of energetic men that the grass must be greener somewhere else. In the natural order of things, the apostles crying "go!" are always more numerous, or at least more articulate, than the prophets crying "stay!" As a result, the conservative suggestion to look is derided by men who would leap; and because we are by nature a passionate people, much given to epithet and insult, the custom is to fall upon conservative spokesmen as fascists, bigots and reactionaries. The words don't mean anything in particular, but they keep the adrenals flowing.

And because other words have lost their meaning, the conservative finds a major semantic obstacle squarely in his path. His opponent is popularly known—God save the mark!—as the *liberal*. It is a graceful word, of fine and shining connotations; it evokes the Latin *liberalis,* it sings of men once liberated from tyrant's grasp, it suggests all things characteristic of liberty and generosity and freedom. Yet by every precept of political philosophy, it is the conservative of our day who expounds and defends the truly liberal principle; it is the conservative who would free man from the needless restrictions and regimentation of the state. In some bewilderment and frustration, the conservative acknowledges that his opponents have kidnaped his word; in self-defense, he is compelled to wage war against "liberals" and "liberalism," and his efforts to label the opposition as "Socialists" or "statists" seem not to have taken hold. As a result, the conservative is tagged as selfish, the liberal as bountiful. And who shoots at Santa Claus? The enemy camp knows a good thing when it sees it, and the "liberal" label is too good to let go.

Thus the misconception of the American conservative takes shape: He is seen as a stingy fellow, long-faced, cautious, timid. He wears rubbers when the sun is shining, remembering sudden rains; he is prudently clad in both suspenders and belt, against the possibility of embarrassment should one or the other fail. He moves, when he moves at all, with grudging slowness. He is a Jeremiah forever wailing in the habitations of the wilderness, a wet-blanket, a Milquetoast, a bore. Or in another version, beloved of Mr. Block of the Washington *Post,* he is a fat and bloated fellow, unjustly rich (you know he is unjustly rich because he is smoking a cee-gar); his rapacious eye seeks out the "giveaway." You find him trodding upon the lissome maid of Hawaiian Statehood; you see his uncouth and selfish features leering happily at the sight of little children jammed in an overcrowded schoolhouse. In either version, as the funereal prophet of doom or the bumptious apostle of profit, this misconceived conservative is a most unattractive fellow.

Is this wretched being in truth a "conservative"? Are timidity and selfishness the tenets of "conservatism"? Of course not. Lincoln defined the philosophy briefly as "adherence to the old and tried, against the new and untried," but that is too brief. It is true, of course, as Kirk has noted, that the conservative seeks in general "to stand by tradition and old establishments," and "to preserve the ancient moral traditions of humanity." Doubtless the conservative, more than others, exhibits what Gibbon called "the propensity of mankind to exalt the past and deprecate the present." But I have never comprehended that conservatism is ancestor worship and nothing more; nor have I believed that the "old and tried" is necessarily, in every instance, superior to the "new and untried." Sometimes it is no better to honor age in government than in eggs.

By conservatism, I mean a philosophy predicated upon the conviction that certain eternal verities exist; that these truths endure, or should endure, and that respect is due them. Conservatism assumes a divine power, unknown and unknowable, which has created man and equipped him with reason and intellect and will. The conservative recognizes that not all men have the same capacity for reason and intellect, and he knows that if free will is to have fullest meaning, it must embrace both the rewards of success and the penalties of failure. Thus the conservative repudiates the notion that all men are equal, for he sees that demonstrably this is not so; he would not have it otherwise. Conservatism is patient; it perceives that change and progress are not necessarily the same things. Conservatism is prudent; it finds it better, in general, to bear the ills we have than fly to others that we know not of. Conservatism is strong; it holds that a house can be no better than its foundations, and it proposes to build on rock, not sand.

Ceaselessly, the conservative urges that individual man is entitled to the greatest possible liberty consistent with order and responsibility. Here he would not be misunderstood. He does not equate liberty with license. He believes, with Webster, that "liberty exists in proportion to wholesome restraint," and that a profligate excess of freedom will bring the retribution any other profligacy exacts.

Conservatism asks also not to be misunderstood on a closely related point: The conservative is not, as is often said, simply "agin the guv'mint," or opposed to all government. Of course he is not. He recalls what Henry said in the Virginia Convention of 1788, that in creating a government it is best to proceed on the assumption that men will be bad, for it is likely they will be so; thus he accepts the necessity for government, to preserve law, order and property from forces antagonistic to society. This is the first reason for government, as Calhoun observed, to restrain men, just as it is the first reason for constitutions, to restrain governments. Far from opposing law, conservatism insists upon preserving law. It is only through the processes of law, as the conservative above all men must recognize, that the stability of his institutions may be preserved from "the lust for innovation," in Randolph's phrase, that has been the death of all republics.

To say that conservatism respects a divine intent, that it fosters responsible liberty, that it defends sound tradition and upholds order and classes against the leveling goals of the welfare state, is to suggest, per contra, the things that conservatism opposes: Secularism, an impersonal industrialism, most of all (and it is with this evil that the

Southern conservative is most concerned) the statism which tends steadily to overwhelm this republic and to destroy the fabric of federal union.

By secularism I mean something more than merely a decline in religious emphasis or simple piety, though this is part of it: A people who in 1776 appealed to the "Supreme Judge of the World" for the rectitude of their intentions, and placed their firm reliance in a Divine Providence, seem to have mislaid this faith in a Power larger than themselves. Our coins still assert that it is in God we trust, but I wonder if it is so. More broadly, the conservative aligns himself against the materialism and the false values of a society which pays the plumber half-again what it pays the school teacher, considering it more important to have toilets that flush smoothly than children who think clearly .When a football coach draws twice the salary of a professor of philosophy, and alumni buy tackles but seldom buy microscopes, something is wrong. More and more we seem to live in a spiritual Levittown. If our intellects soared as high as our TV antennae—but never mind: The conservative finds that enduring moral values, old precepts of taste and manners and familial right conduct, are beset at every hand; and he struggles for their preservation.

John Crowe Ransom to the contrary notwithstanding, the conservatism of a Russell Kirk does not embrace only "a dull hatred" for industry. What the conservative fears, and rightly so, is the blind veneration of bigness which industrialism exacts of its worshippers. More than others, perhaps, the conservative senses the magnitude of the sacrifices laid before smokestacks. He would not, of course, have the economy return to hand-looms and water-ground meal, nor is he suggesting that much in modern industry is not fine and admirable. What he objects to is the wholesale decline in old ideals—old concepts of craftsmanship, of the inherent value of work, of pride in individual accomplishment. Is time-and-a-half, he asks, the ultimate reward of life here on earth? And is not a terrible mockery afoot when 10,000 union members, striving to preserve the closed shop in Indiana, strike a *liberty bell* as the symbol of their tyrannical aim? Industry, in the old meaning of the word, in the root meaning that gives us *industrious,* is undoubtedly good. It is when industry passes into industrialism, into a social organization dominated by the cult of production, that men are reduced to punchcards and the fruit of their genius to statistical units of ouput. In the drawings of Artzybasheff, one finds the great body-presses of Dearborn cast ominously in images of old Aztec gods, ugly, imperious and powerful; and the conservative reflects that the conveyor belt which brings material riches carries away something of the spirit, too.

To a remarkable extent, it seems to me, the South traditionally has reflected the conservative position in these matters. For all the astonishing growth of Southern industry in recent years, the region remains basically agrarian in its politics, its economy, its outlook. Ours is still pretty much a land of small farms; and though the number of small farmers is declining, their influence remains strong in our councils of state. This attitude of cautious reserve toward industrialism is allied with the Southerner's love of place, and his sense of community; it has its roots in a tradition of man's dependence on the soil and his independence by reason of this. The factory may or may not be permanent; the land *is*. Pines, not chimneys, loom large in the horizon of his recollection. "Conservatism," says Kirk, "always has had its most loyal adherents in the country." And country is the one thing we have most of.

Similarly, the South to this day preserves its deep devotion to things of the spirit, as distinguished from those of the flesh. To be sure, we have sinned against our old gods: The South has its Levittowns, its underpaid teachers, its share of greedy men; our institutions of higher education have suffered the corrosive effects of over-emphasized football. When the centennial of The War arrives, we will shame our fathers by vending kewpie dolls of General Lee and by cozening tourists with fake Minie balls from the Wilderness campaigns. Some of us will. And yet . . . and yet . . . secularism and materialism have not made the inroads in the South that one witnesses elsewhere, and for good reason. It is said, sometimes scoffingly, that we live in the "Bible Belt," in a land of fundamentalist preachers whose people pray to an anthropomorphic God; but if this sometimes results in a Scopes trial or in the rituals of hill country Faith healers, it more often results in a simple and homely faith, in a certainty of salvation and a fear of divine wrath. Southerners are a prayerful people. It is not without significance that in rewriting the very preamble of the Federal Constitution, to adapt it to the Confederate States, the framers of 1860 carefully declared their purpose to establish justice, insure domestic tranquility, secure the blessings of liberty—and then, with solid tradition behind them, inserted a respectful phrase: "Invoking the favor and guidance of Almighty God," they ordained and established a Constitution for the Confederate States of America.

The Southern tradition acknowledges the failure of this invocation. As several of the essayists in this volume have emphasized, the South has known defeat—as no other region has known it. Tragically, palpably, the South saw her prayers spurned, her land ravished, a terrible penance put upon her. In the process, our people came to know the lean and bony face of poverty; we know it still. Lacking outside diversions, the Southerner has been compelled to search within himself; and there he has found a realization, not so widely discovered elsewhere, that money in fact isn't everything. This is not only because there live in the relatively moneyless South a great many people who don't have it and can't earn it, but because a different tradition of values governs our society. There remains in the South an innate code of honor, an inheritance of manners, a certain sense of fitness, an easy patience often misunderstood as indolence.

These are subtle things, not easily defined; but the Southerner senses them daily—in the Virginian's incessant "sir," the Mississippian's deference to women, the courtesies of Kentucky. He knows that efficiency is not necessarily the finest attribute of men or society; that it is not imperative to accomplish all things today, or tomorrow, or even day after tomorrow. Toward the end of the War of 1861-65, South Carolina undertook to build a new state house at Columbia; Sherman's artillerymen amused themselves by firing on the structure, and metal stars, set in the granite, still mark where the balls landed. In the embarrassment of the time, unable to complete the Capitol, South Carolina erected only a temporary dome on top. The dome has been temporary, now, for nearly a hundred years. But life in Columbia is exceedingly pleasant, and South Carolinians do not complain.

The conservatism of the American South, I have submitted, thus exhibits to an unusual degree the characteristics by which the conservative philosophy generally is identified: An indwelling devotion to tradition and good manners, a resistance to industrialism, a coolness to the secularist sirens who sing of material pleasures. But there is, of course, one thing more than this, the political tradition of the South with which this essay is primarily concerned. This is the South's abiding, unyielding opposition to centralism, and to the dead hand of the impassive state. In terms of constitutional exposition, we know it as the doctrine of States' Rights. And at mid-century, that doctrine is flourishing with fresh vitality and renewed conviction.

For the past several years, many of us in the South have been doing our frustrated best to educate the great world outside in a few fundamental truths about the Constitution and what is happening to that beloved compact. Try as we may, the task is rough going. When the literate Southern conservative—and there are some literate Southern conservatives—seeks access to the major media of national communication, he finds the borders closed to him as though he carried typhoid. This is not to say that *Time* and *Life* and *Look* do not carry pieces now and then by approved "Southerners." They do. But almost invariably, the Southerners turn out to be Hodding Carter, or William Faulkner or Robert Penn Warren, whose views are as typically Southern as those which prevail in, let us say, South Amboy, New Jersey. In the three years following the Supreme Court's decision in the school cases, three Southern conservatives breached the paper curtain: Clifford Dowdey penetrated the *Saturday Review;* Tom Waring made *Harper's,* Herbert Ravenel Sass made *Atlantic.* Mr. Dowdey's piece came almost immediately after the court's opinion, before the magnitude of the mandate was wholly recognized. Some eighteen months later, Mr. Waring's essay struggled into print weighted down by the longest, most apologetic editor's note in magazine history. A year later, Mr. Sass appeared not as a member of the lodge, but as a guest speaker imported for Brotherhood Week. Look, mom, said Mr. Weeks, we're tolerant! And Mr. Sass was hustled off stage.

These acts of charity were better than nothing, of course, and we are grateful for them. Otherwise, the viewpoint of several million Southerners would have been suppressed, outside their own domain, almost entirely. The South has come to recognize, a little bitterly, that newspapers of the North with rare exceptions will suppress their own race troubles. When a bomb goes off in Montgomery, it is page one news for *The New York Times;* but a flaring race riot in Buffalo rates page 32. The newspapers of Detroit are hell on race friction in Mississippi; they carried scarcely a line when hundreds of white persons picketed a new Negro neighbor in Detroit itself. During all the trouble of 1956-57 in Clinton, Tennessee, the Northern press spared nothing to report the bigotry, so-called, of a severely provoked white community; but when a husky 21-year-old Negro, one Alfred Williams, being then and there a senior student in Clinton High School, pulled a switchknife on a white boy and was thereupon expelled, we searched almost in vain for some slight coverage of the incident in the press above the Potomac. The Associated Press moved the story on its A-wire for morning papers of February 14. It was not news fit to print for *The New York Times.* We are reminded of the problem in freshman physics: The tree that falls in the desert, does it make a sound? In theory it does; but if no one is there to hear it?

Now and then Southern spokesmen produce a little noise; now and then a Southern missionary is permitted to cross over Jordan, in order to acquaint college sophomores of New England and the Upper Midwest with "the other side." Such junkets are at once exhilarating and depressing: After months of sitting with fiddle at rest, overwhelmed by the din of liberal timpani and impatiently asking "now?", "now?", the Southern States' Righter finds it good to play a few solo measures. But lecturing on the Tenth Amendment before these bright-eyed students is like plowing fresh clay. The Fifth Amendment—that, yes, the Fifth they have heard of. But the Tenth? Theirs is a generation that knows not Joseph. The Tenth Amendment, the Doctrine of '98, the demonstrable basis of State sovereignty—these things are mysteries to be ranked with quantum physics and the French subjunctive.

Yet there is nothing obscure about the States' Righter's concept of the Constitution. The gospel does not demand of its disciples that they be metaphysicians or constitutional lawyers either; it asks only that they read and comprehend the English language. What the States' Righter says is that if the Constitution be read from beginning to end, just as it came from Philadelphia late in the summer of 1787, from "We the people" in the preamble to the final ratifying clause of Article VII, it will be perfectly apparent that what the States created was a federal union of separate sovereign States, each individual, each State (as the Tenth Amendment makes clear) *respectively* possessed of all powers not delegated to the general government by the Constitution nor denied by the Constitution to the States. That is not so difficult a doctrine.

The Supreme Court itself stated the facts neatly in *Lane County vs. Oregon,* when the court, three years *after* the War for Southern independence, said this:

> The people of each State compose a State, having its own government, and endowed with all the functions essential to separate and independent existence. The States disunited might continue to exist. Without the States in union, there could be no such political body as the United States.

That was precisely the basis on which the union was formed. If nine States ratified, the Constitution would be binding as to them. But if Virginia, New York, North Carolina and Rhode Island had failed to ratify—they were Numbers 10, 11, 12, and 13—the United States of America would have come into being anyway; and Virginia, New York, North Carolina and Rhode Island might be to this day as politically separate as any Luxembourg or Belgium. Under the Articles of Confederation, the States had asserted nothing so explicitly as their separate, individual sovereignty. This sovereignty they retained under the Constitution of 1787. Whenever three fourths of the States wish to do so (whether or not the three fourths contain a majority or a minority of the whole population), they may wipe out Congress, provide for a dual executive, dissolve the Supreme Court, or make any other change they please. This power to make and unmake is what is meant by sovereignty; and it resides not in the people as people en masse, but in the people-as-States.

Paraphrasing Holy Writ, it may be said of the sovereign States: Before the Union was, we *are.* Madison put it this way in *The Federalist:* "Each State," he said, "in ratifying the Constitution, is considered as a sovereign body, independent of all others, and only to be bound by its voluntary act." The volition to bind certainly would appear to embrace the volition to unbind. A sovereign people, capable of exercising the power to ratify, must also possess the power to rescind. This was the sound reasoning advanced by the Southern States in 1860; it is sound reasoning today, and until the Constitution be rewritten to abolish the States, it will remain a sound position. The bloody war of 1861-65 did not prove the North right as a matter of law, only superior as a matter of arms. It also follows from this line of reasoning that the States which are parties to the mutual compact should be, in the last resort, the final judges of its violation. When the final arbitrament of contested powers is effectively conceded to the Supreme Court, an agency of the general government, and as such an agency created by the States themselves, the agent becomes superior to the master. In that moment of concession, the whole structure and meaning of our government are distorted; the people within their States no longer are sovereign—the court has effectively assumed sovereign power, and we exchange government by the people for government by judicial oligarchy.

The Southern States' Righter does not plead his case on the law alone, but on the merits also. He cherishes the conviction—it is an age-old conviction in the South—that strong State governments are infinitely more to be desired than a strong central government. He knows the people can restrain government when government is close at hand. At the State level, the reins of power run straight from hand to bit: Citizens of Virginia alone choose a Governor of Virginia and an Assembly that acts for Virginia alone. Jefferson's Capitol at Richmond offers both a political and spiritual home, to be possessed with a fierce sense of exclusive possession.

In sharp contrast to this friendly closeness of State government, the Southern conservative soberly contemplates a central government which grows increasingly more remote. He cannot untangle the harness that once was expected to control the creature. Responsibility here is diffuse; everybody is accountable and nobody is accountable. Who is the rider, who the ridden? He journeys to Washington and finds the committees of Congress full of strangers; the vastness of marble hearing rooms reduces the intimacy of his own chambers at the State Capitol to a shabby insignificance. He visits Washington not casually, as master, but suppliantly, as servant; and he uneasily comprehends that his most personal domestic affairs have become subject to the authority of men politically beyond his reach. His Federal government seems no longer to derive just power from the consent of the governed;

he does not recall delegating such vast powers. Power, he recognizes, has simply been assumed. And the conservative passionately conceives this to be wrong.

This dedication to the essential rightness of State responsibility, this concept of the State as the basic political entity of the American structure, is as old as the South itself. It was a favorite thesis of Jefferson, who saw the assertion of State powers as a great bulwark against the one calamity he feared even more than disunion—the greatest calamity of all, "submission to a government of unlimited powers." He believed steadfastly that "the States can best govern our home concerns."

In their original resolutions of ratification, the Southern States made this view explicit. South Carolina, ratifying in May of 1788, declared flatly

> that no Section or paragraph of the said Constitution warrants a Construction that the States do not retain every power not expressly relinquished by them and vested in the General Government of the Union.

Virginia, in June, urged twenty amendments to the Constitution, and the very first of these wanted it made clear

> That each State in the Union shall respectively retain every power, jurisdiction and right which is not by this Constitution delegated to the Congress of the United States or to the departments of the Federal Government.

North Carolina, in August, asked twenty-six amendments; and again, the assertion given highest priority was an assertion couched in language identical to that employed by Virginia. (It is not intended to suggest, of course, that the Southern States were alone in demanding a plain explication of the State-Federal relationship. The first amendment asked by Massachusetts was "that it be explicitly declared that all Powers not expressly delegated by the aforesaid Constitution are reserved to the several States to be by them exercised." New Hampshire strengthened the language of Massachusetts with a reservation of "all Powers not expressly & particularly Delegated." New York, and later Rhode Island wanted it made plain "that every Power, Jurisdiction and Right" not clearly delegated to the general government "remain to the People of the several States, or to their respective State governments to whom they may have granted the same.")

These various State resolutions promptly resulted in the Tenth Amendment. This amendment consists of a single sentence, only twenty-eight words long; it is in no way obscure. *The powers* (not rights, as in the Ninth Amendment, but powers) *not delegated to the United States* (the verb is delegated, not "surrendered," or "granted," or "vested in," but merely delegated) *by the Constitution* (not by inference, or by any notions of inherent powers, but by the Constitution alone), *nor prohibited by it to the States* (prohibited by the Constitution, that is, by its specific limitations, and not by mandate of any court or Congress or executive, but only by the Constitution itself), *are reserved to the States respectively* (not to the States jointly, but to the States individually and respectively), *or to the people* (because there may be some powers the people will not wish to entrust even to their States).

This is the ark of the covenant. And whether the Tenth Amendment is read in the context of 1790, or as a living, vital part of the Constitution today, its meaning is perfectly clear: The sole powers of the Federal government are powers delegated to it by the States through the Constitution; and all powers not delegated, or prohibited by the Constitution to the States, are reserved to the States separately to be exercised by them—*for good or ill*—according to the wishes of the people within their States.

I emphasize "for good or ill," because this right of individual States to do what other States may regard as wrong is essential to any understanding of the Federal Union. The diversity of beliefs across this broad land, the infinite variety of local conditions and problems and traditions which contribute to diverse political viewpoints, form an enduring characteristic of the United States of America. All the miracles of communication and transportation cannot wipe out this diversity, nor substitute a regimented oneness in its place. Is legalized gambling wrong? It is Nevada's right to sanction it if she pleases. Was it wrong to permit the distillation and sale of whisky? Many persons thought so, but it did not become constitutionally a wrong until the long dark night of prohibition descended in 1920. Is it "good" for

18-year-olds to vote? Georgia thinks so, and that is Georgia's right and power. In this Republic, what the States choose to do in their reserved fields is their own business, *for good or ill,* until the Constitution itself be amended by the States themselves to establish a rule applicable to all alike.

The abiding prayer of many Southern conservatives is that this individuality and responsibility be preserved; their continuing apprehension is that local government will be reduced to impotence by gradual consolidation, and the States in essence will be destroyed by judicial erosion. This is seen as a perversion of law, but more than this: It is seen as a surrender to a remote statism, a submission to some massive Orwellian control too powerful ever to be restrained. There is a tyranny of the majority. Nothing was recognized more clearly than this when the Union was formed, and a dozen provisions were inserted in the Constitution to forestall it. Now these provisions are being circumvented or ignored; and this is being done, as Plato long ago imagined it would be done, in the name of liberty: "Tyranny springs from democracy," he said, when liberty magnified and intensified overmasters necessary restraints against license. "The excess of liberty, whether in States or individuals, seems only to pass into excess of slavery." Understanding this, conservatism pleads for a system of government kept close to the people governed, subject to their wishes, responsive to what they perceive to be their own needs. This is the sort of government envisioned by the wise men, genius-struck, who fashioned our Constitution. We will abandon it at our peril.

This body of political tradition, cherished in the South of Jefferson, Calhoun, Upshur, Stephens, Byrd, and Byrnes, underlies the resistance of Southern States to the Supreme Court's decree in the school segregation cases. When the Fourteenth Amendment was ratified in 1868, it never was understood by anyone that the amendment, of and by itself, would prohibit any State from operating racially separate schools. Irrefutable proof of that proposition is to be found in the demonstrable fact that for many years thereafter, States both North and South operated such schools. The Congress itself provided for separate schools in the District of Columbia. The "privileges and immunities of citizens of the United States," it was agreed, embraced no right to an integrated public school; neither was it comprehended that any person was being deprived of "liberty" without due process of law, nor that "equal protection of the laws" required admission of white and Negro to identical classrooms. This clear understanding, repeatedly affirmed by the highest courts of the land, established a plain and lasting interpretation. The States were entitled to rely on its permanence. What happened on May 17, 1954, was that the Supreme Court undertook to accomplish by judicial fiat what the Tenth Amendment declares can be accomplished by the Constitution alone: The court undertook to prohibit the States from exercising a power they had reserved to themselves respectively. This is not "interpretation" of the Constitution; to all practical intents and purposes, it is substantive amendment of the Constitution, and the power to amend lies not with the court, but solely with three fourths of the States.

Southerners are unhappily aware that the court's decision, on its merits, probably is approved by a substantial majority of all the people of the United States. It is likely, indeed, that the court's position is approved by three fourths of the States. But the first proposition is immaterial and the latter, at this writing, is not demonstrable. Nothing political is ever done in the United States by a majority of the whole people; and until an amendment to the Constitution is actually proposed to the States, no fresh constitutional obligation can be implied.

When I say that the South is "unhappily" aware that its insistence upon racially separate schools is opposed widely in other States, I am suggesting simply that an overwhelming majority of the people in the South believe in the prudence and wisdom of essential race segregation within the Southern States. They feel an excellent case can be made for utilizing the powers of their States to preserve, as far as may be possible, the integrity of the white and Negro races. Much persuasive evidence could be offered to suggest that neither race in the South, where we are accustomed by the mores of generations to thinking in terms of race, is yet prepared for the social intimacy implicit in massively integrated schools. What is imperfectly understood outside the South is that compulsory integration of our schools has little to do with education *per se;* it has everything to do with the structure of our society. The court is undertaking to do by revolutionary mandates what can be accomplished, if at all, only by the evolutionary processes of time.

When this book of essays first was planned, it had been my intention to offer a justification, on the merits, of school segregation in the South. The two years between conception and publication have served to convince me, a dozen times over, that such justification exists, but these two years have also persuaded me that in the present climate of opinion, it would be useless to propound it. Such is the emotional frenzy created by our antagonists that considerations of reason, observation, and experience would be speedily shouted down. At the moment, the tendency of many of our Northern critics, deploring segregation, is to cry: "This is immoral; *therefore* it is unconstitutional." In time, perhaps, they may come to understand the distinction between that which is "moral" and that which is "lawful." They are by no means necessarily the same thing. What most Southerners believe to be moral, Christian and constitutional, our critics conceive to be immoral, unchristian and unconstitutional. To argue questions of morality and Christianity requires, at the least, a quiet room and a spirit of intellectual receptivity; but on these issues, few persons, North or South, are quiet, and none is receptive.

I draw a certain faint encouragement from these facts: That when the Eighteenth Amendment came before the States in 1918, ratification was achieved by astonishing majorities. An industrious statistician found that the vote in the various State Senates was 1,310 for, 237 against; and in the various lower chambers of the States, 3,782 for, 1,035 against—a preponderance of 78.5 percent dry. Alcohol was regarded so universally as an evil that few persons, three years after prohibition began, ever dreamed the amendment would be repealed. In time, of course, it was repealed; people came to discover there were worse things than alcohol. As this is written, some three years after the court's decision, only the most sanguinary Southerner dreams that one day the court will reverse itself, or that corrective action will be taken by Congress or by constitutional amendment. Yet as Washington, New York, Chicago and Detroit learn more of the blessings of race-mixing, who can say? Concepts of what is moral and what is Christian have a way of changing; and in any event, these are private, personal subjective matters. I pass them by.

The constitutional question is something else entirely, and here the Southern conservative hopes keenly to win support beyond his homeland. Wholly aside from the merits of school segregation as such, divorced from "moral" or "Christian" considerations, there stands a formidable problem in constitutional law. What are the limits, if any, upon the power of the Supreme Court to "interpret" the Constitution? Where in a government of checks and balances can one find an effective check upon the court? If the individual justices' "sense of judicial self-restraint" is in fact the only rein upon the court, has not a government of law been abandoned to a government of men?

These are questions of far-reaching importance, transcending the immediate issue of school segregation in the Southern States. Thoughtful attorneys elsewhere, no friends of segregation, are troubled by the trend; and in a calmer day, when it may be possible to criticize the court without being labeled "anti-Negro," more of them will speak frankly of the violence done to the stability of law on May 17, 1954. Viewed strictly from a constitutional standpoint, the South's position is basically sound and right. Regardless of what happens in Southern schools, that position ultimately will be vindicated.

It will be vindicated or the whole nature of this Republic will be drastically changed—and I believe, changed for the worse. The United States will cease to be a union of individual States, and will become instead a consolidated nation. Virtually all government will center in Washington. The responsibilities of State and local administrations will dwindle to the merest sweeping of streets, the clipping of public parks. Immense, unapproachable, unreachable, the monolithic structure of Federal government will dominate men's lives and control their destinies. Already we are far advanced toward subjection to the omniscient state.

If this leveling sweep of the bulldozer society can be checked at all, it will be checked by a vigorous conservative force—by counter influences pleading the cause of individual responsibilities within an incentive society, by political leadership advancing the constitutional prerogatives of the States. Such an incipient force exists now within the South. The conservative instinct survives there; it survives not strongly, but at least stubbornly, and it offers a brake upon a society plunging rapidly into a statism only dimly foreseen.

"The empire of Rome," Gibbon tells us, "was firmly established by the singular and perfect coalition of its members." So, too, was our own Republic. And "the decline of Rome," Gibbon adds, "was the natural and inevitable effect of immoderate greatness." Not of greatness: Of *immoderate* greatness, of excesses of power and wealth and envy and ambition, of a lust for authority that must consume freedom in its flames. We can follow Rome. If the forces of conservatism are obliterated, that melancholy end will soon be inescapable; we will have traded the rights of man for the dispensations of the state, and found the pursuit of happiness an illusory blind alley that leads to nothing at all. If the lasting South can prevent this, or help to prevent it, the influence of Southern conservatism one day will be counted not bigotry but blessing. There, men may say, was the anchor by which we rode out the storm.

The Contributors

ROBERT RAYMOND BROWN, Bishop Coadjutor of Arkansas, was born in Garden City, Kansas. He was graduated from St. Mary's University, San Antonio, Texas, and the Virginia Theological Seminary. He has served in Episcopal churches in Texas and as rector of St. Paul's Church, Richmond. He now resides in Little Rock, Arkansas. He is author of *The Miracle of the Cross* and *Friendly Enemies*.

JAMES MCBRIDE DABBS is a native of Sumter County, South Carolina, and attended the University of South Carolina, Clark University, and Columbia University. From 1925 until 1937 he was head of the department of English at Coker College, Hartsville, South Carolina. Since then he has been a farmer. He has contributed essays to the *Yale Review, Virginia Quarterly Review, Sewanee Review, South Atlantic Quarterly, Southern Review, Forum, Scribner's,* and the *Christian Century*. He is an elder of the Presbyterian Church (U.S.). He now lives at Mayesville, South Carolina.

CLIFFORD DOWDEY is a native of Richmond, Virginia, and attended Columbia University. His first novel, *Bugles Blow No More,* was the story of the siege of Richmond during the Civil War, and his other novels have also been concerned with Virginia history. In 1946 he turned to non-fiction in *Experiment in Rebellion,* and followed it up with *The Land They Fought For,* a narrative study of the Confederacy. His most recent book is *The Great Plantation,* a study of pre-Civil War Virginia plantation life. He is at present working on a three-volume narrative history of Lee's army.

RICHARD BARKSDALE HARWELL was born in Washington, Georgia. He was graduated from Emory University. He has been assistant librarian of Emory University, executive secretary of the Southeastern Inter-Library Research Facility, and director of publications of the Virginia State Library. His books include *Confederate Belles-Lettres; Confederate Music; Songs of the Confederacy; Cornerstones of Confederate*

Collecting; and an edition of General Richard Taylor's *Destruction and Reconstruction.* His anthology, *The Confederate Reader,* appears this fall. He is now executive secretary of the Association of College and Reference Libraries, with headquarters in Chicago.

ROBERT HAZEL is a native of Indiana. He was graduated from the George Washington University and the Johns Hopkins University. He has published two novels, *The Lost Year* and *A Field Full of People,* and has contributed poetry to *The Provincial, Poetry, The Hopkins Review,* and *New Directions 12* and *14.* He is author of a critical essay on Erskine Caldwell which appeared in *Southern Renascence.* In 1956 he held the Saxton Fellowship in fiction. At present he teaches at the University of Kentucky in Lexington.

K(URT) V(ALENTINE) HOFFMAN was born in Muehlhausen, Saxony. He was educated in Connecticut and graduated from Yale University. Except for one year as a Vermont farmer he has been a newspaperman for 37 years, in New York City; Juneau, Alaska; Seattle, Washington; Elizabeth, New Jersey; Staten Island, N. Y.; Newark, N. J.; Bennington, Vermont; and since 1946, has been associate editor of the Richmond, Va., *Times-Dispatch.*

RONALD F. HOWELL, a native of Birmingham, Alabama, attended the University of the South, the University of Strasbourg, and the Johns Hopkins University, where he was awarded the doctorate of philosophy. He is now assistant professor of political science at Emory University. He has contributed essays to the *Journal of Public Law, Ethics, Georgia Review, Journal of Politics, Anglican Theological Review,* and the *Emory University Quarterly.* In the summer sessions of 1955 and 1957 he was visiting lecturer in political science at the Johns Hopkins University.

ROBERT D. JACOBS is a native of Vicksburg, Mississippi. He attended the University of Mississippi, the Louisiana State University, and the Johns Hopkins University, where he received his doctorate. He has taught at Johns Hopkins and, since 1953, as assistant professor of English at the University of Kentucky. He is co-editor of *Southern Renascence,* and has contributed essays and reviews to *Modern Language Notes,* the *Journal of Southern History,* the *Hopkins Review, American Quarterly,* and *The Provincial.*

JAMES JACKSON KILPATRICK was born in Oklahoma City, Oklahoma. He attended the University of Missouri, and in 1941 joined the news staff of the Richmond, Va., *News Leader.* In 1949 he succeeded the late Douglas Southall Freeman as editor. He is author of *The Sovereign States* and has contributed essays and articles to the *Reader's*

Digest, and *Human Events.* In 1956 he was awarded the Sigma Delta Chi medal for distinguished editorial writing.

LOUIS D. RUBIN, JR. is a native of Charleston, South Carolina, and attended the College of Charleston, the University of Richmond, and the Johns Hopkins University, where he was awarded the doctorate of philosophy. He has taught at Johns Hopkins, the University of Pennsylvania, and Louisiana State University, and was executive secretary of the American Studies Association. In 1956-1957 he was associate editor of the Richmond, Va., *News Leader* and is now associate professor of English at Hollins College. He is author of *Thomas Wolfe: The Weather of His Youth* and co-editor of *Southern Renascence.*

FRANCIS BUTLER SIMKINS is a native of Edgefield County, South Carolina, and attended the University of South Carolina and Columbia University, where he received the doctorate of philosophy. For over half of his life he has taught history at Longwood College, and has also served as visiting professor at the University of North Carolina, Louisiana State University, Princeton University, and the University of Texas. He was winner of the Dunning Prize of the American Historical Association. His books include *The Tillman Movement in South Carolina, South Carolina During Reconstruction, Pitchfork Ben Tillman* and *A History of the South.*

WALTER SULLIVAN was born in Nashville, Tennessee, and was educated at Vanderbilt University and the State University of Iowa. Since 1949 he has been a member of the Vanderbilt English Department. He has written a novel, *Sojourn of a Stranger,* and has contributed fiction and criticism to various magazines.

RICHARD M. WEAVER, a native of Asheville, North Carolina, attended the University of Kentucky, Vanderbilt University, and the Louisiana State University. Since 1951 he has been associate professor of English at the University of Chicago. His books include *Ideas Have Consequences* and *The Ethics of Rhetoric;* he has contributed essays and reviews to a number of periodicals.

JOHN ELLINGTON WHITE was born in Anderson, South Carolina. He attended school in Staunton, Virginia, and at Washington and Lee University, Kenyon College, the State University of Iowa, and the Johns Hopkins University. In 1954 he became a member of the English faculty of the University of Richmond. He has been awarded a Fellowship in fiction by the *Sewanee Review* for 1957-1958. His stories and essays have appeared in *Story Magazine, Quarterly Review of Literature,* the *Sewanee Review,* and *The Provincial.*